RELENTLESS

Grace Changes
everything!

meggi
oct/2018

Also in the
DREAMS OF FREEDOM
series

I WILL NOT GROW DOWNWARD: MEMOIR OF AN ERITREAN REFUGEE

MY LONG AND PERILOUS ESCAPE FROM AFRICA'S HERMIT KINGDOM

By Yikealo Neab

THIRTY YEARS of conflict with a powerful enemy never broke the spirit of the Eritrean people. After winning freedom from Ethiopia, a young Eritrean man dreams of starting a new life, building a home, and teaching his children what it means to be the masters of their own fate. But all too soon, the fighting resumes. Rounded up and forced into military conscription, subjected to inhumane conditions, and made to serve a despotic leader in an army fighting a war nobody wants, he will have to sacrifice much just for a chance to get back what he lost - his family, his freedom, his birthright. But will he succeed? Or will he simply lose everything in the end?

I Will Not Grow Downward offers an exceedingly rare glimpse inside the highly secretive and brutally repressive regime known as Africa's North Korea.

DREAMS OF FREEDOM

ONE FAMILY, two powerful accounts of love, heartbreak, and determination from one of the world's most isolated and tyrannical governments in modern history.

It's 1991, and a bloody thirty-year conflict with Ethiopia has ended, earning Eritrea its first taste of freedom in over a century. But peace is a flower too easily crushed. Soon, the small Horn-of-African nation finds itself in the familiar grip of a new despot— their own beloved war hero and leader. Under his rule, families still healing are torn apart anew, and suspicion and desperation grow. In the midst of deepening oppression, one man and one woman, separated by circumstances beyond their control, will risk everything to save their children from this life of violence and give them the future they once imagined for themselves.

RELENTLESS
AN IMMIGRANT STORY

ONE WOMAN'S DECADE-LONG FIGHT TO HEAL A FAMILY
TORN APART BY WAR, LIES, AND TYRANNY

Wudasie Nayzgi

with Kenneth James Howe

BRINESTONE PRESS

BRINESTONE PRESS

Cover photo credits: Depositphotos.com
Cover and interior design: Kenneth James Howe Copyright © 2018

NOTE: This is a work of memoir. All of the events in this book happened, although some dialog has been changed for purposes of clarity and brevity. Also, due to the sensitive nature of the story, the author has elected to publish under pseudonym. Therefore, selected names, dates, and identifying details have been altered to protect the privacy of the individuals involved. Otherwise, the experiences described herein have been rendered as faithfully as possible. The depictions of personal interactions are from the author's best recollection.

ISBN-13: 978-1-72-399176-9 (pbk.)

DEDICATION

I lived in a small town in Ethiopia after I graduated from college in Addis Ababa. It was hard for me to find a good place to rent, since I was new to the area. A coworker directed me to a family who were well respected by the town's residents, but they warned, "You will be lucky, if they have a vacancy."

At first, the matriarch of the family resisted my request. She warned me that they don't like noise disturbances and frequent visitors, since they were in mourning. I assured her I was looking for a quiet and safe place and would have no visitors. I knew that her reluctance arose from me being very young. I also suspected she resented my family's origins, being Eritrean. Eventually, she gave in.

I came to learn that she had recently lost her son. He was an army officer who trained pilots and had lost many of his students in the long war between the government of Ethiopia and the Eritrean freedom fighters vying for independence. Discouraged by their deaths, he decided to go to the warfront in person to find out why his students were dying in such large numbers. He never came back. His mother went into deep mourning. In accordance with tradition, she wore black rags from head to toe, slept on the floor, and confined herself to her house, detached from any social interactions.

When I heard her only son died in Eritrea, I couldn't help but feel some guilt by association.

Yet the good lady took me in as her own. She made sure I had fresh *injera* every day. I was invited to have dinner with the family and made to feel at home at all times. I was amazed how a deeply mourning mother, who lost her precious son in Eritrea, could embrace an Eritrean girl as her own. She never vented her grief in front of me or her anger at me.

After Eritrea won its independence from Ethiopia, Eritrean mothers were told about their sons and daughters who never came back home. I witnessed the same resilience in those thousands of women as in that gracious Ethiopian lady who took care of me years before. I came to realize that Mothers are the rocks and pillars of every society. Their resilience has no bounds.

Hence, I dedicate this book to all mothers who lost their children, their husbands, and their brothers and sisters in the Ethio-Eritrea War, a conflict that consumed hundreds of thousands of lives. Their resilience knows no limits.

አዴታት ኤርትራ
ንዘልኣለም ክበራ!!!

Wudasie Nayzgi
September 5, 2018

CONTENTS

CONTENTS *(cont'd)*

FOREWORD

There are pains that the body is capable of forgetting. Childbirth, for example. Or the pain of broken bones. Of poor choices and wasted opportunities. These things inevitably get erased from our memory. Life is so unavoidably full of little happenings — both joyful and otherwise — that such pains fade away to nothing in our minds. They cannot withstand the erosive effects of time. They have limited power to define us.

But then there are those pains that persist, no matter how long one lives, or how fully. They become so deeply etched beneath the skin of one's soul that they defy even the most vigorous attempts to rub them away. There is the agony of broken hearts. There are the aches of personal betrayals and stolen dreams. Some pains, no matter how hard one tries to forget them, can never be diminished, whether by the passage of time or the richness of circumstance. We learn to live with them. They become a permanent part of us.

There is a proverb in my native Tigrinya language, both warning and admonishment. It goes like this: *Haki tseraba mot keraba.* It means, if you speak the truth, you will gather many enemies. Telling the truth invites risks— sometimes even life-threatening risks. But truth is absolute, whether spoken out loud or hidden away. Like certain pains, it cannot be erased.

Our truths make us who we are. If we keep silent about them, we allow their pain to shape us. Let them free, and we free ourselves of their burden.

It is a fact that we are a guarded people. We Eritreans tend to hold our truths close to our chests for fear they will be leveraged against us. Centuries of colonial rule, of bloody wars spanning multiple generations, and betrayals by those to whom we have entrusted everything, have taught us this. Yet we are also a generous people by nature, appreciative of what we have and willing to share it with those who lack our fortunes.

How can both of these things be true? How can we be both open and closed? Every coin has two sides. Which side it shows depends on how it lands. Each toss is a gamble. Many years of struggle against our oppressors have taught us heartache and sacrifice. We know that lies never do good; they don't build, only destroy. That is one side. But the strife has also given us compassion and strength, a boundless capacity for forgiveness, and an appreciation for truth. So, we can toss the coin and wait to see which side lands up, or we can set it down with intent. The side we choose to show reflects who we are beneath our scars.

We are a people with an indelible pain. That is the truth forever etched into our souls. It is the only truth that matters. What good does it do to bury it? *Haki zeraba mot keraba* say my people. Tell the truth, and gather your enemies.

Well, I say let them come. Let them see how the pain they have inflicted has made me who I am:

Relentless.

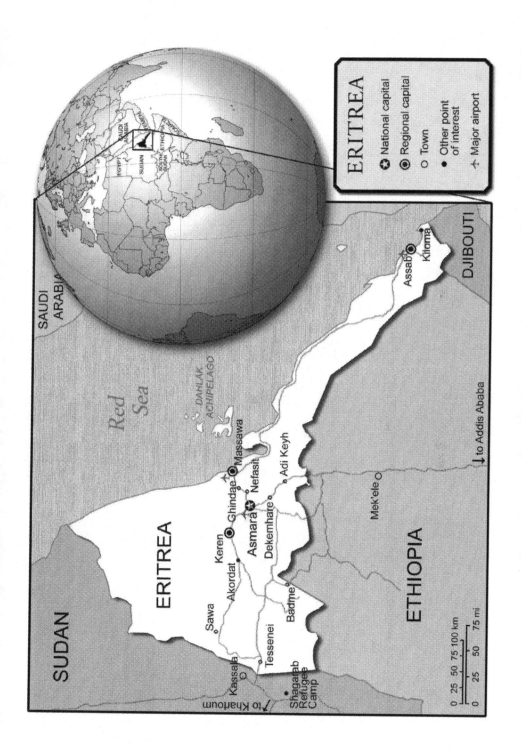

ERITREA

- ★ National capital
- ◉ Regional capital
- ○ Town
- • Other point of interest
- ✈ Major airport

SAUDI ARABIA

Red Sea

DAHLAK ARCHIPELAGO

SUDAN

ERITREA

Sawa ○

Akordat

Keren ◉

Ghindae ◉ ✈ Massawa

Asmara ★ Nefasit

Dekemhare ○ • Adi Keyh

Kassala

Tessenei

Badme ○

Shagarab Refugee Camp •

to Khartoum ✈

ETHIOPIA

Mek'ele ○

↓ to Addis Ababa

Assab ◉ ✈
Kiloma •

DJIBOUTI

0 25   50 75 100 km
0   25   50   75 mi

xiii

PART ONE
SALVATION

ANOTHER WAR

Titi's body trembles every time the animal-like growl of another explosion reaches her ears. She's only two, far too young to fully understand how truly terrifying this is, yet old enough to be scared nonetheless. To her, they are just ominous noises, like thunder, which she doesn't like, either. She only knows it's worse because of the fear she sees in my eyes whenever she looks up from the security of my lap, no matter how hard I try to hide it from her. It's all the clue she needs to be terrified.

We hadn't heeded the warplanes at first, not until the sound of the first blasts came and drummed the air about our heads like the flapping of giant wings. We heard their engines in the clouds high above, but we hadn't thought they'd come to drop their bombs on us. It has been a while since the last attack by air, and we've grown complacent from the frequent flights of our own jets taking off and landing at the military runways on the edge of the city.

"*Hush!*" I whisper, and pull my daughter's tiny shivering body tight against my side. The rumble of another explosion finds us, even here behind the mortared stone walls of the compound. The sound stays with us, as if trapped, just as we are. The sun shines high overhead, leaving only a sliver of shade for us to cower in. Dust and gravel vibrate beneath our feet. The buildings shudder and moan. "Keep still. Hush," I say, as more debris sifts down. Larger shards loosen and fall, clattering on the colorful tiles I had washed just this morning. "Don't fuss."

Another rumble.

"That sounded like it was near the airport," my neighbor says. Her voice finds its way through the electric buzz of panic in my head. "Let's hope they come no closer this way."

Titi burrows in tighter against my side and whimpers. I try to think of something happy to tell her, a story maybe, memories of a time when we didn't have to worry about such things as bombs falling and walls crumbling. But I can't seem to extract the right visions from my mind. Our peace was hard won, yet far, far too brief, ended abruptly by renewed fighting with an old enemy. The new terrors it brings make our memory of peace feel more like a dream, and we've woken up to find nothing has changed. It's a sad truth that too many years of my life have been defined by conflict and upheaval, of death, persecution, and visions of torture, so that I can't help it when these are the images that vie for attention in my mind. They're woven too deeply into the fabric of my consciousness.

For Titi, who was born into the brief interlude between wars, this horror is strange and new to her. It breaks my heart to imagine her growing up with such memories as those I thought we'd banished for good. It saddens me to know that the freedom her parents and grandparents fought to win might have been for nothing.

"It'll be over soon," I promise her. I'm talking specifically about today's airstrikes. As for the war, it will likely continue long into the foreseeable future. The last one spanned thirty years, and this new one has only just begun. The first war reluctantly gave us our freedom; the second war cruelly reminds us that it can just as easily be snatched away again.

So I hug my daughter even closer and cover her ears with shaking hands too numb to feel. I don't want her to hear the whimpers escaping my throat.

NO TRANQUILITY IN PEACE

She was born in 1996, my daughter, after a particularly difficult pregnancy left me bedridden for months. By then, five years had passed since Eritrea defeated Ethiopia, our provincial caretaker, and we gained the right to rule ourselves. In 1993, our independence became official by referendum and Isaias Afewerki, the same man who led our military to victory, became our nation's first president. We thought we'd be well on our way to becoming a fully self-realized nation by now, but after centuries of subjugation, it seems the process is far harder than we'd ever imagined.

Nevertheless, slower than expected progress is far preferable to war. For the first year and a half of my daughter's life, at least, Titi did not have to face the same struggles her parents experienced their entire lives. She was lucky enough to be born into a time of peace and possibility. The day she arrived, we fully expected her to have a long and prosperous life free from the troubles that plagued our own.

My husband, Yikealo, and I were like most of our fellow Eritreans— we still hadn't acquired many of the riches we once imagined we would have by now, although we did manage fairly well as it was. We learned that winning one's independence doesn't automatically bestow the same benefits upon its citizens that those in mature democracies enjoy every day. These things take time to establish. It's not easy for a young government to build a modern nation out of the rubble of a thirty-year war using only the discards of a century of colonial occupation.

We lived more comfortably than some, less so than others, so we had few complaints. For the first year of Titi's life, all that mattered to us was that we were steadily moving forward, improving our lot, and that our daughter was strong, healthy, and safe. We were building a home and filling it with happiness. We were blessed. Titi was meeting all of her developmental milestones. She had no health challenges to speak of. She was eating properly. We had no reason to suspect anything might be wrong.

Shortly after her first birthday in the late fall of 1997, I took her to her pediatrician's office for a regular checkup. She'd been acting lethargic and fussy, signs that I mistook as a viral infection. We were in the middle of our main rainy season, so I suspected she might have the flu.

Doctor Mehari happened to be a good friend of mine from our days living in Ethiopia, before the end of the War for Independence, so he spent extra time and care in examining Titi. For much of the visit, we engaged in the usual light banter, discussing old times, current events, and future plans. But this time, while listening to Titi's chest, his face clouded with concern. The look brought the conversation to an abrupt end.

"It's probably nothing," he told me, after he'd sent Titi out to the waiting room with a nurse so we could speak alone. "I certainly don't think you should worry about it before we have a chance to run additional tests, but you should know I heard a faint murmur in her heart."

It took me a moment to recover from the shock of those words. "I don't understand how I am not supposed to worry," I said. "Isn't that serious?"

"Not necessarily. It might just be a leaky valve. It's quite possible it could heal on its own as she grows. She's still very young, and her organs have lots of time to mature. But there's a chance it won't heal and could become more serious as she gets older. The only way to be sure is to run more tests."

I remember feeling like a boulder had landed on my chest and was crushing the air completely out of me. I couldn't move. For several seconds I couldn't speak. A thousand thoughts crowded into my mind, and none of them was good. I wanted to scream out in frustration, "How can my precious baby girl have a heart problem all of a sudden? What did I do to deserve this? What did she?" But all I could do was whisper a plea: "Can you do the tests?"

He shook his head. "Unfortunately, we don't have the proper machines here. The best I can do is send you to my colleagues at one of the hospitals in Ethiopia. I can help arrange this, if you like."

Ethiopia? I thought. *You want me to go back there now?*

I had believed that part of my life was fully behind me.

Like many Eritreans did during the war, my family had left their ancestral homeland to escape the bloodshed. It might seem illogical for a people to flee *toward* those who are oppressing them, but aside from our geopolitical differences, Eritreans and Ethiopians are more alike than not. Our cultural histories intertwine and extend back many centuries. We were both impacted by European imperialism at the first part of the Twentieth Century. Then, after the Axis powers were defeated in the Second World War, the United Nations took us out of Italy's control and handed us over to Ethiopia for caretaking. As a provincial entity of the Ethiopian Federation, we had no government of our own to speak of, although Emperor Haile Selassie promised — falsely, as it turned out — to lead us toward eventual self-governance. Ten years later, he dissolved the Federation and annexed our lands into his own. So started the long war, which survived the emperor's own ouster in 1974. It was only after his successor was himself overthrown in 1991, and we gained our freedom, that Eritreans began to move back home in large numbers. Some came willingly, eager to begin building on our victory, eager to escape second-class treatment in Ethiopia and elsewhere. Others were forced to return, pushed out by lingering resentments and distrust, as well as the political and cultural upheaval that followed Ethiopia's own rebirth.

After the war ended, the new leaders of both our countries vowed to work together. They had previously allied with each other in the rebellion to defeat Mengistu Haile Mariam, the man who had wrested power from the emperor a decade and a half earlier before becoming an even crueler autocrat in the years that followed. The relationship between our two newly formed governments continued to be highly cooperative through the time of Titi's diagnosis, at least publicly. We had a good standing relationship with Ethiopia, but it didn't mean I was eager to return to Addis Ababa, where I had grown up. I knew I'd face the same challenges I encountered growing up there.

"Just give it some thought," the doctor told me. "In the meantime, I recommend regular checkups so we can detect any changes to Titi's condition."

I went home devastated. That night and every night after that, I couldn't sleep without being tormented by terrifying visions. I spent every waking moment worrying that my tiny daughter might suddenly collapse in a faint, her weakened heart abruptly giving out from the strain. In the weeks that followed, I became overly protective. I watched her obsessively. I experienced emotional cycles of helplessness, anger, and fear that wore at me both physically and emotionally. I had a tendency to break down into tears at random moments throughout the day. My work and personal relationships began to suffer.

My first instinct was to deny the truth. I reasoned that my doctor friend had to be mistaken in his diagnosis. After all, he'd rendered it after listening to Titi's heart for a mere few minutes using nothing more sophisticated than a stethoscope. Also, if she had been born with the heart defect, and it had been present all along, then why hadn't he heard the murmur before now? He'd explained that it might have been too faint before, but I wanted to believe he'd simply misheard this time. A simple error made once seemed far more likely than repeated failures during each of his earlier exams. And given how vivacious Titi had always been — she even recovered much of her usual vitality within days of the examination — I couldn't see how she could possibly be suffering from something so potentially detrimental to her health.

It was only after my initial shock wore off that I could see how foolish I was being. I just wanted to believe my daughter was healthy and had always been so. The diagnosis forced me to confront entirely new challenges that I was poorly equipped to handle. First, there was the reality of our archaic medical system, one of many aspects of our lives that had yet to benefit from modernization. Then there was our personal financial situation. How could we afford to travel to another country, much less pay for any surgery that might be required? But perhaps the most foolish part of it all was how embarrassed I felt, as if Titi's diagnosis was somehow the result of my failure as a mother. The fact that we were in this predicament at all reflected poorly on my abilities to provide and care for my child.

It was completely illogical, but shame so consumed me that I refused to confide in anyone except my husband, Yikealo.

I eventually came to my senses and accepted that the doctor knew what he was doing. I understood then that I couldn't take any chances with my daughter's health or delay in her treatment. I still prayed the problem would disappear on its own as Titi grew, but I also decided that the proper course of action was to face it head on. I would learn everything I could about her condition and do whatever I was asked to ensure it got fixed. No expense or sacrifice would stop me.

Following the doctor's advice, I began planning Titi's medical trip to Addis Ababa to seek a more definitive medical diagnosis and a plan for treatment. Only then did the immensity of the enterprise and potential obstacles come fully to light. How would I get permission for unpaid leave from the NGO where I worked as project administrator, especially since I had no idea how much time I would need to be away? Then, how exactly would we pay for it? My salary was already a pittance, and so was my husband's from his government accounting job. And where would we stay while there? Although I grew up in the Ethiopian capital, my whole family and nearly the entire Eritrean community had returned here years ago, so I no longer had the same connections, and certainly none that would help me out for what might be an extended period of time. There were hotels to stay in, of course, but they would be far too expensive should we need to remain more than a few weeks. It would be cheaper to rent a room in a house, but who would rent to us if I couldn't even tell them how long we planned to stay? It might only be a few days; it could be months. I hoped it would be the former, but I had to be prepared for the latter.

Yikealo was very supportive throughout the entire process. When I decided we'd go to Ethiopia, he told me not to worry about the expenses, that it would all work out. "Take it one step at a time," he said. "First, we should find out which hospital will be our daughter's best option."

Meanwhile, Doctor Mehari continued to monitor Titi's heart for any changes. Thankfully, the condition didn't seem to be getting any worse, nor was it negatively affecting her development or physical activity in any obvious way. Yet despite all this, I would be lying if I said I was relieved. I just wanted it to go away.

Between our work responsibilities and caring for a very young child, it took some time to find a good hospital and required dozens of phone calls. At that time, in early 1998, the internet wasn't widely available in Eritrea, and personal cell phones were unheard of; we were still years behind everyone else in the world in regards to technology, so we had to do everything by mail and by telephone from home. It took a while to find the right hospital, but once that was settled, we began searching for accommodations.

Now we just needed to work on a way to pay for it all.

THE SHINE IS NOT SO FINE

Before our daughter's diagnosis, Yikealo and I had discussed starting our own business. Our goal was to work for ourselves and become financially independent. Now that our country was liberated, business opportunities should be limitless. At least in theory. We knew we needed to start small, and Yikealo had previously identified several "startup" options we could explore. One included taking over the lease of a small market. Running a store wasn't our long term goal, nor was it the best use of our respective university degrees. It was simply a means to an end, a stepping stone to something far greater, like owning our own retail business. Or a chain of businesses. We hadn't started on this pathway sooner because of the uncertainty in our lives, particularly as it related to our government's resistance to private enterprise. We kept postponing our plans hoping for more favorable economic and political conditions to arise; we didn't want to risk leaving our relatively stable jobs for such a chancy venture.

Titi's diagnosis forced us to reevaluate our assumptions.

While the level of risk going independent was high, so was the potential for reward. That was our thinking, and our situation had changed enough to shift the balance in favor of taking that risk. We'd need more money sooner than we expected in order to pay for Titi's medical expenses. Either we stayed in our jobs and never made enough to pay for anything beyond basic necessities — and thus never got Titi the treatment she needed to fix her heart — or we invested our meager savings now to go into business for ourselves. For better or worse, we felt like we had no other choice.

It made more sense for Yikealo to leave his job and have me stay put at the NGO where I was working as a project manager. His college degree in accounting better prepared him for operating a market, including inventory control and all of the accompanying financial aspects, than did mine. I wanted to join him in the venture, but we needed at least one reliable income just to survive. I would leave my job only after we started realizing consistent profits.

One day, just as Yikealo was starting to negotiate a transfer with a store owner, the entire staff in my office was called in for an emergency meeting. I arrived a few minutes early, and as the others trickled in and took their seats around me, I overheard them talking. We were a fairly young group of Eritreans, mostly college educated with a mix of backgrounds, but all eager to help out our country. Not surprisingly, everyone was trying to guess the reason for the unscheduled assembly. Some relished the idea that we might be awarded a large new government contract. The seasoned workers among us were more circumspect, though. *"Melkena aberena,"* they fretted, repeating a somewhat ominous adage that had grown more common in recent months. It reflected the impatience some had with the government and its glacial pace for getting things done. *"The shine is not so fine"* is the closest translation. Put another way, the national picture wasn't as rosy as we might have hoped. They worried, and rightly so, that some of our projects would be shut down.

We were used to such upheavals. A fair amount of turnover in our projects was usual, some of which could be directly attributed to the country's growing pains and the frequency with which our political leaders shifted priorities. They were still trying to figure out what was best for us and who in the international community could be relied upon as an ally. They couldn't fund every project, nor was it reasonable to do so. But it made the job hard for all of us, when we were afraid to fully commit to anything because of all the uncertainty.

At last, the head of our division arrived, the only American within our immediate group. From the moment he entered the room, I had a bad feeling this was not going to end well. He was usually upbeat, but this time he wore a grim look on his face as he passed through us toward the front. The chatter quickly quieted. Everyone was anxious to hear what he had to say. It was clear that some of us were going to be negatively impacted, maybe even let go.

"I have . . . bad news," he finally announced in English. "This comes directly from the Government Oversight Office. I'm afraid to say we've been ordered to terminate all activities. This office and all of its functions are to close. Everyone will be let go."

"What do you mean everyone?" someone shouted.

He tried to continue, but the clamor was too loud to speak over. Everyone was yelling at the same time, some in Tigrinya. There were demands for explanations, as if this was a negotiation, and they could argue their way to a compromise. Perhaps knowing the inevitable outcome, others demanded to be immediately placed with other NGOs. The director had to wave his hands at us for several minutes before he could be heard again.

"At this point, we have been given no information, nor any reasons or explanation. All we've been told is that we must follow the directives exactly as communicated to us. It's my job to ensure we comply accordingly."

"When will our last day be?" someone asked.

"The order is for immediate closure. We're to drop everything and close the office *today*."

"Today?" someone else cried. "What of our ongoing projects? We must be allowed to finish them! Our field work. What if we're expecting international visitors?"

"All activities are frozen as of today. Contact anyone you may be expecting, so they can cancel their travel plans. If you can reasonably wrap up your project in the next several hours, please do so. Otherwise, I ask that you use the time to write up your final reports, detailing your projects' current statuses and any closing instructions as much as possible. Everything will be submitted to the Oversight Office for review. No exceptions, I'm afraid. We have no choice in the matter."

He paused for a moment, clearly as frustrated about this as we were. He looked like he wanted to say something, but then thought better of it. "This is coming from the very highest levels, but without reason or explanation. I wish we could have been given more warning, but I only found out about this a few hours ago. I'm sorry. I'll be available to assist you any way I can through the end of the month, but I'll be leaving soon after."

"Leaving the country?"

He nodded, triggering a wave of alarmed glances and whispered exchanges from everyone else in the room. What could all this mean?

Nobody knew.

And so, just as my husband was preparing to leave his own government job for a risky venture, I found myself out of mine. The moment the meeting was adjourned, I called to tell him the bad news. The telephone rang several times before he answered. I prayed he hadn't taken any action yet.

Without my income, we would be totally dependent on his. Without either, we would be in serious trouble.

After I told him what happened, he replied that he hadn't made any commitments. He still had his job with the government. It was disappointing to us both that things had turned out the way they had, but there was nothing we could do about it. We'd have to delay our plans a little longer, at least until I could find a new job. I hoped it would happen quickly.

But what worried me most was the capriciousness of the government's decision, which didn't bode well for our future. After all, the programs I'd been overseeing offered opportunities and assistance to Eritrean citizens. How could taking them away possibly be good for the country?

After weeks of searching in vain for a new position for me, we decided we couldn't delay any longer getting help for Titi. Our financial situation, already tenuous, was growing weaker by the day. We couldn't afford to lose anymore ground. It was late April of 1998, nine months since the diagnosis, and I couldn't live with the constant, paralyzing fear that something would happen to my daughter. I finalized plans with the hospital in Addis Ababa and prepared to get the plane tickets and find a place to stay. We'd just have to go into debt and figure out how to pay for it later. But later never came.

On May 6th, 1998, all hell broke loose on the border. A clash between Ethiopian security posted in a tiny town called Badme and a small group of Eritreans dissatisfied with unresolved boundary disputes resulted in bloodshed. Voluntary travel between the two countries was immediately cut off. The Ethiopian government started deporting Eritrean nationals who had remained in-country or returned there in recent years, escorting them to the borders and dumping them without regard to where they originally came from, or how they were supposed to return to their families. It didn't matter if they were women. It didn't matter if they were children. As a result, many people died, were killed, or simply disappeared.

The deportations continued over the next couple of weeks, even as we prayed our leaders would find a way to avoid full scale conflict. That was a road we'd all been down before and never wanted to travel again. But these former allies seemed determined to relitigate old animosities. They continued to hurl baseless accusations at each other. Neither side was willing to compromise. These were signs that the relationship they shared, which we had always been told was strong, had long been strained for untold reasons. Their squabbling, as it would later be described, was like two old bald men fighting over something as insignificant as a comb. The outcome was that they were willing to spill blood over lands that were, for the most part, simple outposts.

I realized how lucky I had been not to have planned our trip just a few days earlier. We would have ended up dumped in some remote corner of the country with no way to get back to Asmara, and all the money we spent would be lost. *God is good*, I reminded myself. *He watches over us. He saved us from this disaster.*

But as good as God might be, as much as my faith taught me patience and forgiveness, I found myself deeply angry. I'd lost my job, and now I had lost a chance to help my daughter, all because our president had apparently forgotten why we'd fought the last war.

Please God, I prayed each day. *Help him come to his senses soon. And Ethiopia, too.*

I tried to give both leaders the benefit of the doubt. I held my breath and hoped. But less than a month later, Ethiopia's warplanes began threatening Asmara.

WE HAVE BEEN HERE BEFORE

It was clear the two old bald men, Eritrea's Isaias Afewerki and Ethiopia's Meles Zenawi, had gone completely mad.

They'd once shared a common goal — to overthrow Mengistu Haile Mariam's brutal military regime known as the Derg. Now, just a few short years after succeeding in this, they'd turned on each other. Just as it had in the past, the Ethiopian army marched into Eritrea, and we had no choice but to defend ourselves. All I wanted was to protect my daughter from a heart defect that jeopardized her life. Instead, I found myself having to protect her from bombs that jeopardized everyone's.

The ground fighting hadn't yet reached us in Asmara, but if the past taught us anything, it was bound to happen, sooner rather than later. We weren't invulnerable. The killing had already found its way into our homes through our televisions and radios. We were bombarded constantly with images of the dead and wounded. The radio reported which villages were destroyed and listed some of the thousands of casualties by name. At least in the beginning. Then they stopped. It was ruining morale. Unlike before, this was a war nobody wanted.

Without a job to channel my pent-up anxieties, I spent my days at home with Titi, trying to keep myself distracted from the news, protecting us both from the horrors taking place elsewhere in the country. But as much as I tried to shut it out, with the status of the fighting changing on an almost hourly basis, it was impossible not to become obsessed with it. Even when I shut the television off, the neighbors' broadcasts cut through the walls, echoing through the compound, delivering a constant stream of increasingly dire updates:

Here is a new front in the fight, where the enemy is now advancing! They try to break through the defensive lines of our brave army! But our heroic soldiers push them back! They will not yield! They will always defend our homeland!

The news was carefully packaged and delivered in such a way to inspire patriotic thoughts and support for the fight, but there was nothing encouraging in the images of Ethiopian soldiers' torn and bloodied bodies left abandoned in the trenches and on the fields. We could just as easily imagine that they were our own.

On the afternoon of the raid on our Air Force Headquarters, it was the distant explosion that first drew me outside. Our neighborhood is usually very quiet, but in that moment the skies overhead were torn apart by the scream of the jet engines. Several of my neighbors were already on the street, searching the skies. This is what we do now, run out into the streets rather than hide. There is nothing else we can do except confront our fears head on. Young or old, every face around me held some variety of anger or wonder. Everyone was shouting at each other and at the skies.

How many more planes are there?

Where did the first one go?

It came from that direction and went over there.

No, it went in another direction.

Was it a bomb or a crash? Oh Lord, do they mean to destroy us all this time around?

What are we supposed to do?

What can we do? They are going to pour fire on our heads!

Where can we go to be safe?

Nowhere! They are dropping bombs on us, not rain!

I saw some young men standing on nearby roofs. One of them pointed toward the south and shouted, "There! Something's burning in that direction!"

Within moments, a column of black smoke coiled into the air a few kilometers away. Seeing it sent new waves of fear through us. A group of elderly women huddled together wringing their hands. They started praying out loud, begging the Lord for mercy. Some wept openly. Teenage boys ran in the direction of the fire, ignoring our cries for them to stop.

The lack of information was killing me. *Is the attack over?* I wondered. *Are they sending more planes?* I wanted to go and see for myself what was happening, but running towards trouble was the worst thing I could do as a mother, especially with a young child strapped onto my back. But I needed answers: Was anyone hurt? And what of Yikealo? Was my husband safe? On the other hand, I didn't want to go inside, either. If the planes decided to return with more bombs, then the house's thin walls were no protection at all.

In the end, getting off the street, away from the increasingly maddened crowds, was the only thing that made any sense, at least for me and my daughter. So when my elderly neighbor suggested that Titi and I join her, we followed.

She lives by herself in the same compound, my neighbor, and yet we barely know each other. Still, I can tell by the relief on her face she's as grateful for our company as I am. "We've been here before," she says in a hushed tone, as if speaking too loudly will guide the bombs straight to us. "Many times, and we survived. We'll survive this time, too."

She sounds like she's trying to convince herself. I just nod my head in agreement.

Titi eventually falls asleep on my lap, so we continue consoling each other in whispers. The talking provides release. Eventually, the sirens fade into silence. However, this proves to be just as unnerving for my neighbor. She gets up to turn on her TV, setting the volume as loud as it can go. It takes a while before the state news reporters are able to offer up any details.

As expected, the headquarters of our Air Force was the target of the attack, but the extent of the damage is being withheld from the public, probably to keep people from panicking. We also learn that our own jets, undamaged by Ethiopia's bombs, retaliated as soon as our pilots could get them into the air. The sounds we heard after the initial explosions were our own planes heading for Ethiopia, less than a hundred kilometers away. This explains the confusion about which way the planes were heading. The secondary explosions were gas tanks caught in the fire ignited in the initial attack. We don't know what to feel when the reporter announces the Ethiopian jets that dropped the bombs have been destroyed. We want to celebrate, but we fear it will only fuel more retaliatory strikes and escalate the fighting even further.

Yikealo returns home very late that evening, and it's only then that I begin to learn the full extent of the damage at the airbase. It seems that the headquarters building suffered a direct hit and several soldiers were killed. Many more were injured. "We went to see as soon as we could get there," he tells me.

"You might have been killed."

"The attack was already over by then, and our jets were on their way to deliver our own bombs."

Just as feared, the fighting gets much worse in the days that follow. For now, it remains concentrated nearer to the border, but Asmara is not that far away. Plus, there's the constant fear of another air attack at any moment. How does one survive like this? How do we carry on living?

Somehow we manage. The needs of daily life are too great to ignore for long. We have to eat, sleep, work. There is always shopping to do, appointments to keep. The routine forces us to push past our terrors.

Until the next bombs drop.

The attack comes on a day I leave my daughter at home with my mother for a trip into downtown Asmara. This time I'm much closer to the chaos when it breaks out. Public transportation is completely disrupted, leaving me stranded. It takes me several hours just to make my way through the crowded streets back to my mother's house.

When I go inside, I find Titi curled up and asleep on her grandmother's lap. She's wrapped up tight in a blanket. As if she senses my presence, she opens her eyes and immediately wrestles her way free so she can run over to me. I sweep her up in my arms. I can feel her sobs of fright.

"She started screaming the moment she heard the first explosion," my mother tells me. "I couldn't calm her down. She kept saying she needed you. I tried to tell her you'd come back soon, but she didn't want you soon, she wanted you now. 'Mom will put me on her back and keep me safe,' she kept saying. I tried to calm her down. I told her I can carry her like that, too, but she only wanted you."

After the first attack, I'd gotten into the habit of carrying Titi on my back whenever we heard the jets flying overhead. I would secure her with a length of cloth tied about my waist, leaving my arms free in case we needed to run to safety. It was usually just our own planes in the skies, but she had

22

come to associate the noise with the security offered by such close physical contact.

When I realize how scared she'd been, I collapse to the floor in tears. She must have felt like I'd abandoned her. I should have been here for her, instead of far away and in a place where I couldn't immediately get back. She sees me crying and tries to comfort me. She lifts her hand and wipes the tears from my cheeks with her tiny fingers. "It's okay, Mom. The noise is gone now. The shaking noise is gone."

I want to give her the same assurances, but I can't. I know the shaking noise will return, and it fills me with such sadness and desperation. I feel so helpless. It's a cruel reminder of how inadequate my attempts have been to protect her.

REFUGEES IN OUR OWN LAND

We are a country on the move.

Once, I would have gladly shouted this in the streets, but all our progress has stalled. Now, the kind of moving that defines us isn't the kind of movement that advances us. As the fighting explodes along our thousand-kilometer border with Ethiopia, the government issues panicked evacuations, but no plan for managing them. Schools are abruptly shuttered, businesses locked up. Entire farming communities are emptied. People take what personal possessions they can hand carry and leave the rest behind. Abandoned lands and animals fall victim to the chaos and violence. It's a disaster, yet the government is too preoccupied by the war effort to do anything about it. Few people own motorized vehicles, so their easiest option is to take public transportation, but there aren't enough buses to carry so many people at once. The majority must flee on foot.

They come north in waves, clogging the roads, arriving in Asmara in hopes of finding refuge with relatives and extended families. Those who don't have such connections here continue onward, trying to get as far away from the front as possible. Here in the capital city, I see them arrive by the hundreds each day. Most of them are women and children and elderly men who can't stay behind to fight. Those who do remain are absorbed into our army, whether willingly or not.

Eritrea is shaped like a funnel with a long stem whose narrow opening is tilted toward the southeast. Asmara is nestled slightly above the part where the stem meets the cone. From here, it's only about eighty kilometers due south to the border. The news coverage on the television shows us roads lined with thousands of refugees. Many leave with only the clothes they wear and plastic jugs of water in their hands or strapped to wooden staffs carried over shoulders. Children ride their parents' backs, or hand drawn carts, or the backs of cows and donkeys. They're weary, bloody, dirty, and hungry. Many have been walking for days. Some die along the way. Escaping death doesn't mean they are safe. Their homes may be looted and burned. Women and children are assaulted. Some disappear altogether.

A soldier passing through tells me how he and his unit stopped in a small abandoned town and entered a house after hearing the sound of a crying baby. There, they found a woman who had just given birth. No one but her own frail mother had been around to help. The husband had already been conscripted; the rest had gone on ahead. The soldiers helped clean up the baby, then loaded the three of them up in their army vehicle and took them to a safer place, a camp somewhere to the north of Asmara.

The United Nations is actively trying to construct a peace agreement that both our countries can agree to, but it's an excruciatingly slow process. Too many people die while we wait for the politicians to quibble over details. Too many people are uprooted. The cruel irony is that this is all happening just as we were starting to make headway towards achieving our nationalistic goals.

One day, the regional head of the NGO where I once worked, a European gentleman, contacts me over the phone. He says he's coming to Asmara to assess the refugee situation and wants to help organize an international relief effort. "Are you available to assist me?" he asks, and quickly adds that a colleague referred me to him. "I need help making local arrangements— a car, hotel, meals." I hate the idea of leaving Titi alone again, but I need to do something to help the exploding refugee situation. Thousands of my people have been uprooted and are in desperate need of assistance. Our government has proven we can't rely on it to take responsibility.

I meet him shortly after he arrives, and he introduces himself as Henrik. He tells me based on the reports he's been getting that he expected to see a flood of refugees filling the streets of the capital. "But from what I've seen, the city looks almost deserted. Where is everyone?" I imagine he expected to find children sleeping in the gutters and begging for food.

"They are here," I tell him. "Those who stay have family or find shelter with friends."

"But there must be more than this. I've heard of thousands coming here. Tens of thousands. You can't house that many. Where are the rest?"

"They're traveling further north to get as far from the fighting as possible," I respond.

"But Ethiopian forces are pushing south from the Sudanese border, too."

This is alarming news to me. Where will the refugees go if Ethiopia pushes them back? They will have us in a vise, squeezing us from above and below. Will they attack Asmara next and kill us all?

The next day we drive north to see where the refugees might be going. We arrive at a temporary settlement after a couple hours, and it's only then that the scale of our national disaster hits us both. Even though Henrik had come expecting to find this, it still shocks him to his core. And I had no idea it was this bad. The sight that greets us is beyond anything either of us could have imagined. The settlement stretches far over the dry scrubland, over the adjacent hills and out of sight. Here is the sea of humanity my guest had been expecting to find in Asmara, the mass of people displaced from the south *and* the north. His face loses color as he surveys the scene.

There's very little protection from the elements here, not from the sun or the dry winds, not from the swarms of insects. There are barely any shelters. There's no privacy, only makeshift tents made from blankets and clothing draped over poles and tied into place with twine. The refugees cram themselves into whatever shade they can find, as if they'd come and simply dropped everything in the first place there was room. As I walk among them, their eyes turn toward us, some hopeful, others devoid of all emotion. A few children are in a nearby clearing, but their play seems halfhearted. Women cook on open fire pits. People sleep out in the open on the bare ground. Whole families sit in shocked silence, still unable to understand how this could have happened to them.

My heart breaks to see them, to see how dirty and threadbare their clothes are. *This can't be*, I think. *This should be the time for learning, for being in school singing and reading.* They should be at home, safe, sleeping in their own beds, eating their own food, harvested from their own gardens. Instead, they have traveled all this way with almost nothing, no plan, and no idea when they'll be able to return.

If they ever do.

It's strangely quiet for a place with so many people crammed into it. Fear, shock, and despair rob them of their voices. Even their anger has been stolen away, leaving them lost and bewildered.

We find the government aid workers situated near the center of the encampment. A small platform has been set up, and stacks of supplies, mostly sacks of flour and cans of cooking oil, are located nearby. It looks like a lot, until you consider how many people they need to feed. And with so many more arriving each day, I can only see how their hardship will worsen. The aid workers distribute the food and cooking utensils on a set schedule. Beyond this, we learn there's very little support for other basic human needs, no sanitary facilities, no hospital, no security. Water is drawn directly from a nearby river. No one is making sure sewage doesn't flow in and contaminate it. Without someone to take charge and oversee things, I fear this place will quickly devolve into a humanitarian disaster.

One of the aid workers comes up to us and addresses my guest. He assumes Henrik must be someone important, since he's the only white person around. After finding out why we've come, the worker pulls him away to strategize. Left on my own, I wander a little ways into the camp, away from the protective circle of aid workers. I want to talk to these people, but I'm too overwhelmed to start a conversation.

To my relief, Henrik returns not too long after. "They took me to see a new mother who delivered a baby here," he says in a subdued voice. His face is still very pale, dripping sweat. Yellowish red dust smears one cheek. "It was right out in the open, beneath a tree, nothing but a bed sheet underneath her for protection. No medical care." He sits down on the ground on the spot where he's standing and cradles his head in his hands. I don't know if he's going to break down. "I think you should go see her," he whispers, although he doesn't say why. Maybe he doesn't think I believe him.

But I can't make myself go. I'm not sure I would be able to keep my composure. Besides, it's tradition to bring a new mother and her newborn child some kind of gift. Once the family is ready to receive visitors, neighbors will usually arrive with all sorts of goodies to celebrate the birth and assist the new mother as she recovers. The guests take over the household chores for several days.

But here, everything is turned upside down. There are no chores to take on, and no gifts to offer.

"She's not the only one," Henrik says, still not looking up. "They tell me there are dozens of pregnant mothers here. To give birth under such harsh conditions," he says, his voice fading. "How . . . ?" He shakes his head again, but it doesn't seem to help. "What if there are complications?"

He looks up at me, as if he expects me to have an answer. I don't. I'm just as helpless as he is. And the worst part about it is, this isn't the only refugee camp in the country. Common sense says it can't be. And I doubt it's even the largest. There must be dozens more, each of them filled with people in as much need as this, starving, unprotected, sick, pregnant . . . and without hope.

A few dozen bags of wheat and crates of cooking oil aren't going to save them.

GOD'S CHILDREN

Despite the hardships, Yikealo and I strive to carry on with our lives as much as possible. We learned how to do it during the last war with Ethiopia. We have to expect that this war might drag on just as long. We hope it won't.

We're not alone in trying to make the best of a bad situation. Everyone here in the capital is operating on the slim chance the war could end tomorrow, rather than watching and waiting for what we know is more likely to happen, that it will last for years. Businesses continue to operate, although in a far more limited way. Children keep going to school. Hospitals treat the sick and deliver babies. People get married. Funerals are arranged. All while knowing everything could change the very next moment. Or not at all. It's a strange sort of feeling, hoping for the best, yet always expecting to wake up the next morning to find the situation is still the same. Or worse.

The stream of refugees passing through and around Asmara continues, but for now it's not getting any worse. As the government tries once again to negotiate a mutually acceptable resolution to the border conflict, the fighting wanes, and the stream begins to slow until it reaches a trickle. These are all positive signs. The lull nurtures our hope.

With the extra time I have on my hands not working, I decide to resume my studies in business management through correspondence courses offered by a major inter-national company still operating here in Eritrea. I prefer it to waiting around for better times. Soon I'll have to sit for the final examination, which has to be coordinated with other students in the area, mainly company-sponsored employees, since it requires someone coming from the corporate headquarters to administer it. They'll only come if there are sufficient numbers of students ready to test, and only when it's safe to do so.

Then, out of the blue, I'm offered a position as a project coordinator at an agency overseeing the import and export of commercial products. It's not the ideal job for me; however, I accept the position because we badly need the money. The hospital in Addis Ababa is clearly out of the question now because of the war, so we've been considering the option of taking Titi to a different country altogether, which will require even more money than we had originally planned. As much as I hate leaving her behind at home with her grandmother every day so I can work, her physical health is my greatest concern right now, more so than my own emotional wellbeing.

In rapid succession, there are two additional changes of great import to our lives. The first has been carefully considered: Now that I'm working again, we decide it's time for Yikealo to leave his job and resurrect our plans for starting our own little business. He had recently been moved into a different role within the government, but with so much uncertainty regarding our nation's international partner- ships, particularly with foreign businesses, he doesn't believe his job will be around for very long. He negotiates to lease a building close to our house for the market, and he spends the next few weeks preparing to open it. Each day he rises out of bed before the sun comes up. And after spending all day cleaning and repairing, painting, inventorying supplies, and ordering and stocking shelves, he returns long after darkness has settled over us again.

The second event is also not entirely unexpected, although it still comes as a surprise when it happens: I find out I'm pregnant.

I come from a large family, and have always been very close with my siblings, so it was my dream growing up to have as many children of my own as possible. My husband, who also grew up in a large family, shares this dream. In fact, most Eritreans for as many generations as we know have wanted this dream for themselves. In this part of the world, where life is precious and children are blessings from God, large families have traditionally been valued as much as material wealth.

My poor aunt only has three children.

My mother raised twelve kids.

I'm one of seven.

I have ten.

These were typical adult comments I overheard as a child whenever the subject of family size came up. In fact, I've never heard a married couple choosing not to bear any children at all. Socially and culturally, the idea of a childless marriage simply has no meaning to us. Who will take care of us when we're too old to care for ourselves? Who will carry on our values and lineage after we're gone? Children are so important to us that a partner's inability to reproduce is an acceptable justification for divorce.

But circumstances change with the times, and with such changes our values evolve. Or, if not our values, then at least our priorities. And our pragmatism. For my generation, the generation that came into adulthood as its nation transitioned from oppression to opportunity, the generation that migrated from the farms to the cities in hopes of ushering our new country into the modern world, larger families can be more hindrance than blessing. Liberation has given us opportunities our parents didn't have. And responsibilities. We spend more time away from our homes working in jobs that didn't exist a generation earlier. We're more reliant on our incomes to support us, rather than our ability to grow our own food and manufacture our own possessions. Our young country has taken the place of our children. We are its caretakers, and everything we do is for its development and growth. Nowadays, it's not uncommon to see parents my age willing to stop after having only two or three children.

At least here in Asmara.

This, of course, has made our parents unhappy. "Modern women are selfish," my mother-in-law once told me, when I announced we weren't planning to have as many children as we possibly could. "They choose not to have babies. In the past, we welcomed babies into the world as often as we could. We kept having them until they stopped coming." This generational gap has become a source of tension in some families. In the minds of some old fashioned parents, it's the responsibility of a good wife to bear as many children as she can. It's a part of Eritrean culture.

I'll never forget a pair of conversations I had on the subject soon after I finished college in Addis Ababa and had struck out on my own. A man came into my office at the NGO seeking financial assistance. I didn't know him; he was a new client and a complete stranger to me. All I knew from his application was that he had no formal education and worked as a driver.

While I reviewed his case, he asked me if I was married yet. I knew he was just trying to make small talk, but for some reason I found the question intrusive. "No," I replied honestly, although perhaps a bit more sharply than I intended. I'd noticed from his file that he was Muslim and came from a tribe known for marrying out their girls at a very young age. So, culturally, he would place high importance on large families with many children from multiple wives. As a Christian woman in my early twenties, college educated, and still single and childless, I held beliefs that differed widely from his. Although, at that time, I still planned on marrying and having a large family someday, I wasn't ready to settle down just yet. I was an independent spirit, fairly comfortable pushing back against my parents' customs if they seemed outdated. But I also respected tradition. I knew it wasn't wise to break away from it on the merest whim. Because these particular notions remained unresolved in my mind, I was uncomfortable discussing them with a stranger, especially one whose values were different from my own.

"You should be married by now," he said, dismissing my brusqueness with a click of his tongue. "An unmarried woman is like a naked girl in the middle of a crowd. Everyone sees her and tries to grab her and take her for their own. Some wish to protect her; some have other ideas. But a married woman is covered and protected, and everyone knows and treats her with respect. You are not protected."

His brazen assessment of my situation left me speechless. How dare he assume he knew me? I was not vulnerable! Later, however, after I had a chance to calm down and think about what he was saying, I realized how much it actually made sense. An unwed woman draws the attention of many men, and it isn't until one of them marries her that the others lose interest. In a sense, marriage becomes like her clothing. It protects her. It was his way of reminding me that there is value in some traditions, and that flaunting them isn't always wise.

Of course, it didn't prompt me to go out looking for a husband right away. I still wasn't ready to settle down and raise a family. I enjoyed the newfound freedom of my life — as much freedom as I was allowed at the time, anyway — and I enjoyed my work and the company of my colleagues. I didn't want to think about the responsibilities of a husband and raising a family just yet.

Soon after that, another man with a similar background came into my office for a similar reason, to seek financial assistance. He too asked me if I was married. This time I was prepared. *Aha!* I thought. *I won't give him the chance to lecture me.* "Yes," I lied, "I'm married."

"Do you have children?"

"Yes, I have six already," I said, hoping it would be enough to end the conversation there and then. Anyone could easily see that I was far too young to have so many children, but he apparently didn't think it so unlikely.

"That is not bad," he said, nodding approvingly. "You only have six more to go."

"What?" I exclaimed, before I could stop myself. "How am I supposed to feed twelve children?" Did he really think having and raising such a large family in this day and age was easy or practical? When would I ever be able to work and earn enough money with so many children?

"You feed them meat one day and *shiro* the next," he explained.

Shiro is a sort of protein-rich mash made of chickpeas or fava beans. It's served with our traditional flatbread, *injera*. Because it's an inexpensive meal to prepare, we eat it when we don't have enough money to buy meat.

"Sorry," I snapped, "but in our household we eat *shiro* every day! We can't afford to eat meat, not even every other day."

I hoped my outburst would discourage him from continuing this line of discussion, but it didn't. "Then you eat *shiro* one day and nothing the next," he fired back.

I didn't know how to respond to this. I thought he must be out of his mind to lecture me, of all people. I had gone to college. I'd learned to think independently. I had been taught how to plan for the future, one that was starting to look nothing like the times our parents had lived. I was making thoughtful, mature decisions! Who was he to suggest I should just throw caution to the wind and have children, if I couldn't feed them enough food every day?

He pointed at the cabinets lining my office walls. "You see them?" he said. "You have files for everyone. You write in there how to provide for them. In the same way Allah has files, one for each of his children, born and unborn. The difference is, He has already determined how to provide for them before they even come to you. In His plan, He has written everything down, so it's not for you to worry about such details. Allah knows beforehand when each child will come into this world and when it will exit. It's not your decision whether or not to bear them. Your job is to simply welcome them when they arrive."

Once again, I had to give up. How could I argue against this form of logic, especially since my own faith claimed very similar assertions? God — or Allah — is the author of all life. It's something I've always known and had reaffirmed to me many times, both before that day and since. But perhaps more importantly, I've also learned not to worry so much about what other people think regarding my personal decisions, whether it's a stranger or a disapproving mother-in-law.

After Titi turned two, my husband and I began to talk about whether we could — and should — have more children. The end of the old war had changed everything for Eritrea, but so did the start of the new one. We knew it wasn't an ideal time to bring babies into the world, not when planes were dropping bombs on our heads, food and other supplies were becoming scarce, and so many other people were having difficulty just surviving. On the other hand, we also knew for a fact that wars eventually end and the survivors go on. This was something our parents could only surmise, yet it didn't discourage them from having babies themselves. If my generation decided to wait for the perfect conditions, we might lose our chance for good, and there might not be a next generation to build upon the foundations we were laying. Also, neither Yikealo nor I wanted our daughter to be an only child. Titi was already showing signs of loneliness, even at such a young age. I'd seen her talking to herself or to her dolls, as if they were her real playmates. If times were different, if our circumstances were different, I would happily give her a dozen siblings to play with, to care for, to share her life with. We reasoned it would be a fair compromise to ourselves and to her to give her one.

I think about what that man told me years before, when I was still unmarried, about how we shouldn't worry how many children to have or when to have them, only how we will welcome them into the world. We leave the rest in God's hands. This was our thinking as well. We wanted another child. Still, a pregnancy is a very sobering thing to face, even in the best of times.

But, as the old man also said, we can't worry about that. We must simply prepare to welcome our children when they arrive. And leave the uncertainty for God to sort out afterwards.

YOU ARE STRONGER THAN YOU REALIZE

One morning in May, halfway through my second pregnancy, my husband rises before dawn for a meeting with some people he hopes will help us grow our little business. The general store is less profitable than we need it to be, so we've been looking for other opportunities to expand. This meeting could significantly help us achieve more of our goals.

I lie awake as Yikealo dresses quietly in the dark and gathers his papers. Then he's gone, and the silence swoops in again, lulling me back to sleep. The meeting will take place in Massawa, a city a few hours away by bus on the coast of the Red Sea. I don't expect him back until late in the afternoon or evening.

Another hour passes, and I have to force myself to get out of bed. It's becoming harder by the day, as this pregnancy is turning out to be much more difficult than the first one was, and I still have four more months to go before the baby is due. By now, I've completed my coursework and taken the exam, so all I have to worry about is my job. I fight back the exhaustion that takes hold of me and prepare myself for the day. I fantasize about the day I can quit work to deliver the baby, but it's still a long way off, and far too many people depend on my income right now. Thankfully, I've been through this ordeal before, so I know this particular hardship will pass.

* * *

I haven't been able to sit for long periods of time, at least not since my correspondence studies ended. Sitting was all I did for them, it seemed. Work gives me ample excuses to get up and walk around as I need to collaborate with others or find files stored elsewhere, whereas my coursework entailed extended periods of sitting and immersing myself in my books. I'd inevitably lose track of the time, then suddenly realize I needed to get to bed, as I'd have to get up for work in a few hours. Standing up after sitting for so long wasn't easy. My back would be so stiff that I'd sometimes cry out in pain.

When it came time to take the exam, a proctor was called in from England to administer it. English is one of our country's three official languages, although it's used primarily for professional interactions. Tigrinya or Arabic, the other two languages, are spoken at home and in everyday conversation. Some cf the elder generation still speak Italian, a holdover from our days of colonial rule. We learn English in grade school, and our subjects thereafter are taught in English.

There were about twenty of us sitting for the test, which was given in a room at a local office complex. My belly was so large by then that I couldn't squeeze myself behind the tiny desk, so I had to sit at the proctor's table facing the other students. The exam took nearly six hours, and as the time passed the discomfort in my back grew worse until I was bent over nearly double in pain. It wasn't my only distraction. In fact, it seemed like every little noise, every cough and sniffle, every creak of a chair and click of the clock on the wall, conspired to break my concentration. Which is why the scattered gunfire sounding throughout the city was especially nerve wracking to me that day.

It had become a fairly common occurrence, although rarely was it of any consequence. We'd all learned to tune it out. Even our British proctor seemed unconcerned about it, despite pointing out the emergency exits and reviewing the evacuation plan earlier. We were on the seventh floor of a tall building, not at ground level. The chances of something happening to us so far off the street were nearly zero. When everyone was ready, he planted himself at the front of the room beside me with his arms crossed over his chest and instructed us to begin.

Each time the muffled *pop pop* sounds reached my ears, I would jump in surprise and lift my head to glance about the room. The proctor never reacted. Sometimes I'd glance over to the door, half expecting to see it suddenly burst open and men rush in carrying firearms. Logically, I knew there was no immediate danger to us. Once or twice, I caught the eye of another student, who'd quickly return their attention to their test. Maybe it was hormones keeping me so on edge. Or my physical discomfort. Perhaps it was the worry over how this second pregnancy might mirror the first that caused me to feel particularly vulnerable or protective that day, but I was certain the gunshots would grow louder, closer, and more frequent. They didn't.

Still, I was spending far too much time contemplating anything but the exam. I'd imagine scenarios where we were forced to evacuate. It would take me a long time to drag my overburdened body out of my seat and across the room to the exit. How would I make it down the hall and the stairway without collapsing in fatigue or pain? Would the others panic and leave me behind in the chaos? Would they trample me?

I was so worn out at the end of the test that I actually stopped caring about anything, including whether I passed or not. As for the gunshots, they continued to echo over the city, but I no longer heeded them, either. For all I cared, the violence could have followed me home on my heels, and it wouldn't have made any difference. I just wanted to get back to my house, fall into my bed, and go to sleep.

The results arrived a couple weeks after the examination. I had recovered from that ordeal by then, so it was an immense relief to see that I did, in fact, pass. A fellow student called to congratulate me. "I failed," she lamented. She, too, was pregnant, although nowhere near as far along as I was. "I'm not very proud of myself right now."

The next call came from the course coordinator, who invited me to the ceremony where our certificates would be presented. She mentioned that the current batch of students, mainly employees sponsored by their companies, would also be in attendance, and she thought my story would help inspire them to try their best. It seemed that far too many of the test-takers had failed, much to her disappointment, despite having no other excuse.

I told her I didn't think I could make it.

"Why not?"

"I would rather not be in front of people in my present condition."

She refused to accept that. "It's important for the other students to see you, honey," she said. "We want to make the point that there is absolutely no reason for anyone not to pass the course, especially once they see what you endured just to be there. It will encourage them to try harder."

"I'm not sure I have the strength."

"Nonsense. You're stronger than you realize, Wudasie. Your scores prove it."

* * *

The sun is barely up when I leave the house for work, yet already the air is on the warm side of comfortable, and it'll only get hotter as the day progresses. The heat makes everything harder for me in my condition. Now, more than ever, I just want to lie down and not move a muscle. But I can't take a day off from work this early in my pregnancy. We need the money. I know I'll have to leave my job at some point to deliver the baby. I wish it could be today. On the other hand, I pray I last longer than I did for my first pregnancy, when my doctor ordered me on bed rest for the final four months. We wouldn't be able to afford to lose that much income, and it would put far too much strain on Yikealo, perhaps prompting him to take on more responsibility and risk than advisable.

As I wait for the bus, I give a silent prayer to the saints for good news from Yikealo's meeting later in the day. If he's successful and convinces these people to work with him, I won't have to worry about making it another four months.

The morning passes uneventfully. During lunch, I try to rest with my feet up to ease the swelling in my ankles. We live in a fairly temperate climate, and air conditioning is not common, but on this day I wish we had it. I fan myself with a sheaf of papers and try to eat a little to keep up my strength. The constant heartburn and nausea keep me from being hungry. I drink as much water as I can tolerate to stay hydrated, but it means more frequent trips to the bathroom, and even short walks wear me out.

My first appointment of the afternoon arrives late, and when he shows up his face is red. "*Ay ay ay!*" he complains, apologizing for his tardiness. He wipes at the sweat running down his cheeks and neck and into his collar. "It's impossible to get anywhere in the city right now."

"What do you mean?"

"Security officials, soldiers. They're all over the place, rounding up people off the streets. They're taking everyone."

"Everyone?" A chill settles over me.

He nods. "No one is spared."

After our independence, we had no real army; our focus was on rebuilding, not defense. Many of the former freedom fighters — *tegadelti* — assumed leadership positions within the government. Some took more junior roles. The rest went home. So the Eritrean National Service was established, a compulsory service program intended to ensure certain civil projects would be fulfilled, while also maintaining a sort of readiness force in case of hostilities. ENS instruction includes six months of intensive basic military training, after which service members are assigned to a unit, most often in the army, regardless of whether their job is entirely in the area of civil development or not. Our Constitution, which was ratified in May 1997, but never implemented before the second war started, stipulates that everyone under the age of forty is required to serve, both males and unmarried females, and you're supposed to report voluntarily, although few do. The most common reason they don't is family obligations, especially since the War for Independence left so many in need of assistance and too few to care for them. Also, the pay is terrible, and the work is frequently menial and physically taxing. Most new service members end up being recent high school graduates and students taken to finish up their final year of education. The service length is supposed to be eighteen months, but all conscriptions have become open-ended due to the fighting.

With so many lives once more being lost, the army has been working harder to fill its rolls, forcing more people to fight, most against their will. Government officials have taken to sweeping through the cities and rounding up anyone they can in order to meet the army's ever-burgeoning needs. The practice, which we call *giffa*, is largely the same as what happened during Ethiopian rule before we won independence. The emperor, Haile Selassie, and his successor, President Mengistu Haile Mariam, would send their soldiers to kidnap our youth off the streets, force them into Ethiopian uniform, and brainwash them to fight against their own people. That the roundups are now being conducted by our own government is a bitter betrayal of all our country fought to abolish.

Anyone deemed physically capable of fighting is sent straight into military training, usually at the camp in Sawa, a large installation west of Asmara and near the border with Sudan. There has been a lot of public outcry against the *giffa*, as well as the training methods they use at the camps, yet both practices continue to grow. It's not uncommon for soldiers to suddenly appear at random places where people congregate and load their buses with new conscripts.

A surge of panic passes through me when I hear the man's complaint. My thoughts go immediately to my husband. He'll be forty years old soon, the upper age limit for conscription, so we've been especially careful to avoid going places where he could be swept up in one of the roundups. But then I remember that he left town on a bus very early this morning to meet with potential business partners in Massawa, so I'm almost certain he would have gotten out of Asmara before they started detaining people. However, I won't know for sure until he gets back home late in the afternoon or early evening. If the government would lift its restrictions on personal cell phones, I'd be able to call and warn him. And since he hadn't planned on calling until after his meeting in

Massawa, at the very earliest, I'll just have to pray he remains safe until I hear from him.

As the afternoon wears on, more clients confirm that the roundups are still happening and, in fact, have spread to neighboring towns and all the major roads into and out of them. Now I worry about my husband being caught on his return trip from the coast. Hopefully, he'll hear about the *giffa* and decide to stay put where he is.

These distractions keep me from getting much of anything done the rest of the day. In fact, anxiety spreads throughout the entire office. At the very least, we worry this new development means we're losing the war. At worst, we fear for our loved ones and hope to find them safe when we get home.

Making my way to my own house at the end of the day, I try to be as careful as possible. Even though I'm exempt from conscription, it doesn't mean I won't be stopped and challenged, even in my current physical state. We've all heard stories about the roundups, about how long the soldiers detain people and how poorly they're treated. I don't want to take any risks with the baby. Being made to wait by the side of the road in the sun for any length of time wouldn't be good for either of us. So I avoid large groups of people and take side streets whenever I can. I watch for soldiers. I'm wary of trucks and buses.

The *giffa* brings back memories of my youth in Addis Ababa, when we would watch for soldiers coming through our neighborhoods and sweeping people up. Sometimes their targets were young men, which they'd indoctrinate to resist Eritrean fighters and Ethiopian rebels. Sometimes it would be Eritreans with suspected ties to those same resistance fighters. My uncle was taken from his home and imprisoned for ten years. He was regularly tortured. For a while, our family was targeted simply because of our connection to him. That our own young government has adopted the same tactics to fight against the country that once employed them against us is worse than ironic. It's terrifying to imagine where it could lead us as a country. There have been plenty of signs over the years that our beloved leader might abandon his promises in favor of authoritarian practices. One of his first acts was to abolish the free press and imprison or deport journalists who spoke out against him. At the time, we weren't that alarmed. We thought it was more important to speak in a unified voice. It took us this long to realize that such actions aren't favorable to democratic growth.

But now we're at war against a familiar enemy we already know has far superior capabilities, except this time we're doing it without the aid of a resistance movement. This time, our enemies are the ones who are unified. So, what do we do? Unless we win this new war, too, and even more decisively than before, we could lose everything, sending us back to a time when we had absolutely no voice at all. Yes, I hate some of the decisions our government has made, but I can't entirely blame them, either.

The house is empty when I finally get home, exhausted but not yet ready to panic. I call my mother to tell her I'm here, and she arrives soon after with Titi. No, she says, when I ask her if she's heard from Yikealo. But we both know it still doesn't necessarily mean anything negative. If he has heard about the *giffa*, he'll stay off the roads. He may not have access to a phone to call me. He might even have to spend the night hiding in one of the small villages between Asmara and the coast.

But as the hours pass and the light bleeds out of the sky, a terrible foreboding settles over me. I begin to suspect the worst.

When I put Titi to bed, she asks about her father. She wants to know why he isn't home, too.

"I don't know where he is right now, sweetie," I say. "But don't worry. He knows how to stay safe."

"Are you worried?"

I sigh. She's too young to understand what's happening out there. That's a blessing. "Yes, but it's my job to worry," I tell her. "Your job is to sleep well and have nice dreams."

When I wake the next morning, there's still no word, so I'm certain by then that my husband has been caught. Frantic with worry — for him, as well as for us and our future — I call my sister-in-law, Yordanos, who agrees to find out what she can. She tells me to stay home, in case he returns, and to get as much rest as possible. I think she already fears the worst, and knows that if she's right, the days ahead for me will be the hardest of my life. In case she's able to locate him and learns he's been detained, I give her a small package containing some dried foodstuffs, a change of clothes, and a few other necessities to deliver to him. We've all heard from people close to us that the training conditions at Sawa are horrendous and the meals insufficient. He'll need as much help as he can get to survive the ordeal that awaits him.

I spend the day anxiously cleaning the house and trying not to think about what my husband might be going through, but I keep catching myself losing focus, my mood swinging between frantic moments of activity and paralyzing worry. I'll realize sometime later that I've been staring off at nothing, unable to remember what I was in the middle of doing.

Each time the phone rings, I hope it's him. It never is.

When the day ends without word, there is no question in my mind, even though I have still to receive confirmation.

Yordanos returns late in the afternoon of the second day with the grim news. The route Yikealo travelled to get to the coast two days before had been heavily patrolled. Every bus and truck was stopped, and every rider ordered to step out. "The people I spoke with told me no one escaped the roundups," she recounts. "I learned they took everyone to holding centers. I spent two whole days checking them for your husband."

"Where did you find him?"

"At Ghindae. It doesn't appear he'll be released."

The town of Ghindae is on the road to Massawa, halfway between here and the coast, roughly an hour's drive by car.

She hands me a handwritten note on which Yikealo has scribbled instructions for taking care of our little market. There are also suggestions for requesting his release. I don't know when I'll have time to do the former, and I have little hope of succeeding at the latter.

Nevertheless, I immediately head to our region's zonal command to submit a request for my husband's discharge. I cite numerous reasons of hardship, both medical and financial. Before commenting on my application, they ask me if I am willing to sign a statement promising he'll report for service in the first training cycle after the baby is delivered, should my request be granted. This gives me a glimmer of hope. I would rather they not take him, but a six-month delay is better than no delay at all. At least then we'll have time to prepare for life without him for the foreseeable future.

The man reviewing my paperwork takes his time studying my claim. I can tell by his demeanor — imperious, incredibly patient — that he's a former freedom fighter, or *tegadalay*. When he's finished reading, he sets the paper down on the desk and gives me an unsympathetic look. "These are minor, personal problems," he says. "Don't you know that we have to defend our country? How are we going to do that, if everyone decides they're too busy? Whether your husband is with you or not, you will still deliver your baby, so he is going to fulfill his duty to the army without delay."

"But he is almost forty years old already."

"No arguing!"

I walk home in a fog of dismay. At one point I run into a cousin, who asks if I'm all right. My brain is too frazzled to register the look of worry on her face and the anxious tone of her voice. I'm barely able to keep from breaking down and crying. "What's happening, Wudasie?" she asks. "Is something wrong with the baby?"

"They took my husband," I manage to reply. "They're making him join the army."

"Oh no," she moans. "Oh, I am so sorry, Wudasie. What terrible news. And what terrible timing for you. You need him now more than ever for the delivery of your baby. Did you tell them that?"

"It didn't help."

"Look here. I'm worried more about you right now. You're so pale. You look like you're about to pass out. You have to take better care of yourself."

"But how? Now my husband is gone, and it's up to me to care for my daughter by myself while I'm still only five months pregnant and as big around as an elephant. How am I going to work and take care of our market on top of all that?"

"We'll help. Now is the time for family to come together. You have to keep up your strength, for your sake and the baby's. You need to be strong. Your husband won't be here to help you."

I know she means well, and her advice is exactly what I need to follow. But it's not what I want to hear. And I'm worried I won't be as strong as I need to be.

PAIN AND LOVE

The days pass, and I have no choice but to adapt to life without my husband, now nearing his third full month of training. Each night, I lie exhausted in bed and reflect back on the day he was taken from us and wonder where I managed to find the strength to survive. My family is a great help, as is Titi, who despite her young age and her medical condition continues to surprise us all with her tremendous heart. In the end, however, I just can't do it all. After less than a year as owners of the market, I'm forced to make the awful decision to relinquish the building back to its owner. We've lost everything we invested into it — all our time, effort, and money — and we're financially worse off now than when we started, all because of actions outside of our control. I place the blame directly with our president. He alone is responsible for the state of our country. He refuses to heed the counsel of his advisors. And his citizens. He alone makes every decision and directs every arm of the government.

In light of my previous difficulties carrying Titi, my doctor sees me weekly for this second pregnancy. So far I've been lucky to avoid the same complications that forced me into bed the first time. Maybe I've just mentally prepared my body to endure, because there is simply no other choice. Whatever the reason, I've finally reached the point where I'm done. I just want the pregnancy to be over with now. I'm always exhausted, from the moment I wake in the morning until the moment I close my eyes at night. I can barely stand on my feet for more than a few minutes before I need to sit or lie down to rest.

"It's the tenth month," I say to the doctor. "It's time."

"The baby will come when the baby is ready, not when you are. Don't worry. The baby is doing fine. There's no reason to induce labor at this time. Go home and rest. I'll see you again in a few days."

I tell my sister Akberet waiting outside with the taxi that I'm going to walk home.

"That far? You won't make it. Look at you!"

"I don't want a ride." Privately, I hope the exercise and fresh air will help speed things along.

She sends the taxi away and joins me. We walk slowly, as I can't go much faster than a turtle's pace or take more than a few steps before I have to stop and lean on a wall to catch my breath. By the time we reach the street where I live, it's long past the dinner hour. The sky above is gray with clouds, and the afternoon has turned from breezy to downright windy. The smell of rain pinches my nose, brings tears to my eyes. Thankfully, the storm holds off until we reach the house. But the moment we step inside, the clouds open up and it begins to pour down. Too tired to eat, I head straight for bed. Akberet lies down beside me to keep me company. Her voice is a soothing sound against the harsh backdrop of rain and the terrible racket of the wind battering the windows.

My mom wakes me up early the next morning to ask how I'm feeling. She's been staying with me to help for when the labor begins.

"I'm fine," I say. "Tired, but okay." And it's the truth; I am fine. The walk the day before actually helped. I'm a little sore from the exercise, but I feel more energized than I have in weeks, more mentally prepared to meet the day. Or perhaps

I'm just benefitting from the first uninterrupted night of sleep in a very long time.

"So, you're okay if I leave for a little while then? I want to go to church. I will be gone only for an hour or so. Titi's still asleep. I should be back before she wakes up."

"I'll be fine, Mom."

"Are you sure? Your sister had to go to work."

"Go," I say, already drifting off again. "Nothing will happen in an hour."

But I'm wrong about that.

A sharp pain in my belly wrenches me awake soon after. It feels like someone stabbing me repeatedly. I try to sit up, and now it feels as if hot coals are being shoved into the wounds. Wave after wave of pain sweep through me. Between spasms, I become aware of Titi standing next to the bed. I hadn't realized how loud my cries were, or that they'd roused her from her sleep. She looks terrified and begins to cry.

This finally gets me out of bed. With one hand on my belly and the other on the wall, I stumble out of the bedroom. Titi rushes over to my side, wanting to help, but she's too small, and I'm too wracked with pain. There's nothing she can do except cling to me, and nothing I can do but drag us both down the hall. As I pass by the guest bedroom, I glimpse someone asleep in the bed and realize it's my brother, Biniam, who must have come to visit the previous evening and then stayed because of the storm.

"Get dressed," I tell him, panting. "Call a taxi. I'm having the baby. Hurry!"

"Now?" he cries, jumping out of bed.

"Yes! I think so."

"Where's Mom?" he asks, pulling on his shirt.

"Church."

"What? Church? How could she leave you alone at a time like this?"

"Stop panicking, Biniam! Just hurry up and get me to the hospital!"

"*No no no no!* Please, you can't have the baby now. Don't do that to me, Wudasie."

My brother is a nurse, so I should be relieved that he's here. I don't know if he panics because he knows what could go wrong or just because I'm his sister, but either way he's not helping the situation.

While he calls for a taxi, I make my way back to my bedroom and somehow manage to change into fresh pajamas. I also grab the small overnight bag I had packed and waiting. Then I call my sister-in-law, Yordanos, to let her know what's happening. I'm barely able to speak when the contractions come, but she's able to quickly guess what's happening anyway.

Finally, I turn my attention to Titi. Throughout this whole crazy episode, she's been unable to do anything but watch her mother suffer. I find her cowering in a corner of the room, where she's curled up into a ball like a scared animal. She knows I have a baby inside of me, but she's too young to understand why I'm in so much pain. She sees my agony and thinks I'm dying. I pull her close and try to soothe her. It's not easy when the next wave of contractions hit.

My mom returns from church the same time Biniam helps me outside. The moment she sees the gate flung open and the taxi out in front, she understands. "How could this be?" she cries. "You told me you were fine! This is all my fault. I should never have left you alone!"

"I wasn't alone!"

I know she feels terrible. She's been with me for days now, ready to help as soon as I need her, yet the moment she steps away is when the baby decides to arrive. Now, instead of helping take me to the hospital, I need her to stay here and be calm. I already have my brother's hysteria to deal with.

"Take care of Titi," I tell her. I'm between contractions again and able to give her a reassuring smile. But another spasm rips through me and twists my face into a grimace.

After we get into the car, Biniam begs me to hold on. The pain frightens him. He'd rather not see me like this. But I can't hide what I'm feeling. I slump to one side as all the muscles in my belly suddenly contract. "Please, Wudasie," he begs. "Please hold on. We're almost at the hospital."

"I am trying!" I scream. But the truth of the matter is, I'm not in control of anything anymore, nature is. The baby will come when it wants to come. Biniam squeezes my hand and tries to soothe me. I pray we make it in time.

Even through the pain, I know how lucky I've been to make it this far. Yes, things haven't been easy without my husband by my side, but they could be so much worse. I'm lucky, for example, that my brother was in the house. If not for last night's storm, I would have been alone with Titi. Also, I could have been bedridden for the past four months instead of working. It's been truly exhausting, from the moment I get up in the morning until I lie down in bed at night, but I survived it. Even this new pain sends me an encouraging message. It tells me my baby is finally coming. I didn't have the benefit of such a warning the last time.

With Titi, I didn't really know what to expect. At my final weekly examination, the doctor told me I needed to be admitted to the hospital because the delivery was imminent. I didn't feel any pain or pressure. But since it was my first time and I didn't know any better, I did as I was told and checked myself into the delivery ward.

I was there for two long nights, and nothing happened. The boredom was bad enough, but the uncertainty was worse. Was the baby okay? Why wasn't it coming out? I could feel movement, yet I was convinced something was wrong. Between checkups by the nurses, I tried to read, but I couldn't concentrate. Finally, on the third morning, the attending physician decided I had to leave. "Are you here to have the baby or take a holiday?"

"But my doctor ordered me here," I replied. "He said I'm ready to deliver."

"Well, I'm your doctor here in the hospital, and I don't see any indication you're progressing. Go home. Come back when you're really ready to deliver this baby."

"How will I know?"

"You will know."

Naturally, I was unhappy about being sent home, as well as for the ambiguity of his answer. Given the weeks of bed rest I was forced to endure, I just wanted the pregnancy to be over once and for all. I wanted to tell him I wasn't going home until I'd had the baby, but I had no choice. I had to leave. Yikealo called a taxi, and we left the hospital.

The cramps didn't start until a week later, and even then I wasn't quite sure they were the signal I'd been waiting for. A friend's mother visiting us advised me to be patient and wait just a little longer before going back to the hospital. She had delivered a lot of babies herself over the course of her life and was well regarded for her skills in childbirth. "There's no reason for you to rush there just yet. Wait and call me when the labor begins."

"But it's starting now!"

"No, not yet. You're not ready yet."

"The doctor said I'd know."

"You *think* you know. This is your first time, so it's going to take longer. Stay home tonight. Maybe we'll take you to the hospital in the morning."

"But what if the baby comes in the middle of the night?" I worried about having no one around to help me. I had more faith in the doctors at the hospital than in my own intuition.

"If you want, I'll stay with you. If anything happens, I know what to do."

I did as she said and stayed in bed at home. I felt some pain overnight, but she was right— the baby didn't come.

Still, I was very impatient. Against her advice, I checked myself into the hospital the next day. I didn't want to take any chances. Winter had come to that part of the world. It was raining and windy, and the skies were filled with dark clouds. I didn't want to be stuck at home because of a storm.

So I sat in my hospital bed for another day, and still Titi didn't come.

"You need to breathe deep and push hard," the nurses told me, each time they visited my room. I tried to do what they said, but they were clearly frustrated with me. In their opinion, I simply wasn't trying hard enough to make it happen.

In the time I was there, a parade of women came and went, each one occupying the beds on either side of me for a short while. And each one left for the delivery room and didn't return. Every time another nurse came in to check on me, I'd ask if it was my turn, and they would say, "Not yet. Keep pushing."

Finally, early in the evening, one of the male nurses decided the baby wasn't going to come without help. "Obviously, you're not pushing hard enough," he told me bluntly.

He transferred me into a delivery bed and gave me some medicine. Everything happened very quickly after that. He was a tall man, very strong, and I remember him placing his palms on my belly and pressing down very hard. The next thing I knew, there were these tiny baby cries and I was done. After waiting for so long and not knowing what I was supposed to do, it was all over in the blink of an eye.

The nurse held the baby up for me to see and said, "It's a girl." Five minutes later, I was being wheeled into a different hospital room.

In Eritrea, fathers aren't permitted in the room during the delivery. No one but hospital staff is allowed. I remember seeing Yikealo in the hallway right after the birth and the proud smile of a first-time father spread across his face. I'll never forget how happy he looked.

This time, I won't have him with me, not even after the baby arrives. The government took him away from me and sent him to train in the desert. He's not even in Sawa, two hundred kilometers to the west of us, but at a relatively new camp nearly a thousand kilometers away, right at the bottom of Eritrea's funnel near the border with Djibouti. There, he's being taught how to be a soldier— how to fire a gun, how to obey orders, how to march. At a time when he should be celebrating new life, he's learning how to take it.

The taxi finally arrives at the front of the hospital. The contractions have gotten worse. I'm not sure I'll be able to make it inside, much less stand up. Someone lifts me out and carries me inside in their arms. I'm set down on a gurney. In the fog of pain, the faces hovering over me are a blur of colors; their voices sound like nonsense. I try to answer what I think they're asking. I'm not sure the words leaving my own lips are even coherent.

The latest contraction begins to fade as they get me into a room. My doctor appears by my side. "Wudasie?" he exclaims, a look of complete surprise on his face. "When did the labor start?"

"Seven o'clock this morning."

"Less than an hour ago?" He gestures frantically at the staff around us. "But the baby's ready to come out now! Oh my, one hour is a very short time to reach this stage."

"I think it started while I was asleep."

But he's already left me to go wash up. The bed rocks gently as it's wheeled down the hallway to the delivery room. The ceiling lights are a rapid cascade of blinding white flashes passing over me. I hear the sharp snap of someone putting on rubber gloves. A nurse situates herself at the foot of the bed. "Don't push yet!" she orders. "Give me a second!"

But I can't wait. The next contraction slams through me. I can't hold it back.

"I told you to wait! I almost dropped the baby onto the floor!"

What choice did I have? I want to scream. But the pain and anger are already draining away from my body, leaving me exhausted but relieved. After the rush passes, I feel completely hollowed out.

Maybe this is why we have to endure such agony, so that when it finally leaves us, we are completely empty, ready to fill up again with the love that comes afterward.

"It's a girl," the doctor says, holding her up so I can see. "And she's doing perfectly fine."

WHERE IS YOUR HUSBAND?

The nurse wheels me and my new baby girl into a large, open room in the maternity ward. The far wall is lined with beds — at least five in a row — and most of them are already occupied. It's a big change from my last delivery, when I had a much smaller, semi-private room with only one other mother. Back then, I had private medical coverage. Now, it's the government that oversees my medical care, just as it does nearly everyone else's, save for the privileged few with position and money to afford special consideration. It's amazing how much things can change in just a few short years.

"Rest," the nurse tells me. She takes me to the bed in the corner farthest away from the door. "You'll be able to go home in a few hours with your baby."

"When will she get her vaccines?" I ask.

"Not today. You can do it tomorrow at your neighborhood clinic."

I remember from the last delivery that the doctors would come and check the babies during the morning rounds before discharging us, but not in the afternoons. The entire group of babies born the previous night would then be given their shots during first rounds. I know I'm being overly paranoid, but given how we missed Titi's heart murmur for an entire year, I want to be sure one of the pediatricians checks the newborn before we leave. Every time the nurse comes around, I make excuses to stay. I mention the heart defect suffered by my first daughter and demand the doctors check. The nurses eventually give up trying and leave me alone.

That evening, as the ward quiets, I listen to the other mothers who delivered late in the day as they chat among themselves. For some, this is their first child, and they're full of youthful wonder and joy. They seem so innocent to me. But whether it's their first or fifth, they're all eager to share their stories with each other. I can understand this. We are members of a privileged club, one that only other members can fully understand. If I weren't feeling so exhausted and worried about how I'm going to care for my newborn baby and my three-year-old girl at home with my husband so far away, I'd join in their banter. I just keep thinking about how I'll be returning to an empty house tomorrow with no financial means to support myself. Thank God I still have the rest of my family to help me out — my siblings, parents, in-laws, and cousins — but I can't rely on them for everything forever.

The baby is a comforting weight in my arms. She's warm and quiet at the moment, and I'm drowsy. I shut my eyes and try to rest. The other mothers' voices drift in and out of my consciousness.

Is it your first baby?

Is he your first boy?

Is she your first girl?

I hear one mother say that she already has three daughters and that this is her first son. I open my eyes and look over. She's not much older than me. "I wish my husband were here," she says. "He would have been very happy to know that our prayers for a boy were finally answered."

"Where is your husband?" one of the other mothers asks.

"He is a *wetehader* in the army."

"A soldier? Mine is, too," says another, and one by one the others chime in with nearly identical stories. Their husbands are either soldiers, or they serve in some other capacity within the ENS. Not just some of the new mothers, but every single one of them.

I regard them with fresh appreciation. I'd thought my situation was unique. Instead, it's no different from theirs. I should be encouraged by their relatively positive outlook, but for some reason it only adds to my despair.

"Looks like we're all in the same pot," one woman says, without a hint of resentment or irony. Every single one of them acts as if this situation is perfectly acceptable. I want to yell at them that we're husbandless and our babies are fatherless. I can't understand why they wouldn't be upset, at least a little.

"What about you?" someone else asks. I know the question is directed at me, even though I'm not looking at the speaker. I'm the only one who hasn't shared. "Where's your husband?"

"He's training in Kiloma," I quietly reply.

Their silence makes me look up, and I don't like what I see on their faces, as if they know something frightful that I don't. All I've heard about the new camp far in the south of the country is that it's very hot and dry. From the brief letters I've received from Yikealo, I know he's having a tough time, but I'd already expected that. Basic military training isn't meant to be easy, and he's probably one of the oldest in their cycle. But the look on these women's faces suggests it may be worse than I had assumed.

Later, one of the nurses comes in to tell us it's time to sleep. "If you need anything, tell me now," she warns us. "I don't want you coming to my door and waking me up to ask for anything." She brings extra blankets and water for those mothers who request them. Then she departs, shutting the lights off as she goes. This is another difference from my first pregnancy. At that hospital, I had very personalized care and attention at all hours of the day and night. Here, in this government-run facility, where nearly everyone on the staff, from nurses to doctors, is ENS, they are understaffed, undertrained, and underpaid. The nurses have long shifts, and they aren't as enthusiastic about their work as they would be in private practice.

Several hours later, I wake to a strange noise coming from the other end of the room. One of the other mothers is moaning. I listen to it for several minutes, unable to decide if she's asleep and dreaming or in some kind of pain. After a while, I lift my head and stare into the gloom. It's the woman in the bed in the far opposite corner from me, the one with three daughters and her first son. She's thrashing about. I pull myself out of bed and slip over to her to see if she needs any help. She's awake, and her face is pale and covered in sweat. She manages to tell me she's having terrible cramps in her belly, but she doesn't want to wake anyone else up, especially the nurse. I offer her something to drink, which she refuses. Not knowing what else to do, I return to my bed.

The moaning and thrashing grow worse over the next couple of hours. I finally decide that she needs help, so I make my way out to tell the nurse. The door to her room is closed, so I knock.

"What is it?"

"One of the mothers is sick."

"I checked everybody already. No one is sick. Everyone is fine."

"She's moaning. She says her stomach hurts."

I wait, but the door remains shut.

"I think you should come. She's in terrible pain. She's been moaning nonstop for a while."

"Go back to your room. She's fine. Tell her to be quiet. And don't bother me anymore."

I don't know what to do. If I keep pushing, the nurse will get even angrier at me. I have this vague notion it wouldn't be good for any of us. If she complains to her boss, I could bring hardship down on us all, so I return to my bed. I have to trust that she knows better than I do.

The ailing woman continues to moan for the rest of the night. I can't sleep, and I can't imagine the other mothers are able to, either, but they all keep quiet. Then, just before dawn, the nurse finally comes in. She takes her time making her way around the room and eventually stops beside the sick woman's bed. She just tells her to stop complaining. Then she leaves. The woman eventually grows quiet.

An hour later, the doctor arrives for morning rounds. When he sees the sick woman he gets very agitated. He barks out orders to the nursing staff. "The rest of you," he says, waving his hands frantically at us, "you must leave immediately! Out! Out! Get your things. Hurry up! Go home!" As we gather our belongings, he begins to raise the foot of the woman's bed. She's still quiet, but now she's not responding to his attempts to rouse her. "Hang in there," I hear the doctor quietly but urgently say to her. "Please, stay awake for me." He taps her cheek with his palm, trying to get her to respond. "Stay strong for me. I'll help you, but you need to wake up!"

Moments later, we're ushered out into the hallway and into another room, where a different doctor quickly examines us and our babies before ordering vaccinations. He doesn't listen to my daughter's heart. There's no time. Minutes later, we're discharged from the hospital. I don't know what happens to the woman with the four children. I can only pray she's all right.

In our culture, babies are named weeks after birth, at the time of their baptism, which occurs at forty days for boys, eighty for girls. Yikealo and I have made two lists of possible names, one for each gender, as we had no way of knowing beforehand if we were going to have a boy or a girl. As soon as I get home, I write a letter to inform Yikealo of the birth of our second daughter. Remembering the reaction I'd received from the other women when I mentioned where he was training, I add a package of powdered milk and a few other items I know he'll appreciate. He needs to keep up his strength and spirit if he's going to endure the harsh demands of the environment and his trainers. I hope it'll suffice.

A couple weeks later, I receive a letter back with a suggestion for a name, but it isn't one we'd had on either list. I don't know where he came up with it, but it's immediately obvious to me why he's chosen it: Natsanet. The name means "freedom," or more appropriately, "a yearning to be free." It's a concept our people have long held deep inside ourselves, a philosophy that drove us to fight for more than thirty years. And it's something we feel we might lose again as the new war with Ethiopia drags on. I wish for freedom for Yikealo, who was taken against his will by our own government to help fight a war none of us wants. It's the perfect name for our child, as she is our future. It is in her and Titi that we place all our hopes and dreams, just as our parents did with us.

REUNION

The officials in the Eritrean National Service think nothing of it when they place immense burdens on us by forcibly conscripting our family members, yet they make almost no effort to ease those burdens by keeping us informed of changes in their status. When Yikealo was first detained, they didn't bother to tell me, his wife, what had happened to him, despite his many requests to do so. My sister-in-law had to go looking for him. Then, in the weeks that followed, while he was being transferred from one place to another, it was only from his handwritten notes sneaked to guards with pleas to have them delivered to me that I was able to track where he'd gone, and often by then he'd been moved somewhere else. I had no idea he'd ended up all the way down south in Kiloma until after he had already arrived.

But it's been nearly six months now, so his basic military training must be nearing its end, if it hasn't already. The army will assign him to a unit for regular duty. My biggest question is, where will they send him? Will they keep him there in Kiloma, a thousand kilometers away from his family? I hear the warfront in the south is expanding. Naturally, I pray they'll send him back north to be closer to us, but the fronts here are even worse. If he's sent to one of them and dies fighting, I may never even know what happened to him.

One day, my brother Beraki comes and tells me he's heard from Yikealo. "Part of the training group from Kiloma has been sent to Halewa Maasker, the Command here in Asmara, for their assignments. He's with them."

"Here?" I exclaim. "In Asmara? Will he be staying? Will they send him elsewhere?"

"I don't know any of the answers. They're still waiting to be told."

Do I dare hope the army will station him nearby? It seems unlikely the ENS would bring him all the way back here just to assign him back in the south again. I'm torn by what I want, what I can't have, and what I dread most. Nearly everyone I know who has a relative in the ENS says they're sending more people to fight as soon as their training is over.

"He says there's a chance for us to see him today," Beraki tells me. "We should go. It might be our last opportunity for a long time."

I jump up and hurriedly arrange for my mother to watch the girls. I can't be sure children will be allowed onto the base. I don't even know if I'll be able to enter, and I suspect not. Beraki offers to drive me there to meet him. He's one of the very few people in the city who has access to a vehicle. Besides commercial trucks and taxis, very few cars are privately-owned. The rest are operated by government employees.

When we arrive at the gate, we're told civilians aren't allowed inside. The guard makes us wait at a distance while he calls over the telephone to let Yikealo know we're here. The sun turns my legs to rubber. After a while, I return to the car to sit inside. We had to park far away from the gate because they're afraid of bombings.

In the hour we are sitting there, numerous people pass in and out through the gate. None of them is my husband.

"I think you should check with the guard again," I tell Beraki. "It's taking them a very long time to bring him out."

But he shakes his head at me. He places the tip of his finger to his lips, advising me not to speak. Winking, he tilts his head in the direction of the gate, toward the figure of a solitary old man trundling slowly and carefully down the road toward us. He's hunched over and feeble looking, so my first glance is cursory. Then it hits me all at once that this stranger is my husband. He's changed so much in just the few months since he left for his business trip to Massawa that I hadn't even recognized him. My mouth drops open, and a cry of anguish rises in my throat. But Beraki quickly shushes me. "Go," he urges. "He's there. Go see him."

The next few moments are a blur. I'm horrified at how much weight he's lost, at the scars covering his bare arms. They weren't there when he left home. It's so upsetting to me that I barely hear a word he says, and he has to repeat himself several times before any of it registers. He tells us that after his group completed their training, most were assigned right away. Many went to the front lines. He was lucky to be among the small number brought here to learn of their final duty stations. He's still waiting, so he can't leave the base just yet. They may decide soon, or they may take their time. I hurry home to fetch the girls and to bring a new change of clothes and other necessities, just in case he's sent far away again.

Titi is almost three and a half years old now. It's been nearly seven months since she last saw her father, and I'm not sure she'll remember him, especially considering how much his face has changed. She does recognize him, but she's suspicious of his appearance. Rather than excitement, she acts shy, like she's not quite sure how to take this. Yikealo tries his hardest to convince her. Only when it comes time for us to leave does she fully accept the truth, and then she doesn't want to let him go. "Come home with us, Dad," she says, wrapping her arms tight around his neck. "We'll give you a bath and change your clothes."

We're amused by the idea, but her comment makes complete sense to me in a sad way. She thinks she can wash away his strange appearance, as if the father she remembers must be hiding underneath this frightening new exterior.

"I can't," he tells her. "I wish I could, but not just yet. Come back tomorrow. We'll see then."

"Will you put on the clothes we brought for you then? I don't like the ones you're wearing now, Daddy."

Some of the soldiers with Yikealo feel bad for Titi, and they try to help by telling her that if she brings her father good food to eat he'll get much better. "Before long, he'll be just like you remember him."

After a few days, once he's been fully processed and cleared, my husband is allowed to leave the base for a short break. He tells me he'll be stationed as a guard in Asmara for now, which is the best news we could have hoped for. On the way home, he falls asleep in the car, and when we arrive at the house he says he just wants to go to bed. But Titi won't let him. She insists that he bathe first. She's still stuck on this idea that his malnutrition and scars can be washed away like dirt off his skin.

After he finishes showering and has dressed in his old civilian clothes again, only then do I truly realize how much weight my husband has lost. His old shirt hangs loosely over his bony shoulders, and his pants bunch up at the waist. He tells me he couldn't stomach the food at the training camp. What they fed them was mostly a thin, flavorless mash of lentil beans, which his stomach couldn't handle. If not for the powdered milk and other items I sent him, he would likely have starved. He already looks it. I want to cry when he tells me this. He must have suffered terribly, but he refuses to tell me how much. All I know is that it's remarkable he survived, and I'm glad he won't have to suffer like that again.

Taking his cue, I don't ask him about the scars that now cover his arms and legs. I don't want him to relive what could only have been terribly painful experiences.

He's asleep the moment he crawls into bed, and he stays there nearly the entire two days he remains with us. He has a lot of healing to do. When he's awake, he gets easily tired. I try to feed him, but he can stomach only a little at a time. It will take more than baths and meals to bring him back to us for good. Assuming he ever does.

Now more than ever, I worry how I'm going to manage. I've been struggling already with just the two children. When I left my job to have Natsanet, my position disappeared, and with it our main source of income. Yikealo's National Service pay is far from enough to support us all; it barely suffices to support him alone. It's really just pocket money, no more, so we can't count on it. The search for treatment for Titi's unresolved medical condition still takes up a lot of my time and attention. And now I must add to it a husband who looks like a living skeleton? He might spend the majority of his time on base, but his being away doesn't lessen my worries, only makes them that much keener.

I know we're blessed to be together again as a family. I know things could be much worse. But my husband's return eases very few of the burdens I must bear.

NO EASY CHOICES

The war drags on. There's no reason to think it will end anytime soon.

One night the shriek of warplanes shatters the placid sky over the city. As we always do when we realize they're not our own, we run out into the street, as if we're yanked out of our homes by the booming echoes of their passing. This time, I have both children in tow. Titi is nearing her fourth birthday. She covers her ears with her hands. Natsanet, now close to turning one, mimics her older sister's behavior.

"Which way did they come from?" someone shouts. "Which way did they go?"

The planes are long gone, and only the echoes of their passing remain, bouncing off every wall and battering us from every direction.

"How many were there? Did you see?"

"Do you know if they hit anything this time? Maybe they struck one of the bases?"

A cold shiver passes through me. Yikealo is at his duty base. I pray he's safe.

"Are they sending more to bomb us?"

Of course, no one has answers to any of the questions. The jets belonging to Ethiopia don't always arrive from the south. Sometimes they circle around. It seems like they do it to keep us off balance. If they simply wanted to remind us we're not in complete control, they have succeeded.

After we go back inside the house, I'm unable to get back to sleep. I spend half the night on the telephone trying to get information. All I receive from my friends and family is speculation. Nobody seems to know anything, even though everyone believes they do. Rumors become facts with each retelling, creating a new sort of reality. Some people recommend we gather in one neighborhood. Others say we should head to a different one. They don't think about hiding, but rather running *toward* where they predict the attack will come. All I want to do is keep my children safe. I consider emptying out our underground water tank and climbing inside of it for protection in case the planes come again and drop their bombs even closer. Houses collapse, after all. Bits and pieces of wood, metal, and stone get thrown around. Walls and ceilings crumble, crushing bones. I think about being buried beneath the rubble. But then I worry the water tank might collapse, too, and the idea of being buried alive beneath the ground is just as suffocating. How can we live like this? In such times, survival always sits at the top of my mind; otherwise, it lurks just below the surface.

The night passes and morning arrives. Despite my obsession with survival, I must carry on as if everything is normal. I continue to worry about Titi. Like the planes flying overhead, ready to drop their bombs at a moment's notice, I fear my daughter's heart could explode without warning, and that would surely destroy me as thoroughly as any weapon our enemy could wield. Every time she stumbles or behaves slightly off, my heart stops. It's a terrible feeling, knowing there is no place I can take her to keep her safe. Just like when the planes come.

It's right about this time that I receive a call from Doctor Mehari, Titi's pediatrician. "The hospital just received new testing equipment," he tells me. "It's mostly to treat the wounded soldiers, but I think you should take her to see the cardiologist there for some tests."

This is just what I've been waiting for, a chance to find out exactly what's happening with my daughter's heart. I don't waste a moment to schedule an appointment.

"What brings you here today?" the cardiologist asks. It's a woman, for which I'm grateful, because if anyone is going to feel sympathetic to my plight as a mother of a sick child in a hospital full of wounded soldiers, she will. A male doctor unfamiliar with me might dismiss Titi's condition as not important enough, especially when weighed against the needs of those fighting the war. Just like when I tried to petition for Yikealo's release at the beginning of his ENS conscription, nothing is more important to them than defeating Ethiopia. They can't understand that just because people are dying for our country, it doesn't make anyone else's personal struggle any less important. We all love Eritrea just as deeply.

"My little girl," I reply. "She has a heart defect." I point Titi out in the waiting room.

The doctor, Simret Seyoum, gives me a doubtful look. "How do you know she has a heart problem? She appears healthy and well fed."

"Doctor Mehari, her pediatrician told me she has a heart murmur. It's been there since she was at least a year old. He sent me here to see about getting some more tests done."

Doctor Simret shrugs. "Okay, then let's see if that is indeed the case."

If I had thought a diagnosis of Titi's heart condition would put my mind at ease, I'm wrong. In fact, the ex-amination definitively establishes the presence of a congenital heart murmur. And at her age now, there's a rapidly diminishing chance it will heal on its own. But while the medical tests confirm Doctor Mehari's suspicion, they yield no options for treatment. As Doctor Simret explains, the surgeons here are simply not equipped for such specialized procedures on such tiny patients. In fact, these types of surgeries can only be performed by outside experts.

"What am I to do then?" I ask.

"Sometimes these experts come to Eritrea on a volunteer basis," she says. "They bring all the equipment they need, perform the surgeries, then move on. The good news is, they prioritize children."

"How often do they come?"

"Once, sometimes twice a year. But they stay only a week or two before heading to another country. Those who need a procedure to save their life are taken first."

"But she could die because of this defect, can't she?"

"It's possible. But for now, it doesn't seem life threatening. It's not as bad as I've seen in some other children."

"Have you seen many?"

"Enough. It is a major problem in this country."

"Then what options do I have, besides the traveling surgeons?"

"You could send your daughter to another country. I've heard about a program by a different humanitarian organization that sends patients in need of surgery to Germany."

"And you think that's something I could do for Titi?"

"Maybe. But you should understand that the government imposes heavy restrictions on applicants into this program. Only the patient can go. No one else, no family member or friend, is allowed to accompany them, even if the child is very young." She shrugs. "Not even parents."

"Why not?"

"I can't say for sure," she answers. "Money, perhaps. It is very expensive to fly people to Europe."

But I think I see something in her eyes that tells me she knows this isn't the real reason. I can guess what it might be. Since our government is imposing the restriction, then it probably has something to do with our leaders' increasing paranoia about people leaving the country and not coming back. Travel has become more difficult for everyone over the past couple of years; navigating the bureaucracies in charge of granting visas can be infuriating, and the paperwork can be daunting. I recently experienced this myself when I went to the United Arab Emirates to see if it might work out for Titi's surgery. I wanted to take her with me, but I ended up having to leave her behind because her visa request was refused.

The restriction against sending parents seems pointless and needlessly cruel. It makes an already distressing situation much worse for both the child and the parents. A child needs their mother and father, especially when in a strange place, doubly so when considering the circumstances. Still, I have to add this option to my list of things to check out more thoroughly. I can't imagine sending my daughter off to a foreign land all by herself, especially if it's for major surgery, but if it turns out to be our only remaining option, then I would be negligent to dismiss it out of hand.

I decide I need more insight on the matter from someone with firsthand knowledge. After asking around, I am referred to a woman who was able to send her son to Germany to correct an issue with his feet. She tells me he's been there for several months already, and she doesn't know how much longer they will have to be apart. "The procedure involves multiple operations," she explains. "And he needs time to heal between each one."

"I would prefer to be by my child's side to provide comfort," I say. "How do you not worry night and day from not knowing what's happening?"

"It was a difficult decision to make," she admits, "but I have faith it will all turn out well. I still worry every night and every day, just as you said. But what other choice did I have? None. I couldn't bear the thought of my son living with clubbed feet his entire life. It's better to take care of it now, while he's still very young. I want him to be able to walk properly like everybody else. I had to make a quick decision, because if I missed the chance, I didn't think we'd ever get another."

"How do you endure the agony of not being with him?" I ask.

"I would rather live with such pain and worry for this brief time than have him live with the pain of never being able to walk like a normal person for the rest of his life."

I realize she's right. When it comes down to it, there really is no choice. I'm more worried about my own pain than I am about my daughter's future. She needs this opportunity. I have to pursue it, for her sake.

Coming to this conclusion doesn't make facing it any easier. *Here is an incredibly brave woman*, I realize. *Can I be as brave as this when the time comes to send Titi away alone?* I try to imagine handing my daughter over to a stranger who will take her to Germany. I picture her all alone in a hospital bed, surrounded by people she doesn't know speaking a language she can't understand, no idea of what's happening to her or how long she'll be there. Or even why. Not having familiar food. The thought crushes me. I hope a better alternative turns up first so I'll never be forced to make such a terrible choice.

Images of Titi all alone haunt my thoughts. How might she react after waking up from surgery and seeing no one familiar? I'm sure she'd feel like I abandoned her. She already has difficulty understanding why her father can't live with us in our own house, or that we can't simply resume our old life as it was before he was conscripted.

My solo trip to Dubai to find medical treatment for her proved difficult enough for her to handle, even though it was only for two weeks. After failing to secure permission for her to accompany me, I arranged to have a live-in nanny come and stay with the girls so they wouldn't have to be sent to my mother's house while I was gone. The woman was young, single, and without children of her own, but she seemed very mature and capable. I also had my mother come during the day to check on them, and Yikealo was able to visit most nights, so my girls still had a lot of family around them most of the time. But when I returned from the trip, Titi was furious with me. She thought I had abandoned her for good, despite everyone telling her otherwise. I'd expected her to feel some resentment, which is why I came back prepared with all kinds of toys and goodies in my bags for both girls, but the intensity of her dismay took me by surprise. She showed me exactly what she thought by refusing all of my bribes. Later, when the two of us were alone, I asked her why she was so angry. I worried that maybe the nanny had mistreated her while I was gone.

"No," she replied. "Everyone was fine. I just don't want you to leave again. I want you to be home with me."

"But why?"

"I thought you left because you didn't like us anymore."

If that's what she believed, then how will she take it if I have to send her away alone? She might think even worse things than that I'd simply stopped loving her. She'd believe I hated her.

There are, of course, far worse things than that to imagine. It's just what I chose to obsess about. I didn't even want to contemplate the possibility of something bad happening during the surgery. If something were to go wrong, I'd never be able to forgive myself.

I make a solemn vow to give the option serious consideration, but only *after* I've thoroughly exhausted every other one first. I call Doctor Simret and tell her to please let me know right away when the foreign surgeons come around.

SUCH AND SUCH

One day, Doctor Simret's office calls to inform me that a group of surgeons is scheduled to arrive soon to Asmara. I'm excited for the news until I learn the call has gone out to everyone on a waiting list, which includes hundreds of children waiting for surgeries of one sort or another. If Titi is to have any chance of being considered, we'll need to show up at the hospital early, before the doors open at six o'clock, and wait along with everyone else, since there's no pre-screening or recommendation process before the surgeons arrive. The team comes directly from the airport, sets up their equipment, does their own triage, and selects who will be treated and who won't.

Taking Titi means I'll finally have to tell her about her own heart condition. Up until now I've kept the news from her.

It may be customary for patients in other countries to be informed about their own diagnoses and treatment options, but that's not true here in Eritrea. You see in movies a doctor telling their patient something like: "I'm sorry, but I have bad news for you. You have *such-and-such* condition. It's a rare form of *so-and-so*. The treatment is *this-or-that*." And the patient will ask, "So, what are my chances?" To which the doctor might respond, "You have *such-and-such* chance of being cured," or "You have *so-and-so* many months to live." Even the very young in other countries know more about their medical conditions and the plans for their treatment than most adults do here. It's a longstanding cultural habit that comes from us wanting to protect each other. We try not to let our loved ones know the truth about their health if it's bad news. We don't want them to suffer unnecessarily.

Instead, these particular details are typically shared only with immediate family members. It becomes their burden to carry. Only if it's good news do we tell the patient. Or, at the very least, we say that the doctors are optimistic. Telling a loved one they have only months to live is simply not done. Why make them feel worse than they already do? When a person is at the end of their life, they shouldn't have to worry. Worry only weakens them; optimism builds their strength and resilience.

This is particularly true when it comes to our children. We try to withhold any kind of bad news from them, but especially if it's about their health. Doctors will only discuss their medical conditions with the parents or guardians in confidence.

Titi has long suspected something may be wrong with her. She's a smart girl and has noticed I treat her differently than other mothers treat their children. I don't allow her to play as rough or for as long as the other parents allow their own children. I'm very careful with her diet. She's begun to ask me why she has to visit so frequently with her doctor and the cardiologist at the hospital. No other children her age do. At least none that she knows. I tell her the doctors want to see her more often because they adore her and can't get enough of her. "They care very much about you." I'm being truthful in this. But I know it's not the answer she's looking for.

When I finally do tell her, she's very quiet. I suspect it will take some time for her to process the information.

On the morning of the visiting doctors' arrival, we get to the hospital early in hopes of being among the first to be seen. I'm shocked by how many other people assumed the same thing. The waiting room is already packed with parents and their children. I see through an open door that one of the visiting doctors is with Titi's cardiologist, who looks like she's assisting with the initial examinations. I take this as a good sign, since she's already familiar with my daughter's case. I hope she'll be able to recommend her for surgery.

I guess that the remaining physicians are already setting up their operating tables somewhere out of sight. I check in, then find a place to sit. We can do nothing but wait our turn.

With each passing hour, more and more people arrive, cramming into the waiting room and lining up in the hallways outside. My hopes begin to fade when I see how many of the children are so much worse off than Titi. From snippets of conversations going on around me, I learn that some of these people have traveled long distances just to get here. We're all desperate for a glimmer of hope; we all want our children to live long and problem-free lives, or as problem-free as can be possible in our current situation.

Has your son seen the doctors yet?

No. Yours?

Yes. They said they might operate. Now we're waiting to see if they will.

That's good news.

I hear they're from America.

All the way here? I hope they pick my girl.

There are too many of us, too few of them, and too little time. They're picking only the most critically ill.

In that case, I don't think my boy has a chance.

Nor mine, but I'm staying anyway, just in case. Maybe this time we'll get lucky.

You've tried this before?

Too many times to count. But we'll keep trying until we get a chance. That's just how it goes.

I heard some children are chosen because their family has good connections.

With the government or the hospital?

Is there a difference anymore?

No. Do you know someone, some high official?

No, do you? Anyway, if that's true, then we're just wasting our time.

Don't lose hope. There is always a chance.

I try to shut the voices out. The more I hear, the more discouraged I become. No one ever told me about using connections to facilitate a spot on the operating table. I want to believe it's only a rumor and not true, because I think it's only right that the most critical children be treated first. At the same time, I just want my child to be fixed, and I would do anything for that. It would be unfair to jump ahead of someone more worthy, but what mother wouldn't grab the chance if offered?

It doesn't matter anyway. I don't know anybody who could help me in this regard. It may even be untrue. I can understand why people might think it's possible. They always want to believe there are other ways, other doors to try. Plus, it's an open secret in our country that those with connections and money get benefits that everyone else doesn't. I wouldn't be surprised if it's the same everywhere for everything.

Each time the door to the examination room opens, the conversation stops, and everyone looks over with a hopeful expression. Each time it closes, that look turns to disappointment for those left waiting.

I feel sorry for the hospital staff. They can't pass through the crowds without being pestered with questions and pleas. I don't know how they can have so much patience, especially when morning turns to afternoon and the hours drag on and people get testy because of the heat and hunger. Children grow fussy. Some throw tantrums. Everyone's level of anxiety rises. Patience runs out, tempers flare. But we don't dare act out on our frustration. Nobody wants to ruin their chance for a miracle.

The ones who are chosen for surgery usually go directly from the examination room to the operating theater. We learn the doctors will be performing surgeries all day and night to help as many people as they possibly can. They'll take only short breaks for food and rest. Those of us waiting to be seen take no break at all. If our name is called and we're not here, we'll have to start all over again at the end of the line. Titi gets hungry, but as I hadn't known what to expect, I didn't bring very much for us to eat. At least my stomach is too tight with worry to want any of the food, so I let her have my share. I'm too anxious, both for her, and for Natsanet, whom I left at home with my mother.

Evening descends, and we're all told to go home and return again in the morning. The surgeons have enough patients to keep them busy for now. Those of us from Asmara and the surrounding areas are lucky enough to be able to sleep in our own beds. But many of the hopeful patients are from much farther away and need to seek shelter in a hotel. Those who can't afford accommodations must find a relative or a friend. I suspect others, with no other options, will simply have to sleep out in the open.

It's a holiday week. Normally, we'd sleep in late, but I rouse Titi before dawn the next morning and drag her back to the hospital for another day of waiting and hoping. She's been so patient with all this, especially after the shock of learning she has a life threatening condition. It makes me both proud and sad for her. Children her age should be out playing with friends, having fun, not sitting quietly for hours on end, worrying that their body might suddenly betray them. Hoping for a chance to be operated on.

I point out another girl on the other side of the room. She looks about Titi's age. Within moments, they're playing together on the floor. It's so much easier for them to make friends at that age.

The girl's mother takes a seat nearby. She wears a black *abaya* that covers her from the shoulders down. The *hijab* on her head is very colorful. We make eye contact.

"Is that your daughter?" she asks.

"Yes."

We talk about how easily children interact with each other, even though they're complete strangers.

"It's remarkable how oblivious they are to what's happening all around them," the girl's mother says. I just nod, because I'm not sure if she means the waiting room specifically, the state of our country in general, or something else altogether. "They don't sense our anxieties or worries," the woman explains. She sighs and shakes her head. "They're blessed, passing through life so carefree. They don't know that being lucky means someone will be cutting into their bodies with a scalpel."

"What's the matter with your daughter?" I ask, changing the focus of the conversation. I don't want to think about surgery, even though that's exactly why we're both here.

"She has a heart condition. I'm praying she gets the chance to have the surgery now. If not, we'll be forced to go elsewhere. That will be a terrible strain on me, as I have so many young children to look after. And now I'm pregnant again." She rests her hand on her belly. "I'm not sure what will happen to the others if I have to go to America."

"America?" I ask, puzzled. "I've heard about a program to go to Germany for the surgery. This sounds similar, except that the government won't allow the parents to go for that one."

"There is no such restriction with this one. Anyway, I'm sure there must be several different programs."

"How would you be able to go there?" I ask. "It's very far, and I've heard the visa process is complicated." In truth, my only real experience with traveling to America is from my sister Aster, who went through the Diversity Visa program more than four years before. "I mean, the expenses must be incredible."

"I have a brother who lives there now. He's been trying to help us for some time. He told me that, Allah willing, he would find a way to make it happen, and he did. But right now it's too much of a hardship for me to go all the way there, so I'm praying the doctors here will choose my daughter so I don't have to."

"And if they don't?"

"Then, because it's our last option, we will go. But first I will deliver my baby. It will be very hard for me to wait that long, but if there is no other way . . . ."

"I would never be able to afford going there," I say, sadly. "It's already beyond our ability now."

"We are the same way. We can't even buy the plane tickets. But at least the surgery is free. They pay for it all. Or most of it, anyway. If we're accepted into the program, then someone sponsors the trip. They pay for the procedure, but not the travel. My brother has volunteered to pay for the plane tickets and our lodging, however long it might take."

"Sponsorship?" I ask. "Who is the sponsor? Is it an NGO?"

"I don't know much about it. I wanted to try my luck here first."

A little while later her daughter is called in to see the doctor. We quickly exchange contact information and promise to stay in touch. She comes back afterward to tell me her daughter wasn't selected.

I tell her I'm sorry. It's so hard not to feel resentment because of our circumstances. I'm glad for the children who the surgeons are able to help. I'm grateful for the doctors volunteering their time and expertise without being paid. And yet I still have a simmering anger inside of me that I can't dismiss or even fully comprehend. I feel so helpless, so dependent on other people. Will today be our lucky day, or will we be like Titi's new friend and be refused? It's a cruel irony that I'm hoping for good luck for my child, especially when it was bad luck that brought us to this point in the first place. Or will the day end with us still waiting, the nurse coming to tell us to go home and try again the next morning?

We wait each day for nearly the entire week before Titi is finally called in for her examination. I want to feel relieved, but I'm too anxious. No matter which way the news breaks, it'll be hard for me to bear. Either my daughter is going to go under the knife right away, or she will be sent home with no chance of having her heart repaired here.

The visiting physician we see is actually German, not American, as people had been saying. He checks Titi with his stethoscope. Then he gives her an EKG. Once more, the diagnosis is confirmed. The wait for his assessment feels like an eternity.

"Your daughter doesn't need emergency surgery at this time," he tells me in heavily accented English. He must expect my disappointment, because he immediately starts to explain that they have too many children and must give priority to the most critical ones. "Your daughter is stable for now. Maybe next time," he adds, and gives me a hopeful smile.

The hospital staff ushers us out. I can't feel anything at first, just a frigid sort of numbness drowning me. But then we're outside and the blinding sunlight hits my face, and I don't know what else to do at that moment. The air is hot, yet it does nothing to thaw the iciness of my shock. All at once I have no strength. My hopes are crushed. What do I do now? Titi tugs at me and eventually manages to get me back to my feet. Somehow, we make it home.

Later, I learn that far more people never even got the chance for an initial examination than those who did before the surgeons flew out. Many of them had waited every single day for the entire week, clinging to hope, only to have it stripped away. The doctors went from the last operation straight to the airport. They didn't even have time to follow up with any of the patients they had operated on.

I WILL PRAY FOR YOU

During one of our visits, Doctor Simret advises me to reconsider the option of Titi going to Germany, rather than waiting for the traveling surgeons to return here. "First of all, there's only a very slim chance Titi will be chosen. They always pick the gravest cases. Second, we don't know when they'll return. Anything could change at a moment's notice." I don't bother telling her that I already tried looking at outside opportunities once before, but it didn't work out.

It was early in 2000. A friend of mine, after hearing of my failed efforts to secure help for Titi, suggested I accompany her to Dubai, where she had previously obtained medical treatment for gall stones. A cousin of hers working for one of the royal families was able to extend an official invitation, which enabled the cousin's employer to sponsor her for admission into one of the hospitals. She believed she might be able to use those same connections to negotiate on my behalf. I agreed to go, even though it didn't sound very promising. We spent two weeks talking to everyone we could think of, but we weren't able to procure a similar invitation for Titi.

"Besides Germany, I have heard about charitable organizations," Doctor Simret says. "You might start with the Christian ones."

A friend of mine is a catholic priest at a school where I once taught, so I ask him if there's a chance the Church might be willing to sponsor a trip to another country for the surgery. He agrees to look into it. After several inquiries, he delivers the bad news: There doesn't appear to be anything available of the sort at the moment.

In 2001, I turn my sights on Sudan, our neighbor directly to the west. Titi is now five years old and becoming more active and more headstrong, which makes me all the more worried for her health. Will her body be able to keep up with her wants and needs? Will we be forced to stop her from playing as vigorously as her friends? I've already restricted her activities, forbidding her from the more strenuous games the other children her age are playing. The older she gets, the harder it will be for me to control her. And the guiltier I'll feel trying.

For the moment, the fighting with Ethiopia has stopped, while the two sides try and negotiate an agreement. We've had a few months of peace, but it's a tenuous thing; it feels like we're all holding our breath, waiting for another explosion of violence. Waiting for the planes and their bombs. Unless the border dispute is resolved, there will always be simmering tensions between our countries, so travel to Addis Ababa is still out of the question. Sudan is the next closest.

Given the geopolitical stalemate, all National Service members, including those who have already fulfilled their eighteen-month obligation, are required to remain on duty and prepared to fight should hostilities resume. This includes my husband. With him still in the army and the threat of deployment hanging perpetually over our heads, I don't want to go too far from home, or stay away for long. Who would care for my younger daughter, Natsanet? Germany and America are too far away. So I'm desperate to find a medical option nearby. Sudan is far from ideal. They have their own geopolitical problems, including a civil war nearing the end of its second decade. Also, their medical system is inferior even to our own. But in some places, like the capital city of

Khartoum, I have heard that the hospitals are more advanced than ours.

I raise the possibility with my closest friends, who immediately try to discourage me. "Sudan isn't the right place for such an advanced medical procedure," they warn, and recommend I look anywhere else first. Still, I persist. I make arrangements to go to Khartoum, where a friend knows a physician.

When I arrive, the first thing she tells me is to look elsewhere. "I can't recommend any hospital here in Sudan, not even in the capital. There are too many problems, and it's very expensive for foreigners. I advise you to focus your attention on Europe instead," she tells me. "Khartoum should be your absolute *last* option, and only if your daughter is in a lot of pain or close to death. Even then," she adds, shaking her head, "I'm not sure I would put my own child in their hands if I had better options. It's not worth the expense. Or the risk."

To hear one of their own make such a claim convinces me not to do it. I'm not so desperate that I can't see reason, nor so stubborn as to ignore the counsel of those who know better. The last thing I want to do is make a bad situation worse.

There have been a few times in my life when my strong Christian faith has been severely challenged, and this is one of them. I've been praying now for four years for help, but everywhere I turn, the door always seems to slam shut in my face. "You must stay strong," Yikealo tells me, after I return home again from Sudan. He wishes he could help find a solution for our daughter's heart defect, but his National Service work prevents him from taking a more active role. He knows how heavy a burden it has been on my shoulders.

"God will answer our prayers," he reminds me. "When He is ready."

While cleaning up some papers at home, I stumble across the phone number of the woman I met at the hospital when we were waiting for the foreign surgeons to examine our daughters. I remember how she'd mentioned going to America if her daughter wasn't selected. I wonder if she's gone ahead with this plan.

I call the number, but I get the woman's mother instead. She confirms that her daughter delivered the baby and then went to America for the girl's heart surgery.

"How is she doing?"

"The surgery is done. My granddaughter is actually doing very well, praise Allah."

"That's good to hear. Who is caring for the other children?"

"I am. Now it looks like our prayers for my grand-daughter's speedy recovery are being heard, so their mother can return quickly. Her children miss her terribly."

When I tell her about my own daughter and ask for more information that might help me pursue a similar course of action, she says she doesn't know the details. All she can offer is her prayers for Titi.

I thank her and ask that she does. I'll take whatever help I can get.

DREAMS OF AMERICA

Many years ago, when I was living in Addis Ababa and teaching a history course to high school juniors and seniors, a colleague and friend told me we were going to America to live. "*All* of us," she added, for emphasis.

"Who do you mean by *all*?" I scoffed. "I know you don't mean me, Aysha."

"Yes, you and me and Hirut and Lemma," she said, referring to two of our best friends, who were also teachers at the same school.

We were a very close-knit group, recent college graduates, single and childless and living in what was, at the time, a relatively safe place. I say relatively, because simply being Eritrean in the country of our longtime political foe came with its own risks, although certainly far fewer than those we'd encounter if we were to live at home. We tended to keep a low profile all of the time, drawing as little attention to ourselves as possible. We seldom spoke out politically, and then only in trusted company.

With Aysha's announcement, I half-suspected she was trying to tease me, rubbing in the fact that she would soon be moving somewhere we all envisioned being populated with beautiful people, tall buildings, fast cars, and money, even though we knew much of that vision was a cliché. She'd spent months working with the American consulate in Addis to secure a family visa to join her sister already in America, and when it finally came through, we'd held a quiet little party to celebrate. More than a few people in our broader circle of friends were understandably jealous of her. After all, America wasn't just the fabled land of dreams and riches, but also freedom and opportunity. Life here in Ethiopia was far from that ideal, and it didn't look like it was going to get any closer anytime soon. At the time, the outlook for Eritrea was just as bleak. But despite all this, I wasn't one of those who looked far afield for happiness. I would have preferred our circumstances to be better, but I'd rather live and work in Ethiopia, even as a second-class citizen, than as a complete stranger in a land to which I had absolutely no ties. I loved our people, our culture, and our traditions enough to put up with the risks.

"Aysha," I said, laughing, "you know I have absolutely no plans to live anywhere else but here."

"Then you had better start planning," she said. "Because you are definitely going one day, I know it."

"Planning for something I don't want?" I teased. "Or do you know something I don't? Are you planning on hiding me in your suitcase?"

She grinned, as if that was her plan exactly. "I had a dream last night where the four of us were in a white car in the middle of a bridge that crossed over a big expanse of water. On one side was my sister, urging us to keep going."

"Your sister in America?"

She shook her head vigorously. "No, my sister here. She was telling us to go, urging the four of us to leave, even while she stayed behind."

"Well, I'm staying here, too."

"No, you were in the car with us! I'm telling you, I saw this in my dream! We crossed the bridge together!"

I rolled my eyes, amused by her little fantasy. But I was also a little sad. Was she starting to have second thoughts about leaving us all behind? Maybe the dream came about because she felt guilty. It was a huge step to leave one's homeland, especially now, when more people on both sides of the border were starting to wake up and see the truth about the Ethiopian president and his cruel policies. But leaving the continent entirely was a much bigger leap. Not only was Aysha abandoning everything she had ever known — her family, her culture — but she was going to a completely different part of the world altogether, one where people like us weren't always welcome. "Tonight, when you go to sleep," I said, trying to make light of her dream without offending her, "make sure you kick me out of the car before you drive off. I think I'll just stay here and keep your sister company."

"But why?" she asked. She seemed genuinely confused.

"I'm not ready to go live anywhere else right now. Someday, hopefully soon, the fighting will end and there will be peace, and things will get better than they are now. Imagine how good life will be then! I can't think how difficult it will be to live in an unfamiliar culture, where we're not appreciated."

"We're already not appreciated here."

I shrugged. How else could I explain to her exactly how I felt? I'd been born here. I was raised here. This place was my home.

"Well, don't say I didn't warn you," she went on, nonplussed. "You know my dreams come true all the time. And this one was very vivid."

"But it's still just a dream."

"Or maybe it's God's will speaking through me. I firmly believe that, someday, we'll all be together again in America."

That was in December of 1988, two and a half years before the War for Independence ended. Two months after that conversation, Aysha was gone.

She called several weeks after arriving in America. By then, one of our other two friends, Lemma, had also left the country for the States. "You see?" she remarked. "My dream is already coming true." I had to remind her that it didn't mean anything. A dream was just a dream, nothing more. Besides, we'd already known Lemma was planning to leave Ethiopia, although he hadn't yet settled on an exact destination. He had two options, the US being one, and was just waiting to see which would come through first. We also knew he had family in America, so it really wasn't that much of a surprise to hear that's where he'd ended up.

"God has a plan," Aysha persisted. "Someday, you and Hirut will come to America, too. I just know it."

"Maybe I'll come for a visit, but not to stay."

"No, you'll come here to live. You wait and see. It'll happen."

Although I am of Eritrean descent, I was born within Ethiopia's borders and had grown up in its capital city. My family, like so many others, had moved there both to avoid the violence taking place in Eritrea and for better educational and career opportunities. But to be perfectly honest, living in Ethiopia was never carefree. In fact, despite their attempts to escape the violence, my family had been subjected to, or witnessed, some of the worst examples of abuse inflicted by the government on our people. In Addis Ababa, my father was once arrested, taken to prison, and tortured. He was released only after a female prisoner in the same jail died, raising a loud outcry that threatened to expose the inhumane practices of the detention centers, which the politicians couldn't afford at the time. My family was harassed off and on over the years. I was teased incessantly in grade school. And then, when I was a freshman in high school, a neighbor of ours, a teacher, was abducted from his house. We never found out the reason why. I and several of my friends sneaked out the next morning to look for him. We found him, along with dozens of others who had been taken. Their bodies lined both sides of a street where many Eritreans lived. The message was clear: Give up this ridiculous fight for independence.

Still, it was impossible for me to think of Addis Ababa as anything but my home, and the thought of putting down roots anywhere else, other than my ancestral homeland, never once crossed my mind. I was like any other young person in that I wanted to see other parts of the world, but only as a tourist. I didn't want to live anywhere but among my own people.

One summer, an acquaintance from college introduced me to her Swedish friends. This was right before the end of the war, and I was still living in Ethiopia. The friends worked for one of the many international relief agencies operating in the country, and they'd fallen in love with our culture. They were particularly taken with our coffee ceremony, which is a highly ritualized, symbolic, and important part of our traditions. And they couldn't seem to get enough of our cuisine. Food is as much a social cement in the Horn of Africa as it is anywhere else in the world, and since my friend was not a very good cook herself — a star on the volleyball court, but useless in the kitchen — whereas I had a natural talent for it, they quickly adopted me into their circle. One day, one of them asked if I ever thought about leaving for a different part of the world.

I remember sensing that the question wasn't as innocent as it appeared on the surface, that there was something else remaining unsaid. Conditions in Ethiopia had deteriorated rapidly in a short time because of the crackdowns spurred by our freedom fighters' run of military victories and the successes of the Ethiopian resistance in the north, and it was apparent to everyone that the current status couldn't be sustained much longer. Something would have to give. The president and his security forces were growing ever more brutal, and attacks against Eritreans becoming more commonplace. But so were attacks against their own people, those who were suspected of being Ethiopian rebels. The country was fracturing, becoming less safe for everyone. Spies were everywhere. No one could be totally sure who to trust anymore. More people were fleeing to other countries to escape the violence. "Why do you ask?" I carefully said, wary I might be stepping into a trap.

"It's just that I've been asked many times by many people if I can help them leave here. Especially those of Eritrean origin. But I've never heard you mention it even once."

"I'm more than happy to travel, but not to live."

He looked very surprised.

"I don't want to live as an immigrant in another country," I explained, and was grateful that he didn't raise the obvious contradiction created by my residence in Ethiopia. I would have argued it was totally different, if he had, but he didn't. "I've heard too many stories about how immigrants are treated as second class citizens. God willing, I'll have a good life and a successful career here." I didn't add: *Or in Eritrea.* I assumed it was understood.

He tried to explain that Sweden is nothing like what I'd described. "It's a very peaceful country, and our people are very friendly, loving, and accepting of those from other cultures. I guarantee you won't be treated like a second class citizen there."

"Maybe so, but I'll be happier here, close to my family."

"Well, maybe someday you'll come to Sweden," he said. Then he smiled. "Just for a visit."

"So you can try again to change my mind?" I teased.

"Maybe."

"Well, I thank you for the invitation. Maybe someday I will visit you. And maybe you can try to change my mind then, but I think you'll have a very difficult time of it."

In fact, I was absolutely sure he would never be able to. No one would.

The war ended soon after that, in May of 1991, and Ethiopia agreed to relinquish control over Eritrea pending a referendum to be held in two year's time. People of Eritrean origin, regardless of where they had been born, how established they were, and how much they had contributed to Ethiopian society, were treated even worse than the second-class citizens I had worried about becoming elsewhere. We were spurned, sometimes viciously. And so, quite unexpectedly and much to my disappointment, the roots I had set down in Addis Ababa were torn up. My family moved back to their homeland. I joined them at the end of that same year, eventually resettling in Asmara. My dreams of a future in the place where I had grown up were wiped away. I resigned myself to reestablishing new roots. At least I was still among my own people, still immersed in a culture I knew.

It wasn't until I met my husband in 1992, and we were married three years later and had begun to establish ourselves, that I finally started to feel at home again. I became pregnant with Titi soon after. My vision of raising a family here grew clearer and clearer. It had taken a while for my dreams to catch up with me, but once they did, I knew that this was where I truly belonged. Nothing could change my mind about that.

In early 1996, when I was still pregnant with Titi, Aysha returned from America for a visit. She couldn't resist reminding me of the dream she'd had all those years ago, or the fact that it was still coming true. The third member of our foursome, Hirut, had made her way to America at last.

"I told you then," I said, once more challenging her conviction that I would soon follow, "I am not going to live in another country."

"You said that when we lived in Ethiopia. Now you're living in Eritrea."

"You know why that is. And anyway, this is my true home. I am Eritrean."

"Well, sooner or later, you'll come to America." She pointed toward the sky. "The big guy upstairs never lies."

"He's going to have to work extra hard to convince me."

"He will."

"Well, then He's taking His time with me, isn't he?"

She laughed. "God's calendar is different from ours."

"If I were you, I wouldn't hold my breath."

"Out of the four people in that car in my dream, you are the only one still here, Wudasie."

"Aha! But now I'm married, and your dream car didn't include a seat for my husband," I said. I patted my belly, which was just beginning to show. It would be another couple of months before I'd start having problems that required constant bed rest, but in those early days I still delighted in the wonders of my impending motherhood. "And it didn't include my child, did it? I would never go anywhere without them."

Yikealo was even more dedicated to making Eritrea our lifelong home than I was. This was where we'd make a living using the education we'd both been blessed to receive. It was where we'd raise a family, teach our children and grandchildren, and one day be buried. This was how we'd grow our new nation, molding it in our own image— by staying put. We knew it wouldn't be easy, but we were sure we would see it happen within our lifetimes. Our children and grandchildren were going to have the brightest future with more opportunities than we could imagine possible anywhere else. Why on earth would we possibly want to leave?

"God doesn't reveal His whole plan all at once," Aysha told me. "You'll see. You will come to America someday."

YOU ARE A BAD MOTHER!

Although many of my family and friends have in the past expressed the same conviction as me regarding staying in Eritrea, as time passed and Eritrea failed repeatedly to deliver on the promise of independence — seemed, in fact, to be resorting to the same oppressive practices we'd experienced before — more people began to grow disillusioned and talked about leaving. In 1996, two years before the Badme incident that sparked the start of the second war, my younger sister Aster won a chance to relocate to America through the Diversity Visa lottery system. She had just finished eleventh grade, and was looking forward to going to college, but the only way to achieve that goal was to first do her mandatory eighteen months in the Eritrean National Service. Although only a couple of years had passed since the ENS was implemented, negative stories about it were already circulating, anecdotes and eyewitness accounts of the harshness of the training sessions, as well as other abuses, both physical and psychological. Not surprisingly, women fared much worse in the ENS than men; many were the subjects of unwanted sexual advances and some were raped. Considering that their abusers were often *tegadelti*, men lionized for their role in gaining us our independence, few in the government were willing to investigate the women's claims or formally charge the abusers. So, Aster decided to pursue her dream in America instead. It was a surprisingly quick process at the time. She applied at age seventeen, and she was gone less than a year later. She became the first member of my family to live outside of Eritrea or Ethiopia.

Titi was born shortly after she left, and when I told Aster about her niece being born, she planned to come back for a visit. I convinced her to wait until she was finished with her studies. She'd already started college and was struggling to make her own way, and I didn't want to disrupt any progress she'd made. A year later, when we learned about Titi's heart defect, I chose not to share that news with her. Part of it was the shame I'd felt at the time and my sense of being somehow responsible for the defect. Part of it was this vague but growing sense of betrayal I harbored, although whether it was directed toward my country, or toward God for placing such burdens on me, I couldn't really say. Maybe it was a little bit of both. I also didn't want my sister to worry about us. She was doing better by then, living on her own, working and still taking classes, really starting to establish her place in an unfamiliar land. She didn't need the burden of my bad news to distract her.

As the years passed, it just became easier to keep it from her.

But after talking with the mother of the woman who took her daughter to America for heart surgery, I decide it's finally time to let my sister in on the secret. She's since gotten married to another Eritrean expat, and they're now living in Chicago. From what she tells us, she has a good life and is happy. But rather than calling her with the news, which would only reduce me to an incoherent babbling mess in seconds, I compose a carefully worded email summarizing our situation. It still makes me cry, but at least Aster won't have to suffer through my nonsense.

A few minutes after I send it off, my phone rings. It's Aster, and I can tell she's crying by the way her voice sounds.

She's never met Titi — partially as a result of my discouraging her, but mostly because the deteriorating situation in my country has kept her away — yet I immediately sense that she feels my pain as acutely as if she were her own child. Somehow, this gives me the strength I need to fill her in on the details. I spend the next hour telling her everything, from the diagnosis to the various thwarted attempts I've made to get Titi treatment. I tell her about the woman whose brother was able to find a medical sponsor for his niece and suggest it might be an option for us.

"This sort of thing is possible?" she asks, surprised.

"If we find a sponsor."

"Then leave it to me," she says. Gone are the tears. My little sister is taking charge again. "If there's one sponsor, there will be others. I'll find them."

The search takes her all over the internet, until at last she locates a hospital in North Carolina, which agrees to take on Titi's case. When Aster tells me the news, I'm floored. In defiance of all my doubts, never once daring to hope out of fear of disappointment, my prayers are suddenly answered. And it isn't just hypothetical; the hospital is willing to bring Titi there, diagnose her, and perform whatever surgery is necessary to ensure she never has to worry about her heart again.

"They still need to work out the logistics," Aster tells me, "but they're absolutely committed to doing this."

I spend the next few days in an excited daze. I can only half believe it's true. I keep expecting to wake up to find it was all just a dream. I also worry that Aster will call to tell me the doctors at the hospital have changed their minds. But that doesn't happen. The opportunity is solid and doesn't fade away. For the first time in a very long time, I allow myself to imagine Titi as a normal child. Now, what once seemed impossible appears as certain as ever.

Aster and her husband work tirelessly with the hospital to ensure every single aspect of the trip is considered. Hundreds of emails are passed back and forth. The paperwork alone within the hospital is mind-boggling. The hospital's insurance company gets involved, which requires lawyers and debates and assessments of risk. Physicians must coordinate with departments, departments with the hospital's executives, who must then meet with the board. They have to work out how it will all be paid, how long it will take, the medical risks, surgical preparation, and post-operative follow-up. Where will we stay? Who will be responsible for performing the surgery? Who will monitor the checkups afterward? Once this is all worked out, we still need to clear the trip through our respective state departments. The process drags on, not for weeks, but for well over a year.

In the middle of all this, my health takes a turn for the worse. My doctor isn't able to offer a definitive diagnosis to explain my nonspecific gastrointestinal symptoms, and instead tries to manage them as best he can with medication. I know a lot of it is stress induced, but the longer I remain ill, the more anxious I become and the worse my symptoms get. At one point, I'm so sick and weak that I tell Yikealo he'll have to take my place when Titi's trip to America is finalized. He tells me he would if he could, but it would be impossible for him to leave. While the ceasefire with Ethiopia has held, we're technically still at a state of war. Neither country has been able to propose a mutually agreeable strategy to resolve the differences that prompted the fighting in the first place. So Yikealo is still bound to the country and the army by his conscription. Not that that's our only hindrance. President Isaias Afewerki continues to enact policies that further isolate us from the rest of the world, including making it even harder for anyone to travel. The government has become a fully functioning authoritarian regime of the type we suffered under as Ethiopian subjects. If I can't take Titi to America, we'll have to cancel the trip altogether.

Eventually, my strength returns, although I doubt it's because of any particular medicine or treatment regimen. I simply learn to exist with a heightened level of anxiety that weighs on me night and day. I adapt. I push on.

On the day we finally receive the actual go-ahead from the hospital, I rush over to the American consulate to submit our visa applications for travel to the United States. After that, we must wait again, as the process of having our requests reviewed and granted involves numerous departments and requires its own stacks of paperwork.

While this is going on, the medical board certificate provided to us at the request of Titi's cardiologist expires, so I have to go through the process of getting a new one. The certificate is mandatory for patients seeking medical care outside the country and must be signed by a team of three physicians who can attest to the accuracy of the patient's diagnosis. They will only issue the certificate if they believe the patient has a grave medical need that can't be met by the hospitals and physicians inside the country.

Once the document is signed, it must be submitted to the office of the Ministry of Health, where it navigates yet another bureaucratic maze for authentication and further approvals. Having already been through the entire process once before, I know to expect the usual excuses and delays, so I'm prepared to push it through using whatever means I can. What I don't expect is the response from Titi's cardiologist, when I show her the final approval from the hospital in America and ask for her support.

"It's not necessary," she informs me. She barely gives the letter from the American hospital a glance before handing it back to me.

"I don't understand," I say, confused. "Are you saying your signature isn't necessary, or the letter isn't necessary?"

"I'm saying surgical treatment is unneeded, so there's no reason for you and your daughter to leave Eritrea. Therefore, there's no need for me to sign for a new certificate."

I'm dumbfounded. Is it possible she has Titi confused with another child? Doctor Simret and I have never had a close personal relationship, despite our many visits to her office, so it's possible she's made a mistake. Hopeful that she's simply misremembering the details of our specific case, I nervously ask her to explain.

"There's no longer any evidence of a defect in Titi's heart," she tells me coldly. "It's healed. Titi doesn't need the surgery, so she doesn't need a certificate from the medical board."

"No evidence? Healed?"

My mind goes blank. For a moment, I can't do anything but stare at the woman. I open my mouth to say something, but nothing comes out. My first instinct is to want to believe her. It would be a welcome miracle, if the defect healed on its own, as Doctor Mehari once suggested it might. But I know it can't be true, so I grow suspicious. Is she lying? Why would she? Maybe she's joking. If so, it's a cruel one.

No, she's never joked about anything before.

Which takes me back to the possibility that it's true. But how could that be? How could Titi's condition have reversed itself so quickly and so completely? And why am I only just hearing about it now? Surely it couldn't have happened since the last checkup a couple months before.

And why didn't she say something about it when I called a few days ago to let her know I needed the medical certificate renewed?

My mind races. I know in my heart that she's wrong. And that forces me to accept that she's lying. It makes no sense at all. Why would she? What happened to compel her to deny us this opportunity?

"Go home," she tells me, and dismisses me by turning her attention to the papers in her hands. "Your daughter's condition is no longer a medical concern."

I'm still trying to understand why she'd treat me like this. Besides being irresponsible and ethically questionable, it seems completely out of character for her to intentionally mislead a patient. I can see from her eyes that she knows I don't believe her. I want to ask if someone is pressuring her to make this decision.

"Out," she snaps, making me jump. "And don't come back."

Rightfully or not, I often take such affronts personally. I begin to wonder if I might have said or acted in some way to offend her enough to make her angry with me. It's easier than accepting the most likely explanation for her deceit, that the government is pressuring doctors to deny travel to everyone, even for those in medical need. Because if that's true, then it means my fight to help Titi has hit a wall that will be impossible to break through.

There was an incident, not long ago, when I brought Natsanet into the emergency room. She was very ill with a high fever and diarrhea. Already a fussy eater, she had stopped eating almost entirely, which made her weak and lethargic. I worried she'd get even more dehydrated than she already was. Doctor Simret, Titi's cardiologist, was the doctor on duty that night. After examining her, she told me my daughter was undernourished. "You are not a good mother," she said, rather harshly. It was a terrible thing to say to a parent who is half scared to death for their child, but I was too focused on Natsanet getting better to really care. Maybe she was having a bad night and just decided to take it out on me. In any case, I wasn't looking for a friend to commiserate with me, but a skilled physician to treat what was happening. And despite her characteristically impersonal bedside manner, she had always done what was necessary in the past, or at least all she could do within the limits of her abilities.

I tried to explain to her that Natsanet was a picky eater. She always had been. I struggled every day to find nutritious things for her to eat. Some days I had to beg and bribe her with every spoonful. "She's been like this since birth. She even stopped breastfeeding at two months, and there was nothing I could do to get her to go back."

But the doctor was unconvinced by my explanation. She ordered a bunch of lab tests, and when they failed to reveal anything definitive, she reiterated her previous claim that I wasn't a good mother.

Other parents I spoke with concurred with the assessment that the doctor was standoffish. Her manner was far more clinical than personal, even bordering on abrasive. She was hard to get close to, to make a connection with. Many had even complained to the hospital about her. Not surprisingly, the complaints always fell on deaf ears. The government doesn't care about feelings, only with facts and figures. How many patients were seen? How much money was saved? How quickly were they released? Until that ER visit, my own dissatisfaction with her never rose to the level where I'd even consider reporting her. It just wasn't worth the effort.

Might that incident explain her treatment of me now? It seemed self-contradictory. If she was so worried about me being a bad parent with Natsanet, how could she justify a decision that prevented me from being a good one with Titi? Or worse still, what could possibly cause her to decide that threatening the life of a child was justified? She might be displeased with how I was parenting my younger daughter, but I just couldn't see that explaining her punishing the older daughter for it. The terrible irony was that she had pushed me the hardest of anyone to take Titi outside of the country for treatment in the first place, after the visiting surgeons decided they couldn't help.

I depart the hospital extremely discouraged. On my way home, I try to think if I have any other options. This doctor is the only pediatric cardiologist in this hospital. It's her diagnosis that the medical board requires to convince it to sign off on the certificate. Seeking another opinion wouldn't be easy, and even if I were able to get one, it would almost certainly be a waste of time. It would just be one person's medical opinion against Doctor Simret's, and the latter would hold more weight.

I call Doctor Mehari, the pediatrician who first discovered Titi's heart murmur, and tell him what happened. "Well, I suppose it's possible that Titi's condition has suddenly improved," he tells me, although without much conviction. "If so, then she'd no longer need further treatment."

"But why would Doctor Simret not mention this at our last examination? Why allow me to go on believing the defect is still there? Also, she knew back then I was still trying to find help for Titi. She's the one who requested the travel certificate in the first place."

I beg him for advice on what I should do. Although I don't come right out and say I think the cardiologist is lying, I do make it clear I think she's acting without Titi's best interest in mind. "I can't just let this go. If she's wrong or confused, my daughter's health is in jeopardy. Also, the hospital in America won't wait forever. If we miss this chance, it could be another four or five years before we get another. If ever."

Doctor Mehari is reluctant to intervene, in part because he works at the same hospital as Doctor Simret and therefore reports to the same senior leadership. He doesn't want to invite trouble from the hospital's administration and possibly even the government. But after he examines Titi for himself and reaffirms the murmur is still there, he agrees to take a peek at her medical records to see if there's a reasonable explanation for Doctor Simret's refusal. "I'll need to tread carefully," he advises me. "I don't want to offend my colleague. These are sensitive issues. And sensitive times."

He calls me back a couple days later to tell me there's a problem with Titi's records. "What kind of problem?" I ask.

"I can't find them," he replies. He explains how there's a process for requesting the medical files from the Records Department. "They're supposed to be returned immediately at the end of each patient's visit, but the clerk told me the folder for Titi was empty. I checked with all the other pediatric doctors in the hospital, but I couldn't locate it."

"Then it's still with the cardiologist. They would have sent it to her when I visited. It's probably still in her office."

"That's what I think. But she's supposed to send it back to be filed right away, so I'm wondering . . . ." He pauses. "By any chance, did you say or do anything to offend her? Can you remember any incident between you two that might affect her goodwill?"

The recent trip to the emergency room with Natsanet comes immediately to my mind. "Why should it matter?" I ask. "No doctor should put their personal feelings ahead of their patient's health, especially one as young as Titi."

"Normally, I would say not," my friend tells me, but he doesn't offer what might be a reasonable exception. "I'll continue to inquire about the record."

It becomes clear that the cardiologist is the one holding onto my daughter's medical file in her office, rather than returning it for storage. Neither of us can say what the reason might be, and my doctor friend doesn't feel comfortable pressing the issue any further. "My advice," he tells me, "is to find some high-ranking official who might be willing to intervene on your behalf, ideally someone in the government."

"But there's a proper procedure."

"Yes, there is, Wudasie. But that doesn't mean it's always followed. See if you can get someone to help."

When I tell Yikealo this, he remembers a relative of his who holds a position of some authority in the government. After we explain the situation to him and ask if he'll mediate on our behalf, he agrees to pay Doctor Simret a visit. He takes my husband instead of me, just in case I'm the target of the doctor's animosity.

Yikealo returns later that same day with good news. The cardiologist has promised to send her recommendation for outside medical intervention to the review board. I'm both astonished and dismayed. The news is all I'd wanted to hear, but it also establishes once and for all what I'd already suspected, that Doctor Simret was lying about Titi's miracle cure.

"We walked into her office," Yikealo says, quickly recounting what happened. He can see how angry I am and rushes to stop me before I can get all worked up. "She and my cousin exchanged pleasantries. Apparently they knew each other from some years ago. Then he introduced me and told her, 'I just wanted to stop by to ask about the status of my niece's paperwork. There are a lot of preparations to be arranged, and we don't want to miss the date they're scheduled to report to the American hospital.'

"The doctor was very accommodating. She had Titi's record with her and pulled it out from her drawer. 'I was just about to finish my report and send it onto the medical board,' she says. My cousin thanked her. He said, 'I told Titi's parents not to worry, since I knew the case was in good hands. But you know how parents are. They worry. But that's their job, isn't it?' Then we left."

So, in addition to her betraying me and Titi, she lied outright to my husband and his cousin about what actually happened in our discussion. Why would she do such a terrible thing? And why should it take such extraordinary measures on my part to compel her to do her job? I want to ask Yikealo's cousin if he thinks her behavior could be explained by policies coming from high up in the government, but Yikealo urges me to drop it. We got what we wanted. We can't allow ourselves to be sidetracked by her motivations.

A few days later, he returns to the cardiologist's office to pick up the signed report to take to the medical review board. This time, Yikealo goes alone, and he finds the doctor beside herself with rage. She screams at him for going over her head. "I don't need intermediation from anyone! You went out of your way to make me look bad in front of a respected senior colleague, and for no apparent reason. I told your wife to be patient, that I was working on Titi's paperwork! Don't you see I have other patients to look after? I can't just drop everything immediately for one person!"

Of course, none of this was true, and my husband knew it. But he kept quiet and let her yell at him, treating it as if the whole thing was my misunderstanding. "I didn't believe a word she said," he assures me. "But getting that report was more important than saving our pride. Nothing else mattered."

I know he's right, but it still offends me.

"Anyway," he goes on, "it's done. Getting the medical review board to sign off on the release now should be easy."

BUREAUCRACIES (I)

The next step in the process is getting the medical board certificate authenticated by the Ministry of Health. After the problems with the cardiologist, one might expect this step to go much more smoothly. After all, the government is a largely impersonal machine operating within an established set of guidelines and rarely deviating from them. At least officially. In any case, there should be fewer opportunities for individuals with grudges to interfere.

But being large and impersonal creates other problems. Bureaucracies are still made up of people, many of whom are underpaid National Service members who don't enjoy their work. They can be frustratingly inefficient. This prompts me to try to speed up the review process by appealing to human sympathies. If they know about my daughter's plight, perhaps they'll push the paperwork through as quickly as possible. I make sure to point out the deadline to the registrar when I submit the forms. "You can see that this is urgent," I tell her. "Is there any way you could do me a favor and push this along?"

The woman gives me a sour look. "You don't dictate to us how to do our jobs." She points to the box where I'm to leave the form. "Put it there. We'll get to it just like all the others."

When we miss the deadline, I blame myself for trying to hasten the process. Later, I think it's because I didn't try hard enough.

Now I have to explain to the hospital in America what happened. I fear they'll simply give up on us, forcing us back to square one. But they're very understanding and are willing to postpone the surgery by several weeks so we can get our affairs in order. It's incredibly frustrating to know that others are so willing to accommodate complete strangers, foreigners even, when one's own government seems determined to find ways to make our lives difficult. It's not the first time I've felt this way, but it does open my eyes to something I'd been willfully ignoring for a while. I'd been growing increasingly disappointed with the path my country is taking, yet I had always remained hopeful we would eventually regain the proper course. After this, I'm not so sure it will happen.

It marks the start of my disillusionment with what Eritrea has become.

We finally get the authenticated certificate from the Ministry of Health, allowing us to apply for exit visas for me and Titi at the Immigration Office. As part of the application, I'm also required to procure a letter of recommendation from my employer. It's only the first of many such requirements for getting permission to travel out of the country, but since my office has provided similar statements for other trips I've taken for both business and personal reasons recently, I don't expect any particular resistance this time around. The statement merely claims that my employer — and, indirectly, the government, as most businesses are connected to the political party these days — doesn't oppose me leaving Eritrea for the stated purpose and time. And who could deny a mother seeking medical care for her young child?

The application usually takes a couple days to make its way from my boss's desk to the head of the division, then finally to the Human Resources department, so I don't expect an answer right away. But a few hours after submitting it I'm summoned by my department head's office. When I enter, I'm startled to find the head of HR there, too. A definite chill hangs in the air. They don't smile. They just instruct me to take a seat.

"We've received your application for a letter of clearance to travel to America," my boss tells me. He's a former *tegadalay* and the gruffness on his face is like a vestigial part of a uniform he no longer wears. "We've decided not to grant it."

"But, why not?" I barely manage to ask. I'm too stunned to say much else. My skin turns to ice. It feels like I am being drowned where I sit.

"It was not my decision," he replies, "but rather my boss's."

His words sound contrite, but his voice is flat, emotionless. He exhibits no remorse or sympathy at all on his face.

"I don't understand," I say. "I've been working in this office for quite some time now. I've always worked hard and done a good job. What possible reason could there be for denying my request? None of my other applications for travel out of the country was denied. What's different about this one?"

"I'm sorry, but I don't have an answer for you. I sent your application to my boss this morning. It came back rejected. No explanation."

"But I need it to help my daughter. You know about her heart condition. Please, it's the only way she'll get better. I mean, we're talking about the health of a child. You know this isn't a vacation."

But all he gives me is a curt shake of his head.

"We do know your reasons," the HR representative says, speaking up for the first time. He shrugs, as if to tell me he would fight on my behalf if he could, but he won't because it won't change the outcome. "We're not saying you can't go, just that we can't endorse the trip."

"How can I go if you don't give permission?"

"We're sorry, but that is the situation as plainly as I can explain it to you."

I sit there for a minute, my eyes shifting between the two men, hoping one of them might suddenly change their mind. Surely the head of HR must know that without the employer statement granting me time off, the government won't even consider my request for an exit visa.

"We understand your disappointment," the man continues. "We'll also understand if you decide to leave your position here with us."

I'm completely dumbfounded. Is he telling me I'm being fired? I feel like I'm getting slapped in the face over and over again. Without a job, how can I get clearance to leave? Without clearance, I can't take Titi to America. "My daughter needs medical help," I plead. It's becoming difficult for me to keep my voice from breaking. I want to break down and cry, because there's too much on the line. But I don't want to show weakness, either. I know it'll just invite their contempt.

Slowly, I take a deep breath and try again. "Look," I say, "I don't want to go, but I have to. Please, could you just ask one more time?"

"As we said," my boss responds without hesitation, "we do know about your particular situation. But for whatever reason, the company has decided it can't give you its blessing for travel. That's coming from the very top, from my boss's boss. We're just following orders."

"Then can I talk to the person deciding this?"

"No. And I wouldn't recommend trying."

Once more, I can do nothing but sit and stare at them, while my mind tries to grasp what's happening. My thoughts are a blur. But the only thing I can come up with is the same question I find myself asking more and more: Why?

"As we told you," the man from HR says. He stands up, sending me a clear signal the meeting's over. "If you disagree with our decision, you're free to terminate your employment relationship with us. Just come talk to me when you're ready to do that. My door is always open."

I'm completely useless for the rest of the afternoon. My mind and body shut down. I get nothing done. Waves of fury pass through me, adding to the frustration and utter helplessness I've been harboring for far too long. The emotions threaten to consume me. I begin entertaining fantasies in which the company reverses its decision, but that doesn't happen. Neither my boss, nor anyone from HR, comes to see me. I just sit at my desk and stare blindly like a statue, while the office buzzes all around me, everyone oblivious to my pain.

Wudasie? Wudasie, what's wrong? Hey, is anything wrong?

I turn, not sure the voice is in my ears or in my head, and find a coworker standing over me looking worried.

"What's the matter?" he asks.

"I-I don't know. I can't . . . ."

"Do you want to talk about it?"

I look around and am startled to see that almost everyone has already left for the day. My coworker waits for me to gather my things, which requires several minutes in my current state of agitation. He then takes me to a local coffeehouse so we can talk. "I saw you go into our department head's office," he says. "Do you want to tell me what happened?"

I explain the situation with Titi, starting with my frustrations with the cardiologist and the Ministry of Health.

I have to struggle not to cry. At last, I finish by recounting the conversation that afternoon. When I'm done, I feel drained, yet also filled with rage.

"I've always known that some people are simply mean, but how can anybody be so cruel as to deny an innocent child such a basic need as this?" he wonders out loud. He happens to be one of Titi's favorites among my coworkers. Whenever I bring her into the office, he spends more time with her than any of the others, talking with her and playing games, buying her treats. He's always been like an uncle to her and a brother to me. Like me, he grew up in Ethiopia, except that he was deported after the new war began, so we share similar life paths. I haven't confided in many of my coworkers about Titi's condition, but he's one of them. "What will you do next?" he asks.

I'm so lost that I just sit there. Finally, he summons a taxi and tells the driver my address.

I skip work the next day. The message from the HR man had been clear enough. I'm not welcome there anymore. But why would my request to take Titi to America drive such a wedge between me and my employer, especially considering my performance record? I just can't understand it at all.

I spend the day in a fog of despair. I'm angry and depressed. I begin to wonder what I did to deserve such unfair treatment. I beg God Himself to answer. "What do you want me to do?" I cry out. "Am I supposed to go or stay? Why does it always have to be so hard?" I feel abandoned. Even He seems to have turned His back on me.

After a few days in limbo, I submit my resignation letter, explaining that I'm only doing as instructed. I truly believe I was forced out, so according to our employee rights manual, I should be entitled to termination pay. But I'm told there will be nothing.

"You can file a complaint with the Labor Office," says the HR representative who takes my letter, a different man than the one I spoke with the other day. He seems to know nothing specific about my situation, which may be why he's so willing to assist me. I can't help feeling like I've become toxic somehow, and if he only knew the particulars of my situation he wouldn't be so obliging. "But," he warns, "it'll still come down to whether the senior managers think you deserve it."

I know he means well, but even I know what he's suggesting. The company is like an elephant, and the Labor Office is its foot, and I am just an ant. The people in charge are all part of the same machinery that was once responsible for running the war. Almost every business is connected to the party these days, whether hospitals, taxis, buses, factories, refineries. Everything's interconnected, and it all feeds straight to the highest point, the president. So if the decision not to allow me to leave Eritrea came from someone high up, I have no chance of winning any challenge to my termination. And little chance of reparations. Employee protections are just an illusion. The government makes the rules because they look good on paper, but they enforce or ignore them as they see fit. When they flaunt the rules, no one challenges them. It would be different in private business. But this isn't a private business. For the most part, private business no longer exists in Eritrea.

"What should I do," I carefully ask the man. "What are my options?"

"Go to the Labor Office and tell them your situation."

"Will you go with me?"

"Well," he says, reluctantly, "you don't need me." In other words, he doesn't want to be personally linked to anyone challenging their superior's decisions.

"But what if I don't file a complaint," I press. "I only want to request a review to see if my termination was handled according to proper procedures. If they say it was done properly, then I'll accept their decision."

"What good will that do?" he asks. "Are you only trying to make a point? If you are, then you are only stirring up trouble."

"Please, I'd be grateful if you could be there."

I don't know why, but he finally relents and agrees to request an appointment and accompany me.

The next day, we go to the Labor Office, but when he sees who I'm scheduled to meet, he tells me, "I don't like this woman. We've had issues in the past. She keeps calling me for this and that, but I'm not ready to speak with her."

"What kind of issues?" I ask.

He dismisses the question with a shrug of his shoulders and guides me to a different door down the hall. "This person is better to talk with," he says, and knocks.

The man who answers the door gives me a stony glare and tells me to wait outside in the hallway. "I want to talk to this gentleman in private." The door shuts in my face.

This is the first clue I have that something isn't right. I wasn't scheduled to meet this man, yet he acted as if he'd been expecting us. The two men talk for a long time while I wait in the hallway. Finally, the door opens and they tell me to come in. I'm told to sit down, but not asked to speak on my behalf.

"I've reviewed your case," the man from the Labor Office says. "There is no change. Consider the matter closed."

"But I—"

"Not another word out of you. Who are you to question such a decision? You think you know better than your bosses? From what I can see, they have been more than fair to you. Yet you try to stir the pot and make them seem like the bad guys? Go back outside and wait while I finish up with this gentleman."

I go to the bathroom to compose myself. It takes a while to make my face neutral again. And when I'm finished and leaving, who do I see in the hallway? The HR man speaking with the woman he'd wanted to avoid earlier. There's no sign of tension between them at all, no animosity. In fact, they're joking around like they're good friends. And that is when I finally understand that I never had a chance to win satisfaction. This isn't how the system works. It makes me angry again, but this time my anger is directed inward at myself, rather than at any of them. I was foolish. These people, they're just playing by a set of rules I don't yet understand— not the rules I learned earlier in life, but the new, unspoken ones that dictate how things actually work during such times as these. I had resisted them out of ignorance and idealism, instead of trying to operate under assumptions I now realize are obsolete. I'd always believed that if I worked hard enough and remained loyal enough to a company, I'd get what I deserved. But that's no longer true. It's too simplistic, and not at all realistic. How many times since starting this whole process have I had this fact thrown into my face like cold water? What happened between Yikealo's relative and Titi's cardiologist proves the point. If I am to succeed now, I need to change the way I do things.

But where do I start? And how? I never cared about making the right connections before, and that's left me with very few people with enough influence to actually help me now.

A BRAVE THING

When at last my former employer sends me my release letter, I'm surprised to see that it includes a comprehensive list of all my contributions and achievements — the survey papers I prepared, the manuals I wrote, the workshops I gave or attended — yet it offers no reason at all for my termination. It shows that I have been a dedicated worker with no negative marks. So what do I get for all this effort and loyalty? Released without explanation or compensation, simply for asking to take my sick daughter to America for surgery to repair a heart defect. My anger boils at the injustice of it all. But what can I do? I've already tried to reason with my boss and with our company's HR department. It's like a wall has been placed all around me, blocking me no matter which way I turn.

For the next several days, I don't sleep very well, and when I do sleep, I'm haunted by unsettling dreams. In one, I'm climbing a ladder to reach my sister Aster's room on the highest floor of a tall building. Each time I got close to the top of the ladder in my dream, I'd slip down again. No matter how many times I tried, I could never reach her. "Don't give up," she'd shout down at me. "Try one more time!"

Every night I climb that ladder, and every morning I wake up even more tired and distraught than the night before. "One more time," my sister's voice echoes in my mind. "Don't give up!"

But then one night I make it the entire way up the ladder and climb inside Aster's room. I had already decided the dream reflected my frustration over not being able to achieve what I set out to do. But how does succeeding in my dream reflect the reality of my actual situation now? I still haven't been able to get the necessary permissions we need for Titi to have her surgery in America.

The night after I reach the top, the dream changes again. I'm still climbing a ladder to Aster's room, but this time when I reach the top I don't have the strength to take the last step. I'm stuck, barely holding on. I only have enough strength to call out for help. Eventually, a man appears. "I heard your cries. They drew me here," he says, and offers me his hand. He's very strong, very powerful. After he lifts me up and sets me down on my feet on the rooftop terrace, he says, "You can't always finish a difficult task by yourself. Sometimes you need to find the right person who can lift you that last little bit."

The next day I decide to take my complaints to the highest level in the company, where the line between it and the government blurs. I'll keep banging on doors until someone listens to me. I tell my friend from the office of my plan, half expecting him to discourage me from pushing too hard. It seems like people are becoming less willing to speak out against the many ways we're being oppressed. We've forgotten how to resist, how to stand up for our rights. But to my surprise, he encourages me to do it. "You're not the only one to be treated so unfairly," he says. "Our bosses act as if we're ants doing their work for them. For the sake of everyone in the office, tell them how you feel for all of us. You have nothing to lose."

"Nothing to gain, either," I counter. I'd already accepted that the job is forever lost to me. The best thing for me to do would be to move on. But I can't. Something is telling me I won't move forward until I can put this behind me.

"Maybe not. It's possible they might reconsider your termination."

"I don't want that. Even if it were possible, I wouldn't come back now, not after everything that's happened."

"Then do it for the rest of us. We've all suffered in silence for too long, but we have too much to lose if we speak out."

I know exactly what he means. For far too long we've been feeling unable to help ourselves. But I've already lost my job. My travel plans have been denied. What more could they do to me?

The more I think about it, the more I'm emboldened by my former coworker's words. I decide to speak my mind. But when it finally comes time to put my own plan into action, I'm beset with doubts once again. Am I doing the right thing for me? I think the answer is yes, but is it the right thing for Titi? Am I doing this out of some misplaced sense of self-righteousness? Do I really believe I'm giving voice to more than just my own bitterness? The people I'm about to confront occupy powerful positions within the government, and their influence reaches very far. It's already clear I've somehow crossed someone enough to ensure they make my life difficult. I could be making things worse for my family and completely ruin any future chance I might still have to get Titi her medical treatment. Yikealo, in particular, is especially vulnerable because of his position in the National Service; he can't simply walk away from his job as I did. The repercussions would be severe. And yet he's done nothing but urge me onward. He supports my decision and thinks it's necessary, too. "You deserve to be heard," he tells me. "You've always worked hard and deserve to be recognized. Besides, what more could they take from us? They've already taken everything."

Not everything, I think. *Not yet. There's so much more we could lose.*

I have to think long and hard about this. Is it worth stirring up trouble? What will I gain?

Peace of mind, I realize. It'll be the only thing to come out of this.

Resist, the voice inside of my head keeps telling me. *Someone has to.*

When I find myself standing at the door of the senior manager to whom I've chosen to address my concerns, I realize it's now or never. This gentleman occupies a unique position in the government-corporate hierarchy— neither former freedom fighter, nor politician. He was educated outside of Eritrea and returned here after independence. I remember meeting him once before, when I was first hired into the company. Back then, he seemed very approachable, reasonable, and likeable. I sensed that he was honest and forthright. When I told him the ideas I had for various projects, he acted genuinely interested. But since then, we've exchanged little more than the occasional hello whenever our paths crossed in the hallway. I don't think we've said more than a dozen words to each other in the entire time I've been here. He's one of the top bosses, although subordinate to the man who would have had the ultimate say in granting me permission to travel. *But that's not why I'm here,* I remind myself. *Peace of mind. Someone has to say something.*

I take in a deep breath and utter a silent prayer before raising my fist. It all comes down to this, delivering myself to a near total stranger with whom our only interaction probably meant nothing to him. My heart drums heavily in my chest, and my throat suddenly goes dry. "Who is it?" he barks, making me jump.

Did I knock? I don't remember knocking.

I open my mouth, but nothing comes out.

"Come in!"

His eyes narrow slightly when he sees me. I look familiar to him, but he otherwise doesn't seem to know who I am.

"Do you have a moment?" I ask. "I have something I would like to share with you. It won't take long."

The puzzled look on his face turns to concern. The corners of his mouth edge downward into a mild frown of impatience. Noticing it is enough to make me want to turn around and run away, but before I can move, he tells me to sit, and he gestures to an empty chair.

"You may not remember me," I say, skipping over the customary pleasantries, "but we met when I first joined this company. Last week, I was fired. I'm not here to ask for that decision to be reversed. I'm not here for any favors or special consideration."

The tension on his face loosens. Now he's curious.

"I just thought you should be made aware of how poorly I was treated." I hand over the termination letter and point out my list of accomplishments. "As you can see, I worked very hard and diligently the entire time I was here. And I'm not the only one. Everyone in my department does. It's a very good team of professionals, and we've done a lot of good work."

"So?" he asks, wondering where I'm going with this.

"We have never been recognized for our accomplishments."

Again, his face changes as he reads the letter. When he's finished, he looks up, surprised. "You did all these things mentioned here?"

"Yes. And more. But then last week I was terminated for no reason. I was treated like I have contributed nothing of value to this company."

"A week ago? Why didn't you come to me earlier?"

"There's no formal process for making such complaints except to speak to HR. They told me to drop it. They said I have no recourse. I tried taking it to the Labor Office, but they said the same thing: There's nothing I can do."

"And you want your job back?"

"No. I'm here because the senior managers, the bosses of our bosses, don't know about our work. The middle managers always take the credit. We're underappreciated. We're not even allowed to include our names on our research reports or any papers we write."

He stares at me in disbelief. "What papers?"

"If you go downstairs, you'll see shelves in the office of the department head lined with finished reports. I can assure you they bear none of our names, only the names of our departments. We are people, not parts of a machine. Anyway, now you know what's really happening here. It's an unfair situation that negatively affects morale. But nobody wants to speak up for fear of losing their job."

"And what caused you to lose yours?"

"I asked for permission to travel to the US. My daughter needs heart surgery. I was denied."

He's quiet for several seconds. Finally, he shakes his head and says, "I wish you had come to me with this earlier, so that I might have prevented all of this." He doesn't address the travel issue, but neither does he offer me any conciliatory gesture.

"It's too late for me now. As I said, I didn't come to ask for my position back. But you have many good people in that office who are being treated as poorly as I was. Or worse. They won't say anything for themselves out of fear of being fired like me."

I stand up then, because I've accomplished all I came to do, and I thank him for his time. He waits, as if he really expects me to make some kind of personal demand of him. And when I don't, he says, "Well, I appreciate you coming to me with this. It's a brave thing to speak out sometimes. I'll see if there is anything I can change so this doesn't happen again." He pauses, then adds, "I will pray for your daughter's recovery. Good luck."

I leave his office feeling as if a weight has been lifted from my shoulders. It won't change my particular situation, and I don't have much hope it will change for my former coworkers, either. But there is a greater personal benefit I gain by speaking my mind like this: I feel empowered. It gives me the confidence to speak for myself in the future, rather than keeping my troubles silent, or waiting until it's too late to make a difference. This has always been my weakness in the past. From now on, I will stand up for myself and for the things I believe are just.

When I tell Yikealo this, he chuckles. "Weakness? No, you have always been strong like this, Wudasie."

Maybe, but for the first time I begin to understand that this is what it truly means to be free. No one is going to hand you what you think you deserve just because you won the right. You have to go get it if you can. You have to grasp it and hold onto it, and then wield it like a sword. And you can't let it go if someone tries to wrestle it away from you.

WRITTEN IN ICE

Feeling more energized than I have in a long time, I decide I can't let it go to waste. I've been too passive regarding the situation with Titi, despite what my husband thinks. And something the man said as I was leaving strikes me as more than just empty sentiment. Why would he wish for Titi's recovery after I'd just told him I couldn't take her to America for the surgery?

Because there must be another way.

Up until now, I've been told that adults can get an exit visa only after being granted permission from one's employer. I'd never really thought about those people who don't have a job. Or who work for themselves, like farmers. Or who are students. All of these types of people must travel, too, on occasion. Surely, there has to be some way for them to apply to leave the country. It doesn't make sense not to have that option.

A female answers my call to the Immigration Office. "Is it possible," I ask her, "to travel abroad if a person doesn't have a job?"

"There's no employment requirement to get a visa," she replies blandly. "Why would you think there is?"

Of course, now I feel absolutely stupid for assuming such a thing. If I'd just thought about it, I would have recognized the faulty logic sooner. But I'd only applied to travel outside the country during times when I was employed, and so I'd always followed the same process for getting permission.

Embarrassed by my ignorance I try to explain this to her, adding that I'm not working at the moment.

"The requirement of a letter from an employer is only to make sure they're aware of your plans and are okay with you leaving your position for that amount of time. Are you eligible for the National Service?"

"No. I'm married and my husband is already serving."

It's then that the reasons for the requirement suddenly make sense. Since nearly all businesses are now overseen by the government, their activities are considered indispensible for the smooth operation of the country, whether directly or otherwise. My husband Yikealo, for example, recently took on a new role outside the ENS, even though he remains conscripted. It's still linked to the government, which is why the transfer was allowed. The government views every worker essential, even if it doesn't treat us as if we are.

"So, what are the requirements and documents for someone who is not working?" I ask.

"You need to go to your local *zoba* office," she replies, referring to one of our country's regional administrative branches. "Bring three witnesses with you who can testify that you're currently not holding any kind of job and are exempted from national service. And you said you were married and your husband is serving? Are you able to see him?"

"Yes. He's assigned here in Asmara."

"Good. He will need to sign a form that shows you have his permission to travel outside the country. Bring it and the stamped document from your *zoba* office to us here, along with your application for visa."

"That's it?" I ask, almost in disbelief. Had I known sooner it would be this easy, I would have resigned my position the moment I received the medical certificate and avoided the hassle altogether.

After I hang up, I finally understand the meaning of the dream I'd had where I'd been told to ask for help. If I hadn't sought out the man from my former employer, I wouldn't have gained the confidence to question the travel requirements. I also realize now that the head of our Human Resources department might have been trying to do me a favor by instructing me to leave the company. He must have understood that my travel couldn't be endorsed because of political pressure from above. So, by prompting me to sever ties with the company, I'd no longer be bound by such a restriction, and the company would no longer be seen as permitting travel, whether in defiance of the government's wishes or someone else's, someone more personally invested in my failure, like Doctor Simret.

I do exactly as the immigration officer instructed. The only hitch is that I haven't yet broken the news of my job status to anyone outside of the office other than Yikealo, so my first step is explaining to my family and friends what happened, so that I can get three witnesses to vouch for me. It also requires me to divulge a bit more about our reasons for travel than I'm comfortable with. Finally, armed with the appropriate statements, my husband's declaration, and the completed form from the *zoba*, as well as the medical board certificate from the Ministry of Health, I submit three new applications for exit visas at the Immigration Office— one for myself, one for Titi, and one for Natsanet.

Natsanet's application is a last-minute addition, after Yikealo and I agree that it will be far easier for me to take care of her than for him, even with all the other distractions of the trip. His work schedule takes him out of the house very early in the morning, long before the children have eaten breakfast, and he's usually not home again until late in the evening. He is also frequently asked to travel to other towns throughout the country and is gone overnight. But the greatest impediment to his ability to care for Natsanet is that he could be mobilized at any time, depending on any changes to our military stalemate with Ethiopia. If he's forced to leave home for such duty, it would suddenly put a great burden on our parents, and they're all getting too old to be dealing with a fussy little girl who will soon be turning four. Yikealo's father has been bedridden for years from an old stroke, and his mother already has her hands full taking care of him.

Regardless of whether she stays here or comes with us to America, the disruption will be stressful to Natsanet. She's still a picky eater, some days refusing all food except for the sweetest sweets. It's a daily challenge to get her to eat well. Her father simply doesn't have the time and patience to coddle her like I do.

When I had a job, I wouldn't leave in the morning until I was sure she'd eaten something healthy for breakfast. I would come home at noon and spend nearly the entirety of my lunch break preparing a decent meal for her and coaxing it into her. The nanny tries her hardest, but Natsanet is simply too strong willed and won't listen to her.

To a stranger, my younger daughter looks small and frail. Some people might even believe she's malnourished. But we've always given her as much of the right kind of food to eat as she'll tolerate. She simply has no desire to eat more than a few bites— unless it's sweets. Then she suddenly becomes a bottomless pit.

We have asked Doctor Mehari many times if there's anything wrong with her, but his answer is always no. She's perfectly healthy, small but strong, and active enough for her age. I always worry that she might have a hidden heart condition like her sister, but he tells me every time he examines her that he's unable to detect anything of the sort. It's a maddening irony that Natsanet is as healthy as she is, yet appears sickly, while Titi looks like a chubby, bubbly child while hiding a life-threatening condition inside her body.

Maybe my insistence on dragging Natsanet with me to America comes from the guilt I've felt ever since Doctor Simret accused me of being a bad mother. Or maybe it's the blame I place on myself for Titi's heart defect. Whatever the case might be, I know that if I'm not here to give Natsanet the attention she needs, she might fall ill again. Also, I have this secret hope a doctor in the US can examine her with better machines than we have here. It's not that I don't trust Doctor Mehari, but he's limited by fifty-year-old technology. Maybe the doctors in America with their expensive machines will be able to figure out why she has such a low interest in healthy food.

When I arrive at the Immigration Office with all of my documents, I'm suddenly filled again with the suspicion that someone wants to stop me. It doesn't actually matter if I'm right or not, or whether the problems I've had are due to some general governmental dictate. Either way, there are forces working against me. Doctor Simret's initial refusal to renew the medical certificate is proof of that.

I realize it appears paranoid, but it's not totally irrational. This is what we have become, a culture beset by bitterness and distrust, where some people resent others and report on their activities out of jealousy or spite. Or a false sense of patriotism. Or simply for money. In any case, I find myself repeatedly checking over my shoulder to see if I'm being followed or watched. I avoid crowded hallways and meeting other people's eyes out of fear of being recognized. When I'm forced to sit and wait for hours in the waiting rooms overflowing with people, I hide my face behind a book. I'm overly sensitive to how conspicuous my presence here is, as I am the only person my age applying for permission to travel outside of the country. It's a notable difference from my previous experience, even though it was less than a year before. The government is cracking down even more, making it harder for people who might be eligible for the National Service from leaving without special permission from people high up in the chain of command.

Somehow, I make it through the application process without seeing anyone I know. And when all three exit visas are approved, I almost can't believe my luck. For once, the stars all seem aligned in my favor.

The moment I have them in my hand, I'm too choked up to speak. Here at last are the products of far too many hours of waiting, of heartbreak and frustration. Of misinformation, misdirection, and outright obstruction. The bureaucracies I've had to navigate are unnecessarily burdensome. They've become increasingly infected with corruption, egos, and personal agendas. Greater restrictions on foreign travel, both into the country and out, increasingly isolates Eritrea on the world stage. Our president defiantly asserts that Eritrea needs to be more self-reliant, and in theory it sounds reasonable. But in practice, our isolationism only hurts us even more. It discourages outside offers of help, shuts down international NGOs, and bars both religious and secular charities whose intentions are to improve our quality of life. Our government grows more certain by the week that foreign governments are actively trying to interfere in our affairs or use us to achieve their own political goals. There is historical precedent to justify this wariness, from both the West and the East. We've been exploited by so many other countries in the past that it's natural to be distrustful. But this paranoia isn't helping to protect us, it's suffocating us.

The last administrative hurdle for us is securing our entry visas from the US Embassy in Asmara. It must be done soon, since the exit visas expire in a month, and God only knows how long this final step will take. After the difficulty I had simply getting to this point in the first place, I don't want to have to go through it all over again. There's no guarantee the exit visas will be renewed. In fact, I wonder deep down if it was a fluke with no chance of ever being replicated. Someone in the immigration office might have made a mistake. Maybe they were having an especially good day. Or they somehow missed getting the memo. But even if none of those things is true, the longer this process is drawn out, the more likely it becomes that someone disagreeable finds out about my application and puts a stop to it. Also, new regulations are added and old ones amended all the time. Even the most innocuous changes in government guidelines can unexpectedly turn entire processes upside down. We have a recent saying about this: "Rules and regulations are written in ice, they melt and run away when the sun comes out." In other words, we can't count on anything being certain for long.

Part of the process of getting the entry visas is to sit for an interview. When I meet with the agent, I sense that he's worried about our reasons for going. He's an American, middle-aged, nothing remarkable about him. He explains that they need to be sure we have a good sponsor for our trip, someone with provably sufficient financial means to support us while we're there. This includes the surgery. "Medical care in America is very expensive," he says. "You also need to prove that you have a place to stay and that you won't become a burden on anyone."

I hand him the paperwork from the sponsoring hospital, which states that the doctors have volunteered their time and services to perform the surgery without charge, and the hospital is covering many of the other expenses, too.

The agent gives me an astonished look. "I've never heard of such a huge sponsorship before."

"We've been blessed with good fortune," I acknowledge. I don't add that we've also had more than our fair share of bad to balance it out.

"Well, these documents appear authentic," he says, "but I'll still have to verify everything to make sure all of your living and hospital costs are adequately covered. I'll contact the hospital directly. It may take some time."

I want to tell him that we have less than a month before our exit visas expire, but I'm sure he already knows this. I don't want a repeat of what happened with the woman at the Immigration Office, so I simply thank him, adding, "We've been waiting a long time for this treatment."

The next several days pass with excruciating slowness, and the day our exit visas are set to expire inches ever closer. I pray both night and day that all of my hard work and sacrifice isn't for nothing.

At last, the agent calls me in for the follow up meeting. Once more, he shakes his head and reiterates that he's never seen such a generous sponsorship before. "You're truly very lucky for such an opportunity."

"Does this mean everything is okay?"

He smiles. "Well, you've met all the requirements, so I've sent your passports along with my recommendation to be stamped. They'll call you when they're ready to be picked up."

DENIED

If there's one thing that can get us out onto the streets like Ethiopian bombs, it's a religious feast. The day I receive the call from the US Embassy informing us that our passports are ready to be collected also happens to be the *Inda Mariam Nigdet* festival, or Saint Mary's Day in the Christian local calendar. The annual holiday honors Jesus' mother and has particular significance to Asmarinos. Christians from all over the region come into the city to attend services at Kidisti Mariam, Saint Mary's namesake church and the city's largest cathedral. The church is on Arbate Asmara Street, close to the embassy on the east side of town. After the service, family and friends will gather for the *nigdet*, or religious feast. Large amounts of food and *suwa*, a local drink fermented from sorghum that smells and tastes like beer, are prepared. Every door is thrown open, allowing anyone to come in and help themselves. I hate to leave my family during the festivities, but this is the chance we've been waiting on for so long, so I drop everything I'm doing and make my way across the city and into the crowds.

Despite the bright sights, sounds, and smells of the revelry all around me, my thoughts are focused inward, on the upcoming trip. There's always that seed of doubt in the back of my mind that something will go wrong, that our applications for travel will be denied. I notice very little of the celebrations. I'm too full of anxiety.

The day is not a holiday for the embassy, so it's as crowded as usual with people hoping to go to America for one reason or another. As always, there's a long line waiting to get inside, but today it's swamped by the masses of people making their way to the orthodox church. I find the end of the line and wait.

Once I'm searched at the gate and cleared to enter the compound, I take a seat on one of the benches to await my name being called. One by one, those who arrived before me meet with their agents lined up behind their wall of windows. I watch as some jump up with joyful exclamations, signs that their applications have been approved. When the news is not so good, they cry out in anguish and leave in disappointment. I notice that there are far more of the latter, and it worries me. I pray I won't be told bad news. I'm sure it would be the final straw that crushes me for good. Instead, I try not to think about it, for fear of making it come true. I turn my attention to the people celebrating out on the street. I try to let their exuberance buoy me.

"Another rejection," I hear someone beside me say. It's an old woman, heavyset and crouched over. She grunts with each shuffled step, lifts her walking stick and sets it carefully down in front of her, then shuffles forward a little more as she makes her way out. She's speaking to no one in particular. "The same story, year after year," she mutters to herself. "This year I hoped to go see my daughter in America, but they tell me no, yet refuse to give me any reason. What am I supposed to do? Soon, I am going to die. I just want to see my daughter one last time before I pass."

I feel her pain as if it is my own. I don't know why, but her story resonates deeply with me, and the tears well up in my eyes. Perhaps it's her age and the stooped way she walks. They make me think of my own mother, even though she's a lot younger and healthier. I can't imagine how terrible it must be to never be able to see one's child again. I fear the old woman might be right, that she'll run out of time before she has another chance.

I hear my name being called. Suddenly, I dread the answer. Something tells me it will not be good. My legs shake as I make my way over.

"Here's your passport," the agent tells me, sliding it over the counter toward me. I study her face for any signal that anything is wrong. I don't see it, but neither do I see any reason to celebrate. I can't tell what this means, whether it's because she's become numb by the routine, the constant disappointment she is asked to deliver, or the accusations and blame that inevitably get thrown at her for doing this thankless job. "Congratulations," she adds. I spot the new stamp in my passport before it flips shut.

She moves onto the next one, rechecks the inside, then closes and hands it over as well. "And here's your daughter Titi's with the stamp."

I pluck it off the counter.

"Unfortunately, your application for your other daughter, Natsanet, has been denied."

The moment the words are out, my face goes cold and a sharp pain pierces my heart. A loud roar fills my head. I barely even hear my own words as I force them out of my mouth. "But— But how?"

"I'm sorry."

I try to explain that leaving Natsanet here is out of the question. She's physically delicate, and her father is in the National Service. He'll be unable to care for her full time. I beg her to please reconsider.

"The truth is," the woman patiently explains, "the American government is worried that if you bring both daughters to the States, then none of you will return here."

"That won't happen!"

"Nevertheless," she says, shrugging, "we must ensure you aren't using your daughter's medical care as a means to emigrate from here."

"I have no intention of moving to America! Natsanet is only three. Please."

"I am sorry, truly. But it's out of my hands."

I try pleading with her again, but it's clear there's nothing I can say to make her change her mind. She insists the decision isn't hers to make, but rather government policy. She tells me all this with the same stoic look on her face, but I can tell by the shaking in her hands that she's just as upset as I am. I stumble away from the window and somehow make my way through the waiting crowd to the gate.

Outside the embassy's tall iron fence, I'm swallowed up again in the sea of people still making their way to and from the cathedral. Many of them are dressed in the traditional white garments worn for visits to their orthodox churches. I'm blinded by the brightness. Flashes of gold and crimson. Children running past, homemade paper hats on their heads, hand-lettered in Ge'ez with various bible phrases and teachings. My legs work without conscious thought. They take me away from the embassy. How can I be so numb, yet so completely filled with pain? Everyone around me is happy and talking cheerfully, singing our traditional religious songs. But here I am with my heart torn into pieces.

I manage to find my way out of the procession and over to an empty bench on the opposite side of the street, where I cover my face with my hands. For once, I don't care if anyone can see me crying. We're a private people when it comes to our sorrow, at least when out in public. We share our feelings with only the closest of friends and family. But the pain I feel now is too raw, too intense to hold inside or wait for privacy.

Besides, everyone is in such a hurry, too wrapped up in the celebrations, that they either don't notice me, or are too preoccupied to stop.

Somehow, I find myself swept up in the crowd. It draws me into the plaza outside the cathedral of Inda Mariam. Vendors are everywhere, selling religious books, crosses, candles, holy sand, sacred stones, and pictures of Saint Mary. A priest rattles a bell and shouts, "Araki! Araki!" asking for donations for the poor. Before I know it I'm inside the church. All I want is a quiet, private place to pray, to let out my sorrows. But I find no solitude here, and no solace for my grief. Tears of anguish fill my eyes, pour down my cheeks, while everyone around me is singing and dancing. Soon they'll be eating and drinking, while my hunger for peace and comfort remains unfulfilled.

In the midst of all the noise, a dream I recently had comes back to me. In it, Titi and Natsanet are holding hands. They're standing in the middle of an impossibly tall flight of stairs. They're so beautiful together, big and little sister, each clutching the other so that it would be impossible to know which of them is offering the other support. But then their hands separate. Titi turns in one direction and continues on up the stairs, while Natsanet turns in the other and descends. My vision shifts, and I see that there's nothing below my baby girl save an ominous sea of darkness. I remember being so terrified that she would fall into it that I woke myself up, drenched in sweat and gasping for air. It took me a long time to go back to sleep after that. The whole time I worried about the meaning of the dream.

Now I know, and I wish I didn't.

"How is she going to survive this without me?" I whisper, before realizing I have unconsciously already accepted what this means. I've made my decision; I know what I have to do.

The tears come again, prompted by the knowledge that I'll soon be saying goodbye to one of my two little girls. It terrifies me to consider it. What if something happens to her without me? What if she dies? For a moment I hesitate. Am I making the right choice? Should I stay or go? Now I'm no longer sure.

I entreat Saint Mary, my favorite angel, for guidance.

I make a plea to Saint Gabriel to intercede.

I beg God and Jesus Christ to help.

My friend from college who went to America several years ago, Aysha, once chided me for making such demands of our religious icons. "God is smart," she scolded me. "He hides His office from us. We knock at His door and offer up our bribes in hopes He'll open it wide for us to see what's on the other side. But God doesn't want our bribes. He only wants our prayers, and he only gives strength so we can step through into the unknown."

I have prayed diligently since the moment I learned of Titi's heart murmur, yet have my prayers been answered?

The answer is yes, of course they have. Titi has been given a chance to get the medical attention she needs. A hospital has been found willing to provide that care for free, something we would never have been able to afford ourselves. And should I choose, I am allowed to take her and be with her. Yes, my prayers have been answered.

So why does it feel like a cruel joke? Why does it feel like an impossible test with no good answer? Am I just not thankful enough?

Or worthy enough?

I sit in my corner of the church for a very long time while the revelers come and go all around me. No one pays me any heed. The day wears on, and the crowds get smaller. Everyone is now heading off to their various neighborhood feasts to honor the Virgin Mother. The church is all but empty, and I have no choice but to make my own way home, where I must choose between my two daughters.

GUILT AND MORE PARANOIA

My poor girls. I simply can't face them without getting emotional. Without filling up with such guilt that it threatens to come pouring out of me like water. For days I've put off telling them what is about to happen, but now that the departure is imminent, I have to figure out a way to let them know. I have to be certain they both understand they'll be fine. I want so badly to believe this myself, but I fear my true feelings will reveal themselves when I break the news to them. I don't know what to do.

Yikealo tells me to wait. He knows how they'll each respond, and he wants to spare me the ordeal. But keeping it a secret is unfair to them and torture to me.

If there's any relief in the coming days, it's in finally being able to confess the truth about Titi's medical issue to more of our family members. It's been a terrible weight on me for far too long. I don't share all of the details, just enough so they know we have arranged for her treatment outside of the country. As is customary, there's a warm outpouring of support from everyone. They try to assure me that Natsanet will be well cared for and that I needn't worry about her. "You need to focus on Titi now," they tell me. Their encouragement alleviates some of my guilt, but not all of it. Doubt haunts me as I prepare to make the final arrangements for the trip.

And with it the same old worries resurface. What if someone tries to stop us now? If the wrong person finds out we're leaving, they could try and block my way. I don't like feeling this way. I don't like sounding crazy. Yikealo tells me I'm not. "You're being totally rational," he says, and reminds me of all those people we know or have heard about who were arbitrarily stopped at the airport as they were getting ready to board a plane. Someone just comes along out of the blue and denies them from leaving the country, citing some silly reason or another. Sometimes no reason at all. The government can be quite capricious in its actions, even vindictive. When the American head of the NGO where I once worked tried to exit the country after the government shut it down, he was told that he lacked the clearance to leave and was unnecessarily detained. He was eventually allowed to go, but not after the government had made its point: "We decide whether you can come and go, not you." It made me wonder if he caused trouble by complaining about the NGO's closure. Of course, the worse the situation gets, the more people *want* to leave, whether through legitimate means or illegally, which makes the government even more restrictive. It's a vicious spiral toward a familiar and dreaded endpoint.

Even Yikealo advises me to take the necessary precautions, now that we're in the final stretch. He worries that if I book the plane tickets under my own name, it could alert the wrong people of my plans, including my former employers, some of whom might want to retaliate against me for taking my complaints over their heads. With only about a half million residents, Asmara is not so large a city, especially for being the nation's capital, so gossip has the potential to spread quickly. People know people. Some of them have personal agendas. Now that we're so close to the end of the process, it would be foolish of us not to do everything we possibly can to avoid risks.

I share these concerns with a travel agent I know and trust, and she immediately proposes a solution, as if she's dealt with this same problem before. "We'll use a different name to reserve the tickets," she says. "Then, right before you depart, you pay for them under your own name. It's not foolproof, since there's still a small window of time when someone could find out and stop you, but it'll be narrow. You would have to be very unlucky. Or someone would have to be very determined to stop you."

She pauses to give me a chance to explain. While it's true that I've had more than my share of bad luck, and I do believe someone is determined to step in my way, I have no proof of these things, only anecdotes and intuition. So, I just nod. I tell her instead that we already have very little time as it is, since Titi is scheduled to check into the hospital in three days time. So she goes ahead and reserves the tickets for me under a false name. I'm thankful she doesn't press the issue or ask why Yikealo or Natsanet aren't accompanying us. The fact that she doesn't pry gives me some assurance she'll remain discreet about our transaction.

The next day, I'm shopping with another friend for necessities to take on the trip, when who should I come face to face with? The HR representative from my old job, the one who lied to me about helping me with the Labor Office! Once we make eye contact, there's no way to escape the encounter. Tradition compels us to exchange pleasantries at the very least, even if it's the very last thing I want to do right now.

"What are you up to?" he asks, feigning innocence.

"Nothing."

"Any progress regarding your trip to America?"

The question startles me. I hadn't mentioned my plans to him, so he must have found out some other way, which explains his sudden change in attitude toward me.

"You obviously know the situation," I reply, as calmly as I can manage. But inside, I'm thinking: *Such nerve! He certainly doesn't waste any time getting straight to the heart of the matter.* "How am I supposed to make any progress without the proper documents?" I try to sound frustrated and resigned to failure, but I'm unable to fully mask my contempt for him. I can see he senses it, but it doesn't stop him from pushing.

"Maybe you were able to find a way around the requirements."

"If there's another way I haven't already tried, I don't know about it."

He mulls this over for a moment. "So, what will you do for your daughter's treatment?"

I now know his concern for her is just an act. He doesn't know anything about my girls, much less care about their welfare. If he did, then he wouldn't have deceived me in the first place. I don't trust a single thing he says. Inside my head a voice warns me not to give him any clue that the issue of my traveling to America has been resolved. It's obvious by now he's only trying to extract information from me. As for his intentions, I can only guess at what they might be. These days, anyone can be a spy.

"I have no other options," I tell him.

"That's too bad. Well," he adds, quickly extracting himself from the conversation, "I wish you luck. Please let us know if we're able to do something about it. Okay?"

The encounter leaves me shaken, but it confirms to me that my paranoia isn't just imagined. His interest in my plans was clearly more than passing.

My friend, the same woman who accompanied me to Dubai to see about getting Titi medical help there, and one of the few people I've confided in about my experience with my former employer, is astonished at how calmly I handled the situation. "I don't know how you managed not to spit in his face," she says, once we're alone again. "I wanted to do it. The nerve of that man!"

I tell her that I keep reminding myself how much Titi needs this surgery and how close we are after so many years of trying, so I can't risk this for anything. "But it doesn't mean I didn't want to spit at him," I admit. "You can see how much my hands are shaking now."

My anxiety soars to new heights over the next two days, and I'm afraid I'll become too sick to travel. I can't eat or sleep. As each hour passes, I grow ever more convinced we'll be found out. This is our absolute last hope. After this, there's nothing short of crossing the border illegally. I'm so distraught that I wonder if I'll be able to hold myself together long enough to make our flight.

Somehow, I manage.

On the day of our departure, I say my goodbyes, but only to my immediate family, in-laws, and two aunts. Beyond them, I can't be absolutely sure who I can trust not to say anything. Even the most innocent slip of the tongue to the wrong person could derail everything. Next, I go to Natsanet's preschool and wait for her to finish her day. This is my usual routine, and I don't want anyone to think this day is any different than any other.

When she walks out, I can tell she's very tired. Her class spent hours at the zoo, and the heat has sapped her of energy. When she gets to me, all she wants to do is go home and sleep. Meanwhile my emotions are boiling over, threatening to expose the turmoil inside of me. She doesn't know that this is the last time I'll see her for God knows how long. I'm terrified thinking how badly she'll take the news that I'll be leaving Eritrea with her older sister on a big adventure that she can't come on with us. I know it's cruel to wait until the last possible moment, but both Yikealo and I agreed it's actually for the best to do it this way. If she knew of our plans sooner, she might share, despite being told not to. Children do not keep well their secrets; the bigger they are, the harder they are for them not to reveal. I hate that our lives in Eritrea have reached such a state that we have to act this way, keeping such things from our loved ones. But there's nothing we can do about it.

I take her to my mom's house. The plan is to leave her there to avoid a potentially loud, painful, and risky goodbye in public, which might alert the wrong people of our plans. I still haven't figured out how to break the news to Natsanet in a way she'll understand. I hope she'll accept that I'm not abandoning her. After all, I did everything I could to bring her with us. But she's too young to understand her parents aren't always in control, that there are forces greater than us whose interests run counter to ours.

No matter how carefully we tell her, there will be bitter tears and angry words. And after we get back — ideally much sooner than any of us dares to hope — there will inevitably be the lingering resentment to deal with. Two weeks away from Titi was already bad enough; I don't want to imagine what two months away from Natsanet will bring about. I feel like a bird being torn apart in a huge wind that's pulling me in a thousand different directions all at once.

As we enter the compound where my mother lives, Natsanet stumbles over the tiniest of irregularities between tiles. She's so weary from her busy day that her feet drag and her toe catches on the edge. Her hand rips from mine, and she goes down hard and starts to cry. I want nothing more than to just sit and hold her. I want to cry along with her, although my tears would be tears of anguish, of a pain that wells up from deep inside of me rather than being inflicted from the outside. But I have to be strong for her. I pick her up and carry her into the house, lay her on the bed, and rock her until her tears dry up. She falls asleep before we can talk, so I tuck her in for the last time in what I hope will not be too very long.

I linger a moment at the door and watch her chest rise and fall as she breathes. Then I leave without a chance to say goodbye.

Walking away from her is the hardest thing I've ever had to do. I hope it will remain as the hardest thing I'll ever have to endure for as long as I live. I'm supposed to be happy that Titi is finally able to get the medical attention we've been praying for since we first learned of her heart defect six years ago. But how can a mother choose to abandon one of her children, even to benefit another? I know that it happens all the time all over the world, for any number of reasons. Some people must make much harder choices than mine. I'll only be gone for a brief time, hopefully no more than a couple months, and yet it still tears my heart in two. No mother should ever have to face such a dilemma, regardless of the circumstances. The pain is too great. I wonder, how do they survive, the mothers who are forced to leave a loved one behind? How do they carry on? I'm not sure I have the strength to do so.

I ask my mother for the thousandth time to take good care of Natsanet, and for the thousandth time she promises me she will. She gives me a smile and tells me not to worry, but it's worry I see in her own eyes.

Before she lets me go, she gives me a long hug. "Promise me," she says. "Promise me you'll come back."

The request startles me. Staying in America isn't an option. It had never even crossed my mind. Nor had it held any sort of attraction for me. Not even my sister's descriptions of her life there, or my friend's certainty that I would one day come to live with her, could ever make me consider the idea. I know too well the pain that comes from time spent away from family. Each time I left my parents and siblings, I missed them terribly, even when I knew I would see them again soon.

"Good or bad," my mother tells me, "it's far better to live in your own country with your own people, even with things the way they are now. It will change. Please don't make me beg you to come back."

I tell her she needn't worry. Or beg.

I arrive at the travel agency just before the ticket office closes for the day and pay the amount due. Now our real names are printed on the tickets in large black letters. They feel like a banner unfurled into the sky, announcing to the world that we are trying to sneak away. I slip the papers deep into the bottom of my bag, then hurry off back home.

The plane doesn't depart for a few more hours, which gives me just enough time to pick Titi up from the house, grab the bags we've already packed, and drive to the airport. Now is when my anxiety, at a steady boil all day, explodes into something resembling panic. I can't control the shaking in my hands and the pain in my chest. I can't seem to catch my breath. I hide my face from everyone who passes me on the street, avoiding anyone's eye for fear they'll see the truth in my own.

We leave without any fanfare and very few people in attendance. Usually, when someone embarks on such a significant adventure, they're seen off by a large gathering of family members, friends, and neighbors. Everyone wants to extend their well wishes and bless the trip. But we're so wary of someone finding out and stopping us that we steal away like thieves. The Tigrinya proverb — *Ms kolia aytmker; ms kelbi aytithabae* — warns us to keep our plans secret until they've been accomplished, or else they lose their advantage. Ahead of us are still too many opportunities for our plans to be upset, from the check-in agents at the airport to the immigration officials. Those people are all connected to the government, and they don't have to offer any reason for denying our departure. Anyone leaving the country is automatically scrutinized with greater interest. And suspicion. This is how distrustful our country has become of its own citizens. It has created and fed a deadly cycle that grows worse and worse by the year.

Titi is antsy, unable to sit still in the car. She's been bouncing around ever since I told her at the house where we are going, although I still haven't given her the reason why. Neither have I explained why it's just the two of us and not her father and sister. She's too wrapped up in her own excitement to care about such details. For a moment I wish I could feel her joy with the same youthful innocence. To be as worry-free as she is would make this experience so much easier for me. Instead, I have to bear the burden of knowing what awaits her for the both of us. She has no idea how far America is, how long the flight will be, and what will happen to her once we arrive.

We say our goodbyes outside of the airport, which is as far as most family members and loved ones can generally go. My husband and one of my sisters are there, as are my two brothers. My sister-in-law and a close friend are the last to arrive. Titi beams as she doles out hugs; like a typical seven-year-old, she loves being the center of attention. But when it comes time to say goodbye to her father, the reality of what's happening finally resolves in her mind, and she begins to scream unhappily that he and Natsanet must come, too. The tears come then, and now I'm unable to hold them in, either. I can barely see where we're going as we hurry across the road toward the terminal, just the two of us, me leading, and she tugging at my hand to turn me around.

The guard at the main gate gives us a hard, unfriendly stare as we approach, and he tells us to go back home. "There's no travel for you today!" he barks. "You people think you can just go anywhere at any time you choose. It's my turn!"

It takes me a moment to realize he's only teasing. There's a hint of a grin in his eyes, but also an edge of bitterness in his voice. He steps out of his shack and tells Titi, "How about you watch my post and I take your trip instead? Eh? Let's swap positions for a change!"

Titi is so startled that she stops crying. She doesn't know how to respond to this strange man making such a strange demand of her. She turns to me for explanation, and it's all the distraction I need. I'm grateful that she has momentarily forgotten about her unhappiness, but I'm also angry. I'm in no mood for kidding.

The woman at the baggage check-in counter expresses surprise at how little we're bringing with us. "This is all you have?" she asks, when I place our small bag on the scale to be weighed. She checks my ticket again. "Aren't you going to America?"

"Yes," I whisper, fearful she'll announce our names over the loudspeaker.

"Only one bag?"

"Yes."

She looks more disappointed than doubtful. I don't know what she imagines this trip must be for us, but her shrug of indifference suddenly feels fake to me, like she's trying hard not to appear suspicious of our intentions. Usually when people travel to such faraway places, they take heavy bags. They pack everything they can possibly think of that they might need, then add to it all the personal comforts they think they won't find where they're going. All I had packed was a couple changes of clothes and some traditional dry food items for my sister, for when we meet her at the airport in Raleigh. It's a relief when the woman tags the luggage and directs us toward the gate.

At the immigration checkpoint, the agent barely even seems to notice us. He takes our payment, a standard charge for anyone entering or leaving the country, before stamping our passports. He waves us past without comment. The moment we slide through the turnstile, I let out a huge exhale of relief. But we're still not free. There are so many people here coming and going. I know many of them must work for the government. I worry we'll be recognized, so I take Titi and head straight upstairs to the waiting room, where I find seats in a far back corner, away from everyone else. Titi has stopped making a fuss, perhaps because she's picked up on my apprehension. She sits quietly, immersed in her own thoughts. I hope they're nothing like mine. Every time someone walks in our general direction, I expect them to grab us and take us back to security. I listen for our names over the loudspeaker and pray I don't hear them.

"Where are you going?" a man asks, suddenly appearing beside me. He sits down in the adjacent seat and repeats the question when I give him a suspicious look. Why is he asking me this?

He gestures to the old woman beside him. "This is my mother," he quickly explains. "She's on the flight to Germany. If that's where you're going, too, would it be too much to ask for you to assist her on the way there?"

"I— I'm going to America."

"Ah, even better. She's going there, too. But she's alone and doesn't speak any language other than Tigrinya."

I want to tell him that I barely even know what I'm doing myself, so how can I take on the added responsibility? But I can't turn him down. It's my duty to help if I can, so I give him a tentative nod and a wary smile. After a few minutes, he leaves me alone with his mother. The woman doesn't say much. She looks just as frightened as I feel.

After an eternity, we're finally called to line up. The whole time I'm reciting prayers beneath my breath that no one will stop us. It's a painfully long wait to pass through the checkpoint, another slow march down the aisle to our seats. It feels deliberately made to be so, as if to give the authorities as much time to find and stop us. I keep one wary eye on the crowd, half expecting security guards to push their way through and take us away.

On the plane, it takes forever for the passengers to stow their bags and for the crew to prepare for departure. I sink deep into my seat, shut the window beside us, belt us both in, then stare at the back of the seat ahead of me. Only after the plane begins to taxi and the front end lifts up into the air do I realize how tightly my fingers have been gripping the armrest.

PART TWO
LEAVING HOME

SO HARD NOT TO WORRY

The stranger in the aisle seat is talking. I'm not aware at first that she's speaking to me, not until she takes hold of my wrist and gently squeezes it. The unexpected touch yanks me out of my daze.

She's an older woman, although not as old as the one I promised to assist inside the terminal. For a split second I panic, thinking I've already failed in my promise to watch after her by leaving her behind inside the airport. I rise halfway out of my seat and scan the other passengers until I spot her several rows back. All around me are elderly people; the plane is full of them. In fact, I think I'm the youngest adult on board.

By now, we've reached cruising altitude and the plane has leveled off. Titi is fast asleep on the other side of me, her head lolling against the window shade. I have no idea how long we've been in the air. I sit back down.

The woman tells me her name, but even though I hear and repeat it in my mind, it's like trying to capture smoke with a fish net. It's gone from me as soon as I try to snatch it out of the air. Before I can ask her to say it again, she's moved on.

"We're going to Germany," she tells me. "And you?"

"Yes, that's where the plane is headed," I answer, still in a bit of a daze.

"No, I mean, are you off to a different destination afterward?"

"Oh, yes. America. My daughter and I are going to America."

"That's a very long journey."

"Is it?"

She shrugs. "I think flying to Europe is already too far. America is even farther away."

"I guess. I don't really know. This is our first time going there."

"Oh, really?" she says, raising an eyebrow. "Yes, the flight is very, very long, even from Europe. It must be at least eight or ten hours over the ocean."

I remember sitting in the terminal at Asmara and trying hard to figure out from the times on my tickets how long the flight would last, but it was too much for my overworked and emotionally stressed brain to calculate, especially with all the time zone changes. Of course I know where America is on a map. To get there from Eritrea, one must cross the widest part of Africa before flying over the Atlantic Ocean. But I have no sense of how the distance on paper translates to travel time by plane. The farthest I've ever flown before is to the United Arab Emirates, and I thought that took a long time by itself. Of course, most of that trip was long layovers. It's hard for me to conceive of being up in the air on a plane for more than a few hours at a time. How could an airplane possibly hold enough fuel to fly that far?

"And how are you able to take your daughter with you?" the woman continues. "I hear the government is not allowing youngsters to leave the country without special consideration."

I don't answer the question directly, just nod and say, "Yes, we have special consideration." I don't like talking about Titi's medical condition, especially to strangers.

"So, you're going to be with your husband then?" she asks. I'm not sure if she's being nosy or if she just wants someone to talk to.

To be eligible for a travel visa, an Eritrean citizen must either be older than forty or excused from military service for some qualifying reason, like me. This explains why so many of the adults on the plane are much older than I am. There are other exemptions. If you already reside and claim citizenship outside the country and are just visiting family, you have greater freedom to come and go. It's still a risky proposition, though, as they can make it hard for you to leave. Also, if your spouse lives abroad, then it's easier to gain permission to travel, although it can still take years before it's granted. One common scenario is where the husband has already established himself elsewhere, leaving the wife alone in Eritrea with the children. This may be why my seat neighbor assumes I'm going to join my husband. She must think we've already established a connection with America. It also explains why the guard at the gate made the comments he did about people traveling whenever they like. He thought I was one of those "lucky ones" who are able to come and go as they please.

"My husband is staying behind," I say. "He's in the National Service."

Confusion flutters across the woman's face. I can see her struggle with trying to understand how this is possible. Uncomfortable talking about myself, I turn the subject back to her by asking why she's traveling to Germany.

"I'm thinking about moving back," she says. "Me and my two teenagers, a boy and a girl."

"They're already there?"

"No. They're sitting in the back of the plane. We lived there once, but it's been a few years since we last returned. My husband and I settled there before the liberation and came back during repatriation."

The long war with Ethiopia had scattered tens of thousands of Eritreans seeking refuge from the conflict. Those who went to Ethiopia were just a small fraction of the total number who fled. Many ended up stuck in refugee camps spread out all over northeast Africa and the Middle East. Others settled in Europe and Canada and the United States. After Eritrea won its independence, host country governments encouraged Eritrean émigrés to return to their homeland, since they were no longer considered political refugees. Germany was one such country. Their government offered financial assistance to Eritrean nationals to help their transition back. Many jumped at the chance. Filled with a strong sense of nationalism following our victory, a lot of these same people would have returned anyway, regardless of incentives. We were all eager to begin building a post-war Eritrea.

My new friend tells me how she and her husband were among them. They brought their two young children back with them, children born in Germany but now dual citizens, and set up their own private business. Her story echoes my own in enough ways that I start to feel a connection with her. I wonder why she's leaving again now. I have my suspicions, but I still need to hear them out loud.

"We believed life would be good in our own country with our new government," she explains. "We thought our kids would have a better and brighter future here, with their own people and culture, than somewhere they would never really fit in."

I nod, because I completely agree. It's how I've always felt. Having experienced what it's like to live as an Eritrean in Ethiopia, I lost all desire to relive the hardest of those experiences after settling in Asmara.

"Some of our new friends warned us we were making a mistake," she continues. "They said our children had greater prospects for a better future in Germany. They begged us not to make any hasty decisions. But we had to choose quickly. If we waited too long, we would lose out on any financial assistance, so we took the chance. We also had faith in our leaders. After all, they had managed to win victory for us against all odds. We thought we'd settle down here and remain forever."

She sighs sadly and shakes her head. A darkness clouds her eyes, and for the first time I realize she's actually a bit younger than I had originally guessed. She can't be more than a couple years older than me.

"What changed your mind?" I ask.

"It's hard to be patient," she says. "I mean, how many years does it take to really free a people? We thought our country was making progress. We thought we'd made the right decision returning. But then another war broke out, and we started sliding backward again, losing the few freedoms we had. And it's only gotten worse. When the fighting ended, once more we thought things would improve. But the war isn't actually over, is it? It's just a ceasefire. So there's no true peace, no progress. Instead of moving forward, the government drags us toward the same past we ran away from."

I nod, although my first impulse is to defend the country against these charges. To think these things privately is one thing. To hear them expressed so brazenly is disconcerting. We don't speak like this in public. And even at home we keep the worst of our criticisms to ourselves for fear the children might hear and repeat them to strangers. But we're no longer in Eritrea, are we? We're on an airplane speeding north over Sudan by now.

"The hope and progress we wanted for our children are gone," she continues. "What future will they have, other than going to train for the military at Sawa? I would be willing to send my children there — it's our duty to serve our country, after all — but not when there is no endpoint to their commitment. I know people who have served for almost ten years. They still want to get out but they can't. Ten years! It's supposed to be eighteen months, but the government doesn't let them go. I know families whose children have died in the service, not from defending the country, but because of physical hardships and lack of proper medical care and nutrition. How can anyone plan a future if they don't know when they'll be able to return to their own private life? Or even if they'll ever have one?"

I want to stop her. I can't seem to get rid of the feeling the plane will suddenly turn around again and head straight back, where we'll all be arrested and thrown into jail for speaking out against the government.

The woman shrugs. "By the time they're out of the Service, they're too old for university. Too old to marry. Too old to raise a proper family. We all suffered the hardships of war. We all hoped peace would make things better. This is what I hoped for my children and grandchildren. But now all that hope is lost." Again, her face pinches. This time, however, I see anger flashing in her eyes. "I'm just fed up with the whole situation. It's a big mess, and it's only getting worse."

"Are your children old enough to be in the National Service now?"

162

"Not yet, but they're close. It's nearly time for them to go. My son is in tenth grade. He would have to go next year, and to be honest he's terrified. My daughter is one year behind him. Both of them know that life here isn't better! They think we lied to them, that we wanted to return only for ourselves. They're starting to hate us for it. This is what made me realize we were wrong. Eritrea isn't their home. And the Eritrea I see now isn't mine anymore, not when it is like this."

"So, you're moving back to Germany for good?"

"In order to keep the children's legal papers valid, we have to make a visit every few years. But this time they don't want to come back to Eritrea. They're miserable, and that makes me miserable. I don't know if we will return this time."

"And if you don't?"

"Then I will apply to become a political refugee." She sighs deeply. "All over again."

"And your husband, how does he feel about all this?"

"If I am honest, he prefers to stay in Eritrea. He still believes things will get better there. I am not so optimistic myself. I, too, would also prefer to stay here, if things were different. I didn't enjoy being an immigrant the first time around. We had to do it because the enemy pushed us out of our own country. But now I feel like we're being pushed out again, except this time the enemy is our own government. But to go back to being an immigrant?" She shakes her head. "I think it will be much harder the second time around."

"Where are you staying in Germany?"

"For now, with friends. I don't know for how long we can count on their hospitality. If we stay, we'll have to find a place of our own, a job to support myself and my family. I have no idea how to do any of that. I'm lost. But I may not have a choice. I will have to try for the sake of my children."

I catch myself nodding, and it startles me that I would be agreeing with her so soon after wanting her to keep silent. I sympathize with her situation. I feel her anguish, the torment of being torn into pieces. It's a hard thing to face leaving your home, even harder when faced with the challenge of raising a family in a foreign land. It nearly tore my own family apart for good, and it's why I just can't conceive of settling down anywhere else. While the situation in Eritrea has gotten worse in more ways than I can count, it hasn't been all bad. There's so much to celebrate. Yes, we have a lot of work to be done — more than ever — but no one ever promised it would be easy or quick. A mountain doesn't wear away into the sea in a single year. Or even ten.

The conversation inevitably drifts off to other subjects before we lapse into the quiet of our own thoughts. Despite my deeply held convictions on the matter, the woman's predicament has forced me to question them in a way I hadn't given thought to before. Titi is still many years away from National Service, so there are still many years for that particular situation to improve. But if the last seven years can tell me anything about where we will be going in the next seven, then it's hard not to be alarmed over my children's future in Eritrea.

LOST AND HELPLESS IN ATLANTA

Eight hours after leaving Asmara, we arrive in Frankfurt, Germany. The airport is so immense it's like being in the middle of a city constructed inside a building. People are walking everywhere. Beeping carts speed by. There are lights and sounds and smells all around, and people selling everything from shirts to food to books and newspapers of all kinds. These are entirely unheard of in Eritrea, due to restrictions on all media, especially foreign literature. Titi is also amazed by it all. She wants to stop and stare at everything, but we still have to make our way to the other end of the terminal for our connecting flight.

I wait for the airline staff to show up with the old woman in her wheelchair. She's so relieved to see me that she grabs my hand and won't let it go. Once the plane has completely emptied, we and anyone else traveling to the United States are taken to a US Immigration office and told to wait for our entrance interviews.

The agent, a middle-aged white man speaking English, asks his questions quickly and barely waits for our answers:

Who packed your bags?

What's your reason for traveling to the US?

How long are you planning to stay?

Who are your relatives or family members you are going to visit?

Where do they live?

Where will you be staying?

Address?

Phone number?

Do you plan on working?

Any other travel?

The old woman is shaking visibly after she emerges from her interview. She doesn't speak English, so it's a relief to know she managed to get through it, although not without some difficulty. When the agent asked who packed her baggage, for example, she replied that it was her daughters and not herself, which triggered an inspection by the security agents. It's clear that everyone is still on heightened alert a full two years after the attack in New York on 9/11, especially for airplanes heading to the US, and doubly so for passengers coming from areas of the world where there is a lot of unrest, like the Horn of Africa. Satisfied that we're harmless, they finally let us proceed.

As we continue on our way, the woman begs me not to abandon her again. I tell her I won't, but I remind her that I couldn't even help her during her interview. She needs to understand that I also may not be able to help her once we get to the States and we have to check in with Immigration and Customs.

The next flight seems endless, but I'm so mentally worn out, while at the same time so emotionally unsettled, that I feel like a dust mote suspended in turbulent air. I can't settle down. Every time I check our progress, it's like we've barely come any closer to the US, while our home slips farther away behind us. Titi keeps asking if we are there yet, and I have to tell her no. I urge her to go back to sleep. "I'll wake you when we land." But she can't sleep, either. At times, she clutches my hand and won't let go, as if she's afraid I'll leave her. It makes me think of Natsanet, and the ache returns in my chest. I wonder how it went with Yikealo telling her we'd left.

The airport in Atlanta is just as big and loud and busy as the one in Frankfurt. I'm even more exhausted this time, but at least here I can understand what everyone is saying. As before, I wait for the old woman in her wheelchair. Then we make our way to the Immigration and Customs check-in. A young African-American woman instructs us to form two lines, one for US citizens, the other for foreigners.

When it's our turn to speak with the agent, I step up beside the old lady so I can help translate. The agent, a tall African-American gentleman, stops me and asks in a rumbling voice if we're traveling together.

"No," I answer, "but she doesn't speak English. I'm helping her."

"Then please step back into line," he replies, curtly.

I try again to explain that she can't understand English, but the agent calls for a guard, who takes the woman away from us and into a private room. Then he calls on me and Titi to step forward and begins to ask many of the same questions I've already answered before. I do my best to respond truthfully, but now I'm beyond exhausted, and it's hard for me to keep my thoughts from getting mixed up. I mispronounce names and locations. I forget some, confuse others. He asks Titi a couple easy questions, but she has a hard time understanding him, and she's exhausted, too. The responses we provide only seem to frustrate the agent even more than he already is. He makes a big show of leafing through our papers, sighs deeply, then waves us past.

After a while, the old woman rejoins us in the baggage claim area. Her shaking has grown much worse. I worry she might be having a medical issue. "I told my children I'm too weak to come all the way here to visit them," she tells me. Tear tracks streak her face. "But they are just so stubborn. They want to see me before I die."

I remember the woman at the American consulate in Asmara, the one whose entry visa was denied, and I can't help but feel sorry for her for missing another chance to see her daughter. "Your children should have come to see you instead," I say.

"They can't, so it is up to me to visit them instead. But I'm too old now. I'm too sick and fragile, as you can see. And now that I'm here, I don't know what to do or how to speak to anyone. I am scared of becoming lost and helpless in this big place. What will happen to me if I am?"

She doesn't explain why her children won't travel to Eritrea, although there are only a limited number of reasons. Either they're political refugees and can't, or the cost is too high. It's cheaper for one person to come here rather than several children flying to Eritrea. They also might not be able to take much time off from their family and work obligations. I know my sister Aster has had to put aside her studies temporarily to meet and spend time with us.

As we wait for our luggage to arrive on the carousels, the woman asks me to help her figure out where to go for her connecting flight. Her ticket says she's going to Baltimore-Washington International Airport in Maryland. Titi and I are flying to the Raleigh-Durham Airport in the state of North Carolina. I have no idea where the two are relative to each other. "We'll need to ask for directions for the right gate," I tell her.

Her face fills again with alarm. "You don't know the gate already?"

"It's my first time here, too. But don't worry. I'll take you. I need to find out which gate is for my plane."

"You're not going to the same place as I am?"

"No, we're going to a different city in a different part of the country."

"Oh, no!" she wails and starts to shake all over again. "Are you going to leave me all by myself? Oh my God, I'll be lost forever! Oh please don't do that to me!"

I try to explain that she'll be all right. "Nothing bad is going to happen to you. Look, here. See this paper? There's a phone number for you or someone else to contact your family member here in case of emergency."

But my assurances don't calm her. She's so distraught that she can't remember what her luggage looks like. She hands me her keys and begs me to figure out which bags they open. I don't feel right about this, but what can I do? She points to one on the carousel and says, "That looks like it." But it's not hers. One after another, I pull a bag off the conveyor belt and test the key only to find it's not the right one. Each time this happens, I think someone's going to yell at me for touching their luggage. And I have to do all this while keeping an eye on Titi. She's tired, but her curiosity keeps drawing her away from me. Too absorbed in the newness of all there is to experience, she's oblivious to my worries and the dangers of being among so many strangers in such a crowded place. So, even though I don't have my youngest daughter with me, I still feel like I have two children to take care of. Tending to the old woman's needs and watching Titi is causing me to neglect myself. I still need to retrieve my own bag and figure out which gate to go to before the next flight leaves. I don't know what we would do if we were to miss it.

At last we have all of our belongings. The claim area is nearly empty. Everyone else has already gone on their way.

Before reentering the terminal, our luggage must be inspected again by the security officer. Once more, it's up to me to wrestle the woman's heavy bags onto the table and wait while they search through her items. When they're finished, I have to repack it all and fight to close and lock it. They find nothing in her luggage, but they confiscate a package of beef jerky from mine. "No foreign meat," they tell me, explaining that it's a health risk because of mad cow disease. When they're finished, they let us pass.

"You need to be strong and calm," I tell the woman, as she clutches at my arm and begs me again not to leave her alone. "Please. It's not helping if you do this."

"You have every reason to be mad at me," she sobs. "I don't blame you for this. What can I do? I can't help it. I'm weak. I should have stayed home."

Luckily, I'm rescued by a pair of young men wearing airport uniforms, and we're both relieved to learn they're also from Eritrea and can speak Tigrinya. They promise to make sure she boards the right plane. Although I'm grateful for their help, I still feel a sudden loss when the men disappear with her into the throngs of passengers. I hadn't realized how much her company had comforted me, despite the added burden. Focusing on her needs helped me forget how lost and helpless I am myself. With her gone, it feels like another link to Eritrea has been broken.

It takes a while to find our gate, but we eventually make it and board the plane in time. Thankfully, the next flight is very short. We're barely up in the air when the pilot tells us we're already descending. Before I know it, we've arrived in Raleigh, North Carolina, where my sister Aster has flown in from Illinois to meet us.

WORSE THAN EXPECTED

It's been eight years since I last saw my sister. She came to America when she was just eighteen and I was barely even pregnant with Titi, so the two of them have never met. When she approaches us in the terminal, I don't recognize her right away. I can't entirely blame it on my lack of sleep, as her appearance has changed a lot. She's no longer the wide-eyed Eritrean teenager I remember, but a modern, confident, westernized African-American woman.

After hugs and introductions — Titi is shy and fussy — we gather our bags and head out to the car Aster has rented for the short drive to the hotel. When I see the beds, I just want to crawl into one of them and fall asleep. But Aster won't let me. She fusses over the room, complaining that it's not as tidy and clean as it should be. I don't see anything wrong with it, but she's unhappy with the quality of the service and insists on calling for fresh sheets. It strikes me as odd that she would have to do this. All I've ever heard about America is that everything is always perfect and clean and new. But Aster isn't satisfied and apologizes for getting such a cheap room. She says she had to reserve it sight unseen, and didn't know that this one was in one of Raleigh's poorer neighborhoods. "Every city has its good and bad places," she says. "Some areas are better than others. There are poor people and rich people everywhere. You can easily distinguish between the two, because the rich have too much of everything and the poor don't have enough of anything."

As if on cue, someone knocks at our door, and when we open it we find a young black man dressed in shabby clothes. He politely asks if he can borrow a few dollars. Aster hands him some bills, then tells him not to worry about paying her back.

"Does that happen a lot here?" I ask.

"Actually, this is the first for me," she answers, looking both startled by the encounter and embarrassed. I can tell she wants our visit to America to reflect our ideal image of it, but so far my impressions have been far more sobering. It makes me worry about what to expect at the hospital. What if we get there and realize we've come all this way for nothing? "We'll look for a different hotel tomorrow," Aster promises, and clicks her tongue at the stains in the carpet.

After my shower — a blessing after two full days of traveling — I find Aster and Titi sitting on the bed talking to each other like old acquaintances. It's a complete turnaround from her shyness at the airport. Children, Titi especially, are so willing to open up to strangers once they decide to. As Aster is her aunt, there's no question of safety or trust. Scattered around them on the bedspread are packages of cookies and chips, which Aster brought with her. The hour is too late to find a store or restaurant open.

With so many questions to ask about America, Titi shows no signs of slowing down, despite the fact that she must be dead tired. Aster is happy to keep answering them. I lie down on the other bed, close my eyes, and allow their voices to lap over me like waves on a shore. The next thing I know, Aster is rousing me. It's morning of the next day already, and we have to get dressed to go to the hospital.

The December morning is sunny and warm. Everything is decorated for the Christmas holiday— lamp posts, buildings, even cars. The lady at the reception desk in the main lobby at the hospital jingles as she jumps to her feet when we introduce ourselves. She's a short woman with a round face and maybe a little too much makeup. "You're the patient from Africa!" she exclaims with unbridled warmth. "We've been expecting you!"

The physician assigned to Titi's case comes to meet us. He's actually surprised to learn that I speak English as well as I do. Then he takes us around to introduce us to his support staff. Everyone is so warm and friendly that I have a hard time keeping my emotions in check. Everywhere I look, there's fancy machinery, and it all looks shiny and new and very expensive. My worries from last night evaporate away.

Finally, he takes us to his office to brief us on what to expect. "I'll perform my own examination of Titi," he says, "so that we can get the most accurate and up-to-date idea of her condition."

I confess that much of what he says enters my ears, but just as quickly escapes my mind. I try to concentrate, but I'm so overwhelmed with jet lag and the newness of everything that it's hard for me to concentrate. I'm like Titi was at the airport in Atlanta, trying to take in everything all at once. Thankfully, Aster is with us and paying attention. My English is decent, but after living here for eight years, my sister's is much better. She's able to understand most of what the doctor says, and she asks questions for what she doesn't. I know she'll explain it all back to me later.

Before leaving the hospital, we're taken to see the woman who helped coordinate everything between me and Aster, the doctors, and the hospital. I've lost count of how many emails we passed back and forth just between the two of us— enough that I feel like I know her well and consider her a dear friend. She even sent Titi a wonderful email on her last birthday. When I give her the traditional silver jewelry set I brought for her from home, she presents gifts from her own daughter, who happens to be Titi's age.

Aster asks her for a recommendation for a hotel nearby. After hearing about our experience from the night before, the woman tells us she'll call around at some places she knows. "We have several charitable foundations assisting our patients. We'll find a decent place for you to stay while you're here."

The hospital is situated on a huge, beautiful campus with dozens of impressive buildings. From the outside, it appears modern and meticulously well-maintained, yet somewhat impersonal. But it's the warmth of the people who work inside that makes me feel truly blessed. I don't know if it's because of the holiday season, or if it's the way the staff treat their patients all of the time, but everyone is just so kind and welcoming. The nurses and aides are ready with warm smiles and are constantly presenting little toys for Titi to keep.

Her medical examination fills up most of the day, and when the doctor is finished, he tells us the news: "There are three issues of concern."

Three? I'd been told only that there was a faulty valve, which is certainly frightening enough. But now he's telling me it's worse than that?

"The first issue," he says, "is what we call a *patent ductus arteriosus*. It's a fancy name for a naturally occurring opening in the aorta that's supposed to close early in life." He goes on to explain that before a baby is born, the blood doesn't need to go to the lungs to be oxygenated, as it receives the oxygen directly through the placenta. "The *ductus arteriosus* is a hole that shunts the blood straight to the pulmonary arteries, allowing it to skip the circulation to the lungs. It normally seals off soon after the baby is born. If it remains patent, or open, the heart and lungs have to work harder, since less of the blood flow gets to the lungs than is needed. How hard depends on how large the opening is. This can cause damage to the lungs over time."

"How do you fix it?"

"Sometimes they close up on their own. Sometimes they aren't severe enough to worry about. People can live long, normal, healthy lives with a small PDA. In Titi's case, however, there's sufficient leakage that the hole needs to be plugged. Thankfully, it doesn't require open heart surgery. Instead, we'll insert a small device through a catheter in her leg to do the job. Once that's done, there shouldn't be any more blood leaking between the aorta and the pulmonary artery."

"And the murmur will go away?"

"Unfortunately, the PDA isn't the only reason for the murmur. There's a second hole in your daughter's heart, this time in the wall separating the right and left ventricals, the large chambers of the heart. It's called *ventricular septal defect*, and in severe cases it can cause the heart to enlarge, as it has to work harder, resulting in pulmonary hypertension and vascular damage. Treatment in this case is much more invasive. The good news for your daughter is that her defect is small. There's still a good chance it'll close up as she grows older. I recommend we simply keep an eye on it for now."

As much as I hate the idea of surgery, especially open heart surgery, I dislike the idea of going back to Eritrea without having everything fixed even more. What if the hole doesn't close? Or it grows wider? Our country doesn't have the capabilities to fix it, especially if it's the more complicated of the problems. And as long as Eritrea continues along its current path, I don't see the government allowing us to leave a second time. I'm certain that this will be our one and only chance.

He listens patiently while I explain our situation to him. He then tells us he doesn't take the option of surgery lightly. "There are simply too many risks for the possibility of minimal reward. And both the recovery period for the open heart surgery and follow up checks will be much, much longer and intensive," he adds. "From what you're describing, it doesn't sound as if there would be anyone qualified to monitor Titi's post-operative progress in your homeland. I honestly believe our best option all around is to wait and see how she responds to the PDA repair. Open heart surgery really should be reserved for only the most desperate of cases. I do believe your daughter's condition isn't going to get any worse. Give it a chance to improve on its own. It's not worth the risks right now."

I don't know what to say. I know he's right, but as a mother with limited options and limited time, I just want everything to be fixed now, once and for all. "How soon can you do the other procedure?" I ask.

He sighs. "Unfortunately, it's the third issue that needs to be addressed first, since it raises Titi's risk of infection. It's about her teeth." He goes on to explain that dental hygiene has a direct impact on heart health. "We see a lot of these sorts of problems in countries where the water is not treated, regular dental care is unavailable, or nutrition is inadequate. Titi isn't undernourished, but she has considerable issues with her teeth, so I've asked a colleague in Dental to see her. He's agreed to do what is needed to prepare her for the PDA repair, and it won't be at any additional expense to you. Once that's taken care of, then we'll fix the *ductus arteriosus*. Luckily, your daughter still has most of her baby teeth, so there's still time for her adult teeth to come in nice and strong."

Poor Titi. I try to explain to her what will happen over the next few days, and she tries to be brave, especially when the dentist gets to work on her the next day. Thankfully, she's asleep for most of it. But when he's finished with her, I'm shocked to learn that her teeth were in far worse shape than I had imagined. The oral surgeon had no choice but to extract several teeth, leaving her mouth full of holes and her gums swollen. Another six teeth had to be treated for cavities. After Titi wakes from the anesthesia, she's given antibiotics and told she can't eat anything solid, even though she's hungry and begs for food. When I ask when it will be okay for her to have something, the dentist tells us, "Not for at least another twenty-four hours. Her heart surgeon has scheduled the procedure for first thing tomorrow morning."

BETTER THAN HOPED

After a fitful night, I wake up on the morning of Titi's heart procedure feeling sick to my stomach. I can't eat or sit still. If the previous day's ordeal was long and stressful, today's will be far worse. The possibility of something going wrong is so much higher. My hands shake as we get Titi ready. After so many years of preparing for this moment, after all the struggles and heartbreak, I'm ready for it to be done. How could I not be? But I'm also dreading the moment I will be forced to let her go, relinquishing her into the hands of total strangers. I wish I could just pull her back into the bed with me and cover us both up with the blanket.

It's another bright, crisp winter morning, as if the world is trying its hardest to keep me cheerful while we make our way to the hospital. There's an electric feeling in the air that seems to infect Titi, too. She chatters nonstop in the car. I think she's just trying not to be nervous. I mask my face and words to avoid betraying my emotions. I simply smile for her sake and pretend to be confident. Aster, on the other hand, is barely managing. The moment the nurses wheel Titi away for surgery, she breaks down and sobs.

The wait is long and agonizing. We make our way to the cafeteria, where we sit holding hands and sipping burnt coffee from a vending machine. The recycled air smells of grease and eggs and disinfectant. People come and go around us, some of them in patient gowns and trailing shiny chrome poles with hanging plastic bags. There's laughter, murmured conversations, and the soft sound of clinking dishes and utensils. Christmas music plays overhead. Yet all of this simply flows past us. In my mind, I'm thinking only about the possible outcomes for my daughter. They range from the best to the worst. I know I shouldn't dwell on the negative. I know the surgeons will do their best. But I also know I must brace myself, just in case their best isn't good enough.

My thoughts drift. I reflect on the long and difficult road that brought us here, starting from Titi's birth, then jumping to the day we first learned of her heart defect. I think about all the obstacles we had to overcome, all those years of searching for a way to help her and how frustrating it was to be so dependent on people who simply couldn't care less if my daughter lived or died. People who seemed content with making things as difficult for us as possible. I think about the hopes and aspirations Yikealo and I once shared at the beginning of our marriage, and how our lives were thrown into chaos, not just by Titi's diagnosis, but by a few arrogant men whose actions triggered a second war and took my husband away from me. I think about how none of it had to happen. Our leaders could have easily acted differently, for the benefit of all; instead, they fed the violence with their heated rhetoric and unreasonable demands, like a hot wind fans a spark into a wildfire.

I relive the days following the *giffa*, the uncertainty that followed Yikealo's conscription and the months of heartache. I think about the terrible decision of returning the market he'd worked so hard to build, of all the invested time and money we lost. The pain of carrying Natsanet alone, and the bittersweet joy I experienced on the day she arrived. My heart breaks as I remember how small and broken my husband appeared to me the day he returned to Asmara, like a half starved refugee. How could all of this have happened in just seven short years? It feels like only days, and yet those days hold a lifetime's worth of choices and challenges, of broken promises and dashed hopes.

And now, here I am, sitting in a waiting room in a hospital in a place called Raleigh, North Carolina, in this strange, frightening, puzzling place called America. The culmination of all my hopes and efforts. The product of my faith, despite it wavering at times. I could not have done any of it without all of that, as well as the support of my dearest friends and family.

Not to mention the generosity of complete strangers.

It seems too incredible to conceive, yet it's true. Who would have thought the journey we started in 1998 would end up here, thousands of miles away from home, in 2003?

But it's all behind me now. Now, at last, it has come down to this moment.

The doctor comes out in his hospital scrubs and updates us that everything is going fine. The hole has been repaired, and they're just waiting for Titi to wake up again. It's suddenly over, at least this part. There's still so much left to do, but for the first time in a long time, I have the luxury of asking myself, what comes next?

Just make it through today, I silently think to myself. *That's all that matters right now.*

At last, they wheel her out of the surgical suite and into the recovery area. I'm surprised to see that she's already sitting up, her eyes wide but still a bit glassy. I rush to her bedside and hold her tight for as long as the nurses will allow. The doctor tries to update me while I'm there. Somehow, I'm able to listen and comprehend what he's saying. My head feels clearer than it has in a long time.

"She did wonderfully," he tells us. "No problems at all. The PDA is fixed. In a little while, we'll remove her IV. You'll be able to go home tonight."

"Home tonight? Already?"

"Well, home being wherever you're staying for now. We'll need to do some follow-up examinations over the next few days to make sure everything is healing properly."

A few days? Is that all she needs?

A few hours later, the nurse comes in and discharges us from the hospital. After so much buildup, this part feels almost anticlimactic. After five years of waiting for life-saving surgery, she won't even have to spend a single night in the hospital? It feels like a miracle.

Before we leave, the woman who has helped us since the beginning tells us she found a room in a building run by a charitable foundation. The offer comes as a pleasant surprise, especially after the disappointments we've experienced so far with the hotel. The room is in a large fancy building. It's clean and comfortable. It shares a well-stocked kitchen, playroom, and laundry room with other guests of the hospital. We only have to pay a small daily fee, and it includes breakfast and some dinners. But the most heart-warming part for me are the holiday gift baskets placed in the room for us. I'm told they're provided by generous donors. I wonder who these people are, who give so selflessly to strangers they don't even know and will never get to meet. The experience is so different from that past two nights that I'm reminded of Aster's words about rich people and poor people here in America. It seems it doesn't just apply to money, but to richness of heart. Some people just have an overabundance of it. It's a refreshing change after meeting so many people who seem to lack it altogether.

Titi's recovery is nothing less than remarkable. By that evening, she's back to her usual cheerful self, despite being tired and sore. She limps slightly, favoring the leg where the surgeon inserted the needle, and her mouth is still swollen and achy from the dental work. But by the next morning, both her color and her appetite are fully restored, and the achiness is considerably less. At our first follow-up examination, the doctor clears Titi of nearly all dietary and physical restrictions. The next appointment is scheduled for a week later.

With all this extra time on our hands and much less to worry about, we decide it's a good time to do a little sightseeing. I don't want to tire Titi out, so we just go to a nearby mall, where we shop for new clothes. The next stop is the food court, where Titi wants to taste a little bit of everything from all the different restaurants. Aster tells her to be patient. "You'll have plenty of chances to try what you want, honey."

A woman cleaning tables nearby overhears us talking and comes over. I'd noticed her earlier and wondered if she might be a recent arrival in America. I'm surprised to find out she's also from Eritrea. Her name is Abeba and she's been living here with her husband for eight years, just like my sister Aster. In fact, the story has become quite familiar to me by now: They left Eritrea just as tensions between our country and Ethiopia were about to explode. Already disillusioned by the broken promises, restrictions, conscriptions, and the worsening global isolation, they were among the first to emigrate. When I explain to her the reason for my own visit and of our plans to go back once Titi has fully recovered, she gives me a look of utter disbelief. "I have been hearing bad news from friends and family. Why would you go back if it is so bad?" she asks. The question brings to mind my last conversation with Titi's pediatrician. When I told him we were planning to go to America for the surgery, he'd replied in earnest that I shouldn't hesitate one minute longer. "Go. But don't come back, if you can help it."

Before I have a chance to answer her, the woman excuses herself, saying she has to go back to work. But before we leave the food court, she slips me a piece of paper with her phone number on it. "We should get together on my day off," she says. "It would be nice to talk to someone from home without worrying about who might be listening."

"You miss it?" I ask.

She nods. "I miss some of it. How could I not?"

After the two young men in the airport in Atlanta, and now her, I'm starting to appreciate just how many of my fellow countrymen must have left Eritrea over the years that I've already met three of them. With the woman from the plane going to Germany, I now see how many of us have become scattered across the world. It's not just my sister or a few acquaintances anymore. And after hearing the same reasons over and over again why they left, my reasons for going back are starting to sound more like stubborn excuses.

At our next appointment, a week after the surgery, the doctor declares that Titi is well enough to go home. In this case, he means wherever home might be here in the States, since he thinks Titi will still need months of continued follow up examinations by a cardiologist to monitor both the plug and the remaining untreated defect. We won't get the same quality of care back in Eritrea, so my sister books the flights to take us to her home in Illinois, where she lives with her husband in a town outside of Chicago. "I'll try and find someone there to do the exams," the surgeon tells us. Then he gives Titi a hug and says he won't be seeing her again. "It was a great pleasure to meet you. You are a strong little woman, just like your mom and aunt."

Before leaving Raleigh, we call Abeba, the lady we met at the mall. She invites us over to her apartment, where we meet her husband and three children. They tell us that they first tried to settle in the United Arab Emirates, but her husband won a scholarship to attend school in the US, so they came here instead. "We had only one child then, a boy," she tells us. "But we didn't have papers to bring him, so we had to leave him with his grandmother in Eritrea. We tried for years to bring him over once we'd settled, but there was always something else blocking us, some new rule change or someone else reviewing our case. They'd suddenly renege on an earlier promise, so we would have to restart the entire process all over again."

In the end, they were able to bring him over, but it took five whole years to make it happen. Five years! The same amount of time that has passed since we found out about Titi's murmur. By then, the boy had changed. He barely remembered his parents. And he now had two siblings born here whom he'd never met.

"Five years," I repeat in disbelief. I can't imagine being separated from my family for that long. I've been away only a couple weeks, yet even as busy as we have been, I still miss my husband and Natsanet terribly. And I still have another month or two ahead of me before we know for sure that the device placed inside Titi's chest is stable enough for us to return home.

"Our son was so angry when he finally came that he didn't want anything to do with us for a long time," the woman says.

All three of her children are playing with Titi in another room. I can hear the casual burble of their voices, the relaxed laughter. It's a joy to hear Titi's mixed in with theirs.

"He had no way of understanding how we could possibly leave him behind for so long. He was especially bitter about his younger siblings, jealous that they had everything he'd been denied. He didn't understand why it made any difference that they were already born here and he wasn't. He was too young to know how complicated immigration policies and procedures are. He just felt like we'd abandoned him." She shakes her head. "It took him a long time to forgive us. And a long time before he didn't resent his siblings or think they had taken his place in our hearts."

This makes me think about Natsanet again. I'd already worried myself sick over the possibility she'd resent me and Titi, so hearing this about the boy makes my heart sink even more. Natsanet's a little younger than the boy was when his parents left him behind, too young to understand why I had no choice, either. I could tell her the reasons why things turned out the way they did, but they wouldn't mean anything to her, just like the woman's son couldn't accept their reasons for leaving him behind. Will Natsanet think I favored her older sister over herself? It seems unavoidable. She already feels this way a little bit, just by virtue of being second-born. She never received the same kind of attention from her grandparents and aunts and uncles that Titi got. Titi was the first, so they lavished attention on her. Of course, Natsanet came to accept this as the way things are, that she deserved less simply because she had the misfortune of being born afterward, once the novelty had worn off. For instance, whenever anyone would bring anything over for the children, she'd automatically assume it was only for her older sister. And when it turned out not to be, she still wouldn't truly believe she could have any of it, much less an equal part.

All of a sudden, I get this suffocating feeling in my chest. The prospect of spending even one more day away from her seems much too long. I want to go back home now, but Titi needs to fully recover first. She's still at risk. If the device they inserted to block the hole shifts, it could cause a life-threatening complication.

I'm stuck between what I know I have to do for one child and what I want to do for the other.

CULTURE SHOCK

Aster tells me that December can be very cold in the part of Illinois where she lives, but when we get off the airplane in Springfield it's raining rather than snowing. The sky is dark gray in the middle of the day, and the air is chilly and breezy. The weather is a depressing switch from the warmth and sunshine of North Carolina. "Just wait until you see the snow," Aster says, as if that will cheer me up.

I don't have any desire to see anything as wet and cold as that, but Titi begs her aunt to take her. "Where is it?" she asks, looking all around.

"It's not here yet," Aster says. "Winter's late this year. But we won't need to drive very far to find it."

"Now?"

"Soon, honey. Be patient. There are so many other things to experience first, like the big city of Chicago. And Lake Michigan."

My brother-in-law meets us at the airport, then drives us straight to their house. They have a nice car, and they've bought a nice place in a quiet new development. It's not a short trip, but he drives very fast. I'd been told everyone here in the States does, and it appears to be true. "People are always in a hurry to get somewhere," Aster comments. The surgeon in Raleigh told me the same thing, after I told him we'd be flying to Illinois. He talked about the fast cars and traffic jams in Chicago, but I hadn't quite realized how fast and how many he'd meant. Once again, I'm like Titi— naive about how things really are here. In some places, everything is just as I'd always imagined or thought I knew from books and pictures, new and clean and fancy; in other places, the places we never hear about, everything just looks old and dingy and uninviting. We pass through one area where the trees are bare and everything looks dismal and gray and the ground is swampy, and I think to myself, "I would not like to live here." But as dreary as it is, I still try to take in as much of it as I can, whether it's the drabness or the flashy bright colors. I don't know how much time we'll have before we have to go back, and I want to remember it all.

There are houses everywhere in this part of the town where they live, each one almost identical to the next. Aster's is no different, just one of many that all look like boxes with windows. I can't imagine how they keep track of where they live without getting lost.

The first thing I notice when we walk inside her house is that the living room and kitchen are joined into one large spacious area. Back home, the kitchen is in a remote part of the house, far from everything else. This serves to keep the strong aromas of cooking away from where we socialize. Also, the kitchen is where the family unit spends most of their time, not visitors; guests are rarely invited there. Instead, food is brought out fully prepared on a nice plate and served in the living room. Here, everything is just the opposite. Everyone wants to be in the kitchen, and anyone is welcome to just come in there and make themselves at home.

Soon after we arrive, Aster's cousin on her husband's side begins preparing food for us all while we settle in on the couch in the living room. She had arrived the day before to help get the house ready to receive us. This is another break from our tradition; guests aren't expected to wait while the food is being cooked. That would be unthinkable back home. Aster laughs when I mention this. "You'll get used to all the differences," she says. "I actually like it much better. It's so much less formal."

But I don't. Formal is just another word for tradition, and there are parts of it I don't want to lose.

The next several days are filled with new experiences like this. Even our walks around the neighborhood are enough to prove how so very different everything is here. In the fronts of the houses and in back, the yards are covered in grass. It looks artificial, cropped so short and close to the ground. At the moment, the grass is more brown than green from the cold, but Aster says it will turn verdant in the spring, once the weather warms again and the ground thaws. "By the end of May, you'll start hearing lawnmowers everywhere. People take such pride in their yards." She laughs at the puzzled look on my face. Expanses of grass simply aren't known in Eritrea. They aren't very practical.

I'm also surprised at how detached all the houses are. Most are single units, self-contained, with no shared walls or common areas. They're separated from each other with large buffers of space. It feels off-putting to me, unwelcoming. Aster points out several apartment buildings in other neighborhoods, where people live in close proximity to one another, but I still don't get the sense the residents of these buildings are anymore social than those who live in houses.

The edges of individual properties are marked by low fences, shrubs, or nothing at all. In Asmara, most properties in the city are enclosed by tall brick or stone walls, and entry into the compound is gained through heavy gates with thick metal bars or wood, although they are rarely ever locked. Inside the walls, the ground is covered with cement or tiles, which makes them easy to clean. It's where most of our domestic life takes place. And much of our business and social interactions, too. Here in America, business is conducted somewhere far away from home. In fact, for much of the day, the neighborhoods appear largely deserted. Even in the evenings, the streets are emptier than I'm used to seeing. Very few people take advantage of the abundant sidewalks and footpaths. I can't help wondering if it's because of the cold weather, or if the situation remains the same during the summer. I realize I won't be around to see for myself.

One of the more amusing things I find are the garages. Every house has one facing the street. They're supposed to be used for storing cars, and some are even large enough for more than one. But it seems that people use them to store cardboard boxes and extra furniture instead. It's a hint of the material excessiveness I've heard so much about. The cars are parked outside in driveways or on the side of the street in front of the house. And speaking of cars, there are so many of them everywhere, in the neighborhoods, on the roads, at the store. There must be at least one for every person.

Maybe more.

On Christmas Eve, we take the train down to St. Louis to see the Gateway Arch. Even after reading about the famous landmark in books and seeing so many pictures of it, I'm still amazed when I finally get to see it in person. Some of the experience matches my expectations from the images I've long held in my mind. Yet there is so much more I hadn't expected, too, and I realize that this essentially describes my whole American experience so far. There are parts that match the movies we watched back home, but there are so many other parts that seem completely unfamiliar.

Even Titi, whose knowledge of this country is very limited, is confused at how often reality doesn't match her expectations. "Where are all the tall buildings?" she asks, as we drive through smaller towns on our way to the bridge that crosses the Mississippi River. She uses the Italian word *palazzo*. "Where are all the palazzos?" She thinks they cover all of America.

Aster tries to explain that we'll see them once we get into the city. "There are some skyscrapers there. You'll see them. But not as many as in Chicago. Or New York."

Everyone is in such a festive mood, and everywhere we go we hear Christmas songs playing. All the stores are decorated with ribbons and bright colorful lights. People are walking around with their arms full of giant bags and wrapped-up presents. We see a huge Christmas tree in the middle of a park. Titi is awestruck by it all. She thinks she's in a fairytale land. Back home, we celebrate Christmas with lots of feasts. We have a Christmas tree and sweets and some decorations and lights. But we don't exchange gifts, only cards. Children get new clothes to wear for the coming year. Adults eat and drink and socialize.

That evening, Aster takes us to see the Christmas lights on the houses in a neighborhood nearby. One of the homes has so many lights it looks like someone dumped a giant box of them over the place. Scratchy Christmas songs play through hidden speakers. People come from miles away to take pictures. It's incredibly gaudy and nearly overwhelming. But it's also beautiful and heartwarming.

As the days pass, the differences between life in America and life in Eritrea stack up. One of the most striking for me, although less obvious at first, is how restricted children are here from roaming about on their own. They're watched constantly by adults, taken by hand or by car from one play area to another. They're accompanied by adults if they walk to school, or else they get on a bus and are driven door-to-door. At home, older children in the neighborhood are responsible for watching over the younger ones. School children walk together to classes, sometimes long distances away. Not so here. I'm told that there are greater risks here. For example, the streets aren't safe because of all the traffic moving so quickly. Strangers aren't considered safe because they might want to harm the children. Back home, Titi was free to wander over to our neighbors' houses and play with other kids her age. She walked to school from her very first day. I remind Aster that we also had dangers growing up — real dangers like abductions and murders — but they never stopped our parents from letting us be kids. We learned quickly how to take care of ourselves.

Aster just shrugs and tells me it's better to adapt to these different customs, rather than resist them. So, I have to constantly remind Titi not to leave the house without my supervision. Not to leave the front door wide open whenever she comes in or out. At home, we would keep the doors open whenever the weather is nice. Neighbors and friends are welcome to come in and out all day. The doors are closed and locked only at bedtime. Here, we lock the doors all the time, even when we're home and awake. It's no wonder why nobody ever stops by for a visit.

Instilling this vague sense of danger, or at least of caution, into Titi's mind comes hard for me. I don't want her to be afraid of anything, yet I want her to be safe from whatever threats Aster believes are out there. I can't challenge my younger sister's wisdom; she's been living here longer and knows better than I do. It's equally as hard for Titi to understand. Why is everyone suddenly assumed to be dangerous by default? Why here, especially when everyone seems so warm and friendly? She has to learn to let the answering machine get the phone whenever it rings instead of picking it up. She can't open doors whenever someone knocks, but rather must wait for an adult to see who it is. I even have to discourage her from talking to strangers who return her warm smile whenever we're out in public. Each time I do, she gives me a disapproving look and says, "Oh Mom, you're becoming a mean person. That lady was just being nice to me."

In Eritrea, when you meet an acquaintance, there's an expectation — almost an obligation — to greet each other and engage in conversation, even if it's just to exchange pleasantries. We clasp hands. We share a hug and kiss each other's cheeks. Not so here. Physical contact is sparing. Shaking hands usually only happens in formal situations or when meeting someone new, and hugging is reserved for the closest of friends and family members. Here, you're not expected to share your food with people sitting next to you. Eating is much more casual, and more of an isolated part of a larger experience. Food is not so much a vital part of the American social life as it is a backdrop to it. There's also less ritual to meal preparation and eating. In Eritrea, everyone sits around a single platter of food and shares the experience together.

Our customs — habits for me and Titi — are hard for us to simply set aside. Part of me wants to resist doing so for fear that we'll get used to our new behaviors and take them back with us as bad habits when we return to Eritrea. But another part of me wants to fit in, rather than stand out. It feels like these two things are silently at war with each other inside of me.

And there are moments when I'm not so sure which side I want to win.

ADJUSTING EXPECTATIONS

Word eventually spreads at home that I'm here in America, despite everyone's attempts to keep it quiet. Absences prompt inquiries— by friends, by Titi's teacher and classmates, by neighbors. Few people know the full details about the trip or its reason, and we'd prefer to keep it that way. It'll be easier to explain after we return. And safer for everyone until we do.

My email inbox fills up with questions from curious friends. They want to know what it's like here. They ask where we've gone and what we've seen. They're actually more excited about me being here than with my plans for returning. I receive numerous congratulations, as if I've achieved a coup of sorts. I guess I have, although it's not the one they imagine. They send me their good wishes and promise to meet when I return, but I get the strong feeling they don't expect that to happen anytime soon, if at all.

Aysha, my old friend from Ethiopia, calls me from her home in Texas. "I heard you were here!" she exclaims, and, of course, she has to remind me yet again of her dream from so long ago. "So, I told you, didn't I? You didn't believe me, but here you are! The big guy upstairs doesn't lie."

I explain to her my reason for the trip and that I'm not staying, but it doesn't make any difference to her. She's convinced my coming here at all finally proves she was right all along. I have to admit that she has a valid point, but it doesn't mean I'm staying.

"Well . . ." she says suggestively. "Who knows what will happen. Right?"

What will happen next is a question I've been asking myself more and more, but my worries aren't for me or Titi. Instead, they focus on how our stay here could be impacting the people we left behind. The longer we remain, the greater the risk grows that my family back home will be harassed. The actual reasons for our coming here matter less than what people are going to assume, which is that we've left out of dissatisfaction with our homeland. What they don't understand is that my feelings for Eritrea never played a role in our coming here. Nevertheless, some people will only see our leaving as proof of our betrayal against the country. For them, it's the equivalent of treason.

By now, everyone in my old office must know we've left, including the representative from the Human Resources department I saw just days before the flight. He'll realize I avoided telling him the entire truth, and even though I never actually lied outright to him, he'll judge my words as deceitful. Will he cause trouble out of spite because of it? If he does, will it bring trouble to Yikealo and Natsanet? I've heard too many stories about friends and family members of people leaving the country being harassed, detained, interrogated. Even imprisoned. Most of the attention is focused on cases where someone clearly left illegally, but it isn't just limited to them. I can only hope my husband is able to avoid these sorts of problems until we're able to return. After all, we didn't violate any laws.

After the holiday break is over, Aster registers Titi at a school in the neighborhood, despite my reluctance to make such a commitment. She says that since we're going to be staying for a while, Titi should continue her education rather than wasting her time sitting around all day watching television. I worry the experience will only make her frustrated and confused, but Aster convinces Titi to give it a try, so there's little I can do but agree. Although she's in the second grade at home, we enroll her in the first grade here, where she'll get more help learning how to speak, read, and write in English.

The school is three blocks away, and I walk with her every day. At first, Titi is intimidated by the language barrier and has a difficult time letting me go. She feels lonely and home-sick. She begs me to take her back to Eritrea and doesn't believe me when I tell her it'll happen soon enough. I explain that I don't want her to be bored or miss out on anything. She accuses me of secretly planning to never take her back. "I'll never get to see Dad and Natsanet and Grandma again."

I walk her back to my sister's house every afternoon, then spend hours helping her with reading and writing. Although she learned the Latin alphabet in Eritrea, she hasn't been taught how to read it yet. And other than a few spoken words in English, she doesn't understand the language. In our elementary schools, most subjects are initially taught in Tigrinya, which uses a different alphabet called Ge'ez script. English is taught as a formal subject in the early grades, but it's not until middle school, when students are fluent, that other subjects are taught in English.

"Did you make a friend at school today?" I ask her each afternoon.

"How can I, if I can't talk to anybody?"

"Are you trying?"

"Yes," she answers, resentfully, but I can tell by her body language that she really does want to make friends. She misses her sister and her friends from home.

One day, the teacher tells me that Titi tried to hug one of her classmates. "I know this is acceptable in other cultures," she says. She herself is a recent transplant from India, so she understands the struggle with learning new cultural norms. "But not here. Titi will need to learn to keep her hands to herself, or else she'll get into trouble."

When I tell Titi to stop, that some people don't like hugs, she takes it personally. I try to explain about cultural differences to her, but she has a hard time accepting what she can't understand.

Still, she tries. After about a month, things start to smooth out. She doesn't fight me anymore going to school and doesn't fuss when I leave her. She seems to be getting along better with the other children, and she isn't as sad all the time. She stops begging me every day to take her back home to Eritrea, although she still asks when we'll see her father and sister. One evening, I pass her closed bedroom door and hear her speaking to someone. I know she's alone, so it puzzles me. Then I realize she's practicing her English by mimicking the things she hears in school and on the television.

On another day, Titi asks why I don't help out in the classroom. "I heard the teacher say she needs help. Sometimes other moms come. You could come and help instead of staying home."

"What kind of help?" I ask, intrigued. Without work to keep me busy, and with both Aster and her husband gone during the day, I'd been finding the long hours alone difficult to fill.

"Grading papers. Helping to make teaching aids. That sort of thing."

When I tell her teacher the next day that I would love to help, she gives me a surprised look. "Titi understood what I said!" she exclaims joyfully. "She's making very good progress learning English! And yes! I'd love for you to help."

I start with small tasks at first, then take on more responsibility as the days gather into weeks. And I realize that it isn't just Titi who is learning, but me as well. I carefully observe how people behave under certain circumstances; I take note of what is appropriate and what isn't. I begin to feel comfortable again. I hadn't realized how depressed I'd become sitting alone in my sister's house. It lifts my spirits to be useful again, which also raises Titi's. The more time I spend in her classroom, the more comfortable my daughter becomes, more socially and academically confident. She starts to recover more of her former joyful demeanor. She makes friends.

Before long, so do I.

"Why don't you consider staying here in the US," Titi's teacher asks me one afternoon. The students had long since gone home for the day, and we are just sitting and enjoying the peace and quiet. "The kids love you. You could become a teacher."

The same answer I'd been giving every time someone asked me that very question reflexively comes to mind: Why would I stay and be a second-class citizen? But for the first time it feels like I'm lying, and the only person I'm fooling is myself. Arguing that I have to go back because that is where the rest of my family lives is starting to sound defensive. Am I really any worse off here than I have been at home?

I still think it would be unreasonable for us to stay. And unfeasible. Everything is so much more expensive here. How could we possibly afford it? I can't work, as it would be a violation of my visa, so I can't earn money. And even if I could, how would I go about doing it? I remember what the woman on the plane told me about returning to Germany. She wondered how she'd be able to find a place to live and a job to support herself and her children. There's a lifetime of basic knowledge people accumulate that an immigrant needs to learn in a very short amount of time.

But it's the costs of everything that really make me pause. I don't shop, so I keep forgetting how expensive everything is. For example, one day Aster finds a ten-dollar bill in her purse. "Let's get coffee and pastries!" I suggest, without thinking. She'd taken us out once before as a special treat, and it reminded me so much of home. In Eritrea, coffee preparation and serving are part of a rich cultural tradition, steeped in ancient rituals and laden with meaning. The region is, after all, the birthplace of coffee going back a thousand years or more. People here in America don't give coffee's history the slightest thought. For them, if there is any ritual or symbolism in it at all, it's something completely different than what we celebrate at home.

Aster laughs at my suggestion and says, "Ten dollars isn't enough."

"What do you mean?" I ask, shocked. At home, ten American dollars is the equivalent of 200 *nakfa*, a significant amount indeed. A cappuccino in Asmara costs about ten *nakfa*, or the equivalent of fifty cents here. As culturally important as coffee is to me, spending much more than that seems absurd, especially since there is no ceremony and it's served in throwaway paper cups. Aster admits that even she doesn't quite understand why people are willing to spend so much for coffee, despite having lived here as long as she has. She tells me how some people won't hesitate to buy a five-dollar cup of coffee every single day, yet complain about spending one dollar for a newspaper that will enrich them even more. And sometimes people buy coffee more than once each day. For them, it's not a luxury but a necessity, a vital — and expensive — part of their everyday routine.

It's another cultural difference between me and Americans that I'll just have to accept without really understanding.

As successful as Aster and her husband have been in the time they've lived here, they still don't have a lot of money to spend on luxuries, much less daily trips to the coffee shop. They both started with nothing after arriving, but now they own a car and a house. But brewed coffee from a restaurant remains one of those luxuries. Ten dollars, whether earned or found, could always be put to better use.

One day, the mother of one of Titi's classmates introduces herself to me. I'm immediately struck by everything about her. She's tall and graceful, possessing a warm smile and a soft voice, yet also strong and confident. "Looks like our daughters are becoming inseparable," she says. And when I answer, she immediately knows from my accent that I've recently come to America. She asks when we arrived. By now, I'm used to the question and no longer feel any concerns telling our story. In fact, it's liberating not to have to worry about who finds out, not like I did in Eritrea. I tell her about Titi's heart condition and how we had to fight for years just to find someone who could perform the surgery. She listens as I explain how difficult it was just to get permission to travel, and she sympathizes when I share how hard it's been being separated from my husband and younger daughter.

I half expect her to ask why I don't bring them here with us, considering my complaints, but she doesn't. Instead, she seems to already understand the private struggle going on inside of me, even if I'm not yet fully ready to acknowledge it.

"You were born here?" I ask.

She nods. "Born, raised, and educated. But the children's father, my ex-husband, is from Nigeria. I have two children with him, a boy and a girl." She looks away for a moment, and I can almost sense her reimagining some past event. There's a fierceness in her eyes that tells me she has her own story to tell. It takes little coaxing for her to share it with me. When she's finished, it's the most incredible and heartbreaking thing I've ever heard.

When she and her ex-husband separated, they were assigned joint custody of the kids. Her daughter, Titi's classmate, was four at the time, and her son was about two. One day, her ex-husband failed to bring the children back after a weekend visit. It took her a while to track them down, only to learn that he had taken the children to his native land of Nigeria. "It was my worst nightmare," she tells me. "I had no idea where he was in that country or how to go about finding them, much less getting them back. But I knew I had to try. For more than a year, I worked with the embassies, but they were either unwilling or unable to help. I eventually decided to quit my job as a psychologist and sell my house so I could go to Nigeria to recover them myself."

She shakes her head at the memory. "I knew roughly where his family was from, so I was finally able to locate the village. But even that wasn't very helpful to me. I tried every single legal channel I could think of after arriving, beginning with the US Embassy in Abuja, but there were so many roadblocks. As soon as I overcame one, another would pop up. And I was starting to worry that he'd learn of my presence in the country and take the children into hiding somewhere else, and I'd never find them again. So I started going about in disguise. I even hired local help to facilitate their recovery. It took a lot of patience and hard work, but I finally got them back."

I don't ask her whether it was legitimate channels or not that worked for her. As a mother myself, I can easily imagine the immensity of her pain and appreciate her fierce determination. Legal or not, in the end the means are irrelevant. Only the outcome matters: the recovery of her children.

"The really hard work started only after I got them back to the US," she continues. "Because they'd been gone a couple years, I had to rehabilitate them — and myself — culturally, as well as emotionally and physically. I thought it would be easy to find that kind of support here in the States, but I was wrong. Afterward, once we'd worked through it all, I decided to focus on using my education and experiences to help other parents in similar situations." She turns and smiles gently at me. "You should know that you and your daughter aren't alone here, should you choose to stay in the US. There are so many networks for immigrants, so many options, charities. America is the land of immigrants."

I realize then that she's offering more than kinship or advice. She's personally offering to help us manage a transition. If we'd had this conversation only a month sooner, I would have politely declined her invitation. But on this day I find myself much more open to the suggestion.

I wonder if maybe I should start taking it more seriously than I have.

Six months. That's how long our visas are good for, starting from the moment they were first stamped into our passports in December of last year. Suddenly, it's May already. Our visas are set to expire, and Titi's recovery continues to be monitored with no set end date.

I hadn't planned on staying in the US this long. I'd hoped the medical care would require only a small number of weeks. I certainly hadn't envisioned us being here more than a couple months, so I didn't give the visa deadline much thought. But now that the expiration date is fast approaching, I realize taking Titi back to Eritrea so soon would be irresponsible. The cardiologist she's been seeing wants to continue following her for at least another six months. The PDA repair appears to have fully taken, and Titi's strength continues to improve. But while the doctor hasn't seen any change in the septal defect, he remains optimistic the hole will eventually close off on its own. It will take time before we'll know for sure, but time is something we don't have.

With each passing day, Titi adjusts more fully to life in America. She's fitting in better at school, learning the language, making friends, growing comfortable in this new culture. Even I am able to better appreciate how much we have here, despite how much more we lack. There are constant challenges to overcome, but they're far more manageable challenges compared with those we experienced in Eritrea— in fact, almost petty. And my new friend was right: There is so much more support here for immigrants than I had ever imagined.

With Titi doing so well, my focus shifts to Yikealo and Natsanet. So far, they've been able to avoid any serious harassment, which offers me some peace of mind. I find myself contemplating with greater frequency and seriousness the idea of bringing them here to live, and less about getting ourselves back. What would it be like for us to live here permanently? What will Yikealo choose to do? Will he agree to come, or stay like the husband of the woman on the airplane going to Germany? What would we do for work? These and other uncertainties weigh heavily on me, along with the very simple question of my loyalty to my country. Eritrea is my home, even if it feels less welcoming by the year. I feel like I'd be letting it and my family down. The decision would be much easier if things were worse off than they actually are, but with the war on pause, it's easy to imagine how things could start improving again.

I share my turmoil with my sister, who tries her best to remain objective, but I can tell she's excited about the prospect of us staying for good. She doesn't realize, as I do, that it may ultimately be impossible to achieve. We had such a struggle just getting permission for me and Titi to come. I already failed once with Natsanet, limiting my chances in the future, and I fully expect to fail with Yikealo as long as he's in the ENS. I see very little chance of him being released from his conscription anytime soon. So, am I just wasting my time fantasizing about it? Am I just delaying a reunion our family needs now just so I can entertain a whim?

The subject has begun to insinuate my conversations with Yikealo on the telephone, although we've never addressed it directly. Emotionally, neither of us is at that point just yet. We would have to be desperate to make such a radical move, and in spite of the hardships he's suffered and continues to suffer, I sense they're not enough to make him turn his back on his country. "Not yet," he tells me, although I can hear the weariness in his voice, so I know he's at least open to the idea.

Realistically, we both know that now isn't the time for him to ask for entry visas. It hasn't been long enough since the American government refused Natsanet's visa out of fear I wouldn't return. Submitting a request now would only validate that belief.

There is another, more practical reason we haven't discussed the option too openly during our phone conversations. There's always the risk that someone could be listening in, which might cause problems for Yikealo and Natsanet. We can't be sure the calls are secure. In fact, it's likely they're being monitored by the Eritrean government.

Ironically, it's these same nagging suspicions that ultimately convince me that bringing my family here is the better alternative to us returning.

Days before our visas expire, I submit an application to the local US Immigration Office— not for a medical extension, but for permanent residence status, which would give us more time to figure things out. Just as important, it will loosen the restrictions on me with regards to work. Titi can continue to be monitored during her recovery, and I won't have to worry about reapplying for extensions. This is how I rationalize it all to myself, anyway.

Less easy to rationalize is the cost. The lawyer's fees alone exceed three thousand dollars. Aster and her husband dip deep into their modest savings to help. They see it as our first concrete step toward establishing ourselves here in America. I promise them I'll pay them back, although I don't know how. Three thousand dollars is more than a lifetime of earnings in Eritrea. But if it takes a lifetime to return the money, so be it.

Next, we're scheduled for an interview in Chicago. Our lawyer accompanies us, as well as a translator she recommends, just in case I have any difficulty understanding the questions. My English is good, but there are numerous legal terms I don't understand. It feels like an unnecessary expense, but I don't want to take any chances at all.

The interviewer is a tall gentleman with blond hair. After listening to me explain Titi's situation, he asks her to sit in a chair outside the interview room so he can speak to me in private. After hesitating, she agrees to go.

"I don't want her to become upset," the interviewer gently explains. "She's a bit young to understand why I have to ask you some of these questions, especially as they pertain to your relationship with your husband and the political situation in your homeland."

Although I understand his reasoning, I still find Titi's dismissal unsettling— not because I want her to be informed, but because I'm still uncomfortable leaving her alone anywhere other than at school. But my concerns are unfounded, as the interview goes much more smoothly and quickly than I anticipate. In fact, I'm able to answer all of his questions without the help of either the lawyer or the translator. When he's finished, he notes that he has nearly all of the information he needs to render a recommendation. "We still need to run this up the flagpole, so to speak," he says, referring to both the approvals higher up in the state department and the background security checks. "Just a formality."

The lawyer also assures me not to worry, but I'm never happy whenever there's any uncertainty. Too many times have I been told something, only to be disappointed when it doesn't turn out to be true. I want badly to accept the lawyer's word. After all, it's her job to know what she's talking about. But experience tells me that anything can happen to upset even the most sure thing.

Before leaving, the immigration agent adds that the residency status, if approved, includes both my husband and Natsanet. "So when they're able to join you here, you won't have to worry about submitting a new application for them."

It's a consolation, although a very small one, as bringing them here remains a remote possibility. The obstacles we face before they have a chance to come are mountains compared to the hills I've already had to climb. It's not like they can just get on an airplane and come here. But I do appreciate what it means. Their names on the permit are important to me. It represents the first step, if even just a tiny one, to a future here in America.

That is, should we eventually choose that path.

And only *if* the residency permit is granted. I'm still not convinced it will be. Past experience has taught me not to count on anything. I'll only believe it after I have it in my hand.

A week passes without word from the Immigration and Naturalization office. Then two. And with each day that ends with our status here in the US still unresolved, my doubts grow. When at last we finally receive the agency's decision a full three months later, it comes in a simple letter informing us that the permit is granted. It's so anticlimactic I have a hard time believing it's genuine.

In August of 2004, after we've been here for nearly nine months, Titi and I become permanent residents of the United States of America. In all, the process took months longer than I had expected and a lot more trips to the Chicago office of Citizenship and Immigration Services than it should have, requiring far more time, effort, and money to accomplish than should be necessary. It proves that bureaucracies everywhere suffer from the same inefficiencies. But one difference between the system here and in Eritrea stands out. Here, I was never asked to pay extra money to "facilitate" the process or guarantee a favorable outcome. I can't decide if that's a good thing or not. Sometimes, fair just feels so impersonal, especially when human lives are on the line.

Now that I'm a permanent resident, I can finally apply for a job. I'm eager to begin supporting myself and Titi, and I launch myself into the process with zeal. But bureaucratic frustrations seem to follow me everywhere, this time in my application for a work permit. On the day of my appointment, I decide to leave Titi in school, rather than bringing her with me as I'd been asked. But because she's not with me, I'm told I have to reschedule. Apparently, Titi must be present for some strange reason I don't quite understand. Do they expect her to apply for a permit at the same time? She's too young to get a job herself. "It's because she's here with you in the country and you're her sole legal guardian and we need to be sure she'll be cared for while you're working," they try to explain. I still don't understand what seems like an odd requirement; nevertheless, it teaches me a valuable lesson. When dealing with governmental agencies, follow any instructions they give you to the last letter, regardless of whether they make sense or not.

A few days after we receive the residency permit, Aysha calls again out of the blue from Texas and tells me she's had another dream. I haven't shared my change in plans, so it's hard not to find her timing a bit uncanny.

"You and your dreams," I tease halfheartedly. She knows I can no longer deny how accurate they've been thus far. "What was your dream this time?"

"You were crossing a bridge over a wide river."

"I thought you said this was different," I tell her. "It's the same dream as before."

"No, it's different this time, because now you've made it safely across. Then you turn around and I can tell you're worried about something. Your family is still on the other side, but instead of going back to them, you beckon them to follow behind you."

When I tell her about the residency permit and my decision to start our lives over again in America, she doesn't seem surprised in the least. "I knew it," she says confidently. "See? I told you it would happen."

I don't have the heart to tell her that it hasn't happened yet. I don't want to take away her triumph with a dose of cold, hard reality just yet.

Now that I've committed to bringing my family here, my next step is to submit the necessary paperwork to begin the reunification process. I have no idea how long it will take. I expect it may be several more months, which is why I dive right into it. The sooner I begin, the sooner we'll be together again. I pray the government of Eritrea recognizes the folly of trying to obstruct us and allows them to come. Their petty refusals only raise ill will, adding to that which too many of its residents already feel toward the government. And now that I'm on the outside looking in, I can say with certainty that they need all the goodwill they can get. I could tell while interviewing at the consulate that the American government has unfavorable opinions about how Eritrea is being run.

I'm aware there will be challenges every step of the way. It's not unusual for separated families to be away from each other for years. I know some people who have totally given up hope altogether. Some couples have been driven to the point of divorce because the strain of the separation and dealing with intractable bureaucracies was too much to endure. I try not to focus on the negatives. Instead, I keep a joyful image of my youngest daughter and my husband in my mind. I picture God clearing the way ahead of us until our paths join again. It's better to start a long journey hopeful rather than discouraged.

The Immigration Office provides me with a list of social service organizations and charities that offer resettlement assistance. I spend hours calling one number after another. Some lines are disconnected. Some don't answer their phones. Others leave me on hold for long periods of time. One by one I cross them out. But then someone picks up at Catholic Charities USA. After I explain my situation, they schedule an interview.

When I arrive at their local office, I'm surprised to see how many immigrants there are among the people applying for assistance. We come from all over the world, but it seems that most are from Africa, like me. I'm told about the types of assistance I may be eligible for and how to apply for them. But I'm also warned not to become reliant on handouts. "The American government — and its citizens — don't intend to support you and your family forever. Nor can we. We all want you to succeed so you can contribute to society and give back to those who follow after you. So, as part of this, you must look for a job to support yourself and your daughter. By demonstrating you're a responsible and productive member of American society, you'll find it easier to get the assistance you need. Having a job is one of the first and most important steps you can take."

I tell him that I actually welcome the opportunity to work. It's been hard for me to be idle and nonproductive during the long summer break that just ended.

"Good. I also advise you not to be too picky about the type of work, either."

I'm assigned various case workers and coaches. I start to receive financial assistance and job search training. For housing, I'm referred to a woman who specializes in placing newly arrived immigrants. "Right now," she says, "we have only one vacancy for single moms with young children. It's a one-room studio in a small town about fifteen or twenty miles outside of the city.

I'm unsure about the distance, since I have no car, no job, no credit cards, and no knowledge about how to get around. I'd hoped to stay as close to my sister as possible.

"It's a nice, quiet little place," she says, sensing my hesitation. "Why don't I take you and your daughter on a little trip up there to see for yourself?"

To my surprise, she's right. The town is pleasant, neither big and crazy, like Chicago, nor too quiet, like some of the farmlands I've seen. Instead, it's surrounded by hills blanketed with trees. She tells us that there used to be a lot more of the forest, but the trees have since given way to more and more residential neighborhoods. The apartment building she takes us to is actually located close to a vibrant downtown area with bus stops and a convenient shopping center, where I can get groceries and look for a job. There are also schools nearby. I can walk almost everywhere I need to go.

Next, she shows us the apartment, which is in a complex of three buildings. Each "house" consists of several personal living spaces, or studios, but shares a family room, dining room, and a large community kitchen on the floor below. "I know it's small," she tells me, "but without a credit history and job yet, you're simply not going to find anything better. At least you'll have some privacy. It also comes furnished with two beds, blankets, bed sheets, towels, and some basic necessities. And there's a daycare center on site."

It is small, but it's more than I ever dreamed of to start out. It certainly meets our current needs.

Several of the people living there recognize my host as she's- showing us around. Like me, they're mostly immigrants; others are single parents escaping other types of persecution or trying hard to pull themselves out of poverty. One person is from Liberia, another from Afghanistan. There's a family from Nigeria. The people in the unit next to mine speak Spanish. They all greet her with the same smiles and hugs, which she reciprocates without hesitation. I'm struck by her warmth. She listens thoughtfully to their updates, whether they're about a job they got, money they've been able to save, or a car they've bought. She listens equally as attentively to their complaints, if they have any. She offers to help, if she can. She's like a mother and sister to us all. It comes as no surprise to me when I learn she's a nun.

Titi doesn't take very well to the idea of being uprooted again. She's just started another new school year and already loves her teacher after only a month. It's hard for her to say goodbye to the new friends she has made. The day I've scheduled for us to move, she cries and begs me not to take her away from them.

It breaks my heart all over again. I know I'm forcing her to leave her best friend behind, the daughter of the woman who had to track her children down in Nigeria. The two of us mothers have become close friends, too, and she also pleads

212

with me not to separate the girls. "Titi can even stay with us during the week, if she wants."

But she understands when I have to decline the offer. We have an incredible opportunity to assimilate ourselves into society, and I intend not to let it go.

Of course, it doesn't help that my own sister disagrees with my decision. "Why move Titi in the middle of the school year?" she asks. "Let her finish. It's more than she can handle." I think the truth is, she's unhappy about the both of us leaving the house. After being here on her own for eight years, she'd forgotten how much she missed having her family around. Even marriage can't fill that hole. We're only moving twenty miles away, but it still feels like we're going to an entirely different country.

Nevertheless, if I stay, I'll never be forced to build a home here. I'll never feel like I've set down roots. It's the only way I'll be able to feel right about tearing Yikealo and Natsanet from theirs.

SETTLING IN

After our moves — the two of us into our new apartment and Titi into her new school — I sign up to attend career training offered by the County Social Services Agency to help prepare me for the job hunt. So far, everything seems to be moving forward at a brisk pace. But then I hit the proverbial wall. I knew having no work history here would make the search harder, but after a month pouring over job openings posted on the computers at the Social Services office and applications mailed or hand delivered to dozens of stores and businesses — everything from retail sales and janitorial to skilled positions more in line with my education — I have yet to receive a single reply. And when a second month passes without an offer for an interview, I begin to despair. How am I supposed to establish myself if I don't work? How can I buy anything? I wonder why no one will hire me. The economy is booming and unemployment is low. Don't my college courses and prior work experience mean anything?

I'm reminded again and again not to be picky. "Start small. Consider babysitting. Or house cleaning."

But I can't afford to work ten hours a week for less than minimum wage. Or ten hours a day for not much more.

One day, a secretarial position opens up at the local public school district. An acquaintance from the job training, an older Afghani gentleman who also happens to be interested in the same job, offers to give me a ride so we can submit our applications together. Even though we're competing for the same position, it's hard to think of each other as rivals. We share a set of experiences that makes us allies. In his case, he left his homeland several years ago after the American invasion and brought his large family here. He's worked on local assembly lines, but now all of the manufacturing companies in the area are closing and the jobs are being shifted out of the country, so he has to look for another type of work.

The first question we're asked when we show up is whether we can type fifty-five words per minute. He shakes his head and shrugs.

"I can type," I respond, "but not to that level of efficiency."

"I'm sorry, but that's an absolute essential minimum requirement."

The woman screening us must notice the look of discouragement on my face, because she tells me to wait a moment. She gives my résumé another look, then asks about my teaching experience. "We have an opening that you might be qualified for. You'd be working in one of the classrooms."

I tell her about the volunteer work I did helping out my daughter's first grade teacher, and she asks if I can come back for an interview and a security check. Neither of us is offered the secretarial position, but by the way my Afghani friend shrugs off the bad news, I realize he hadn't had very high expectations about it to begin with.

A month later I'm informed that I wasn't selected for the classroom job. "But we'll keep your file active for up to a year," the woman from HR tells me. I thank her, but privately I don't think I'll ever hear from her again.

Then, a few months down the road, the school district calls me out of the blue and offers me a position as a personal aide in a Special Needs classroom at one of the middle schools. I'm informed that the child I'll be assigned suffers from severe autism and the job will be quite challenging. At this point, I don't care. I'll do anything I can to get my foot in any door, even if it means getting my toes slammed once or twice in the process.

It doesn't take long for me to realize how different the new job will be from my prior experiences, both in my daughter's classroom and teaching high school students in Ethiopia. The students here — there are seven or eight in total — have such complex individual needs that managing any one of them is a full time job and requires a unique skill set that I haven't developed. Unfortunately, there's no time for learning, as I'm asked to dive right in. Anything I do pick up is either through trial and error or offered as advice by the other aides. Communicating with my charge is the biggest challenge, not because of any deficiencies in my English fluency, but because of gaps in my ability to understand his particular method of communicating. But I learn; I have no other choice. The hardest part is keeping him focused enough to do his schoolwork.

Each morning I rise just as eager to work as the previous day, although with a renewed appreciation of the challenges. I can't help but wonder what new trial I'll encounter that day. And each evening, I go home exhausted but content. I remind myself how lucky I am to have a job at all. I'm earning money. I'm now able to buy my own food and clothing, instead of being entirely dependent on my sister, social programs, and charities. Still, the challenges of the position begin to take an emotional toll on me. I want to help my student out as much as possible, and I'm frustrated by how often I'm not able to do so.

The other aides look out for me. They're mostly younger women with school-age children. We're a truer represent-ation of the community's cultural diversity than the pool of certificated teachers. The aides warn me not to get burnt out, but how can I avoid it when I need this job so badly? I know I'm in over my head. Many of us are. It partially explains the high turnover rate in the department.

One day, I'm told about another position at the high school helping Special Education classes. I don't like to leave a job unfinished, but I have to face the fact that I'm not the right person for this one, so I apply for the transfer. My current head teacher advises me against it. "High school students are much more difficult to handle than middle graders," she warns. "And high school Special Ed students are especially hard."

After some reflection, I decide to accept the offer.

On my first day I enter the classroom braced for the worst. Based on what I've been told about these students, I expect to find them throwing chairs about the room and other types of mischief, but nothing of the sort happens. The students are typical teenagers, not much different than those I taught in Ethiopia. They all have their rebellious streaks. They show the same disrespect and resistance to authority, although in somewhat different ways than I'm used to. The cultural norms are different, but they're still just teenagers trying to find their way in a world that doesn't always seem willing or capable of understanding them or accepting their uniqueness.

My new head teacher is committed to finding a way to reach them. She's an angel who clearly cares very much about her students. She draws from a deep well of experience — over two decades teaching regular classrooms and a family consisting of a mixed-race marriage with a large number of children, half of which were adopted — so she has a lot of patience and an open mind. Somehow it works, because the students respond to her in kind.

It's through her that I meet an Ethiopian immigrant couple who are friends of hers. They invite me and Titi over to their house for a barbecue on Mother's Day. We sit in their backyard while the husband cooks, and she tells me how she fled her homeland as a teenager in the late 1970s. "It was soon after the military coup that ended Emperor Haile Selassie's rule," she tells me. "We all hoped for better from the new leader, Mengistu Haile Mariam, but all we got was the same oppression."

Listening to her speak is almost like looking into the mirror. I recognize in her the same sense of betrayal and disappointment that I've begun to allow myself to feel toward my own country. We both celebrated the end of one reign of oppression, only to allow another to take its place.

"In the unrest that immediately followed Haile Selassie's ouster," she says, "there was persecution and killing. But it only got worse. It became so bad that my family was forced to flee. We sought asylum here in America." She gives me a thoughtful look and adds, "It took a long time for us to adjust, not just to learning a new culture, but to letting go of the guilt we felt, as if we'd been cowards for running away. I expect you'll experience the same rash of feelings. Don't expect your adjustment to be quick and easy. You'll struggle with it every day for the rest of your life."

They now have a teenage daughter in high school. We shared a few moments shortly after we arrived at their house today and before she disappeared into her bedroom with Titi in tow. She seems very well adjusted, but then again, she was born here and grew up never knowing Ethiopia. Yet, despite the age difference between her and my daughter, the two girls took to each other very quickly. It seems that some cultural values get handed down regardless of environment and circumstance.

As I sit here enjoying the company in their beautiful home, it strikes me how truly relaxed I am at this moment. It's encouraging to know that I'm not alone in my journey, and that the challenges I face aren't insurmountable. These people, for example, had to overcome tremendous violence and oppression when they fled Ethiopia. They took an incredible risk by leaving their home, and another by coming to America, a land completely unknown to them. Yet they made a good life for themselves. It's not so hard to imagine it being my own family in a few years, after Yikealo and Natsanet have arrived and settled in. Today, it feels eminently doable.

Another academic year winds its way to a close. I've had some challenging assignments at the school district, but enjoyed them all. Some of the teachers have become my closest friends. I'm constantly amazed by the support they and my employer continue to give me. It's wonderful to be part of a community with so many immigrants. They make me feel like I have an army standing behind me, pushing me forward, supporting me, making sure I don't slide backwards. It's the most incredible feeling in the world.

Titi is also making progress. Although the doctor is still not ready to declare her free of the septal wall defect, and even warns that she may never be, he doesn't see it being much of a problem as she nears puberty. He asks to see her less frequently. Of course, my motherly fears for her health will never go away entirely, but they have gradually lost much of their urgency. And that's allowed me to devote my full attention to reuniting the family here in America. It has been more than a year and a half since we left Eritrea, and while each and every one of those days has scored a permanent mark on my soul, they don't discourage me from giving up. I've gotten used to being patient, to accepting delays and setbacks. Titi still struggles with it, though. Some days are better than others for her. I hope my Yikealo and Natsanet have learned to deal with our separation, too.

I make frequent calls to the embassy, to Immigration Services, to anyone I can connect with as I keep prodding the system along. But there's little they can do. The main obstacles are in Eritrea. Yikealo fights the same fight from there, the same battles I fought when I first tried to bring Titi and Natsanet. I wish I could be there to help him. I feel so helpless being so far away. The best I can do is talk to him over the phone or on email.

Pretty soon, another year passes. Titi has made several friends and is becoming more and more American. One day, she receives an invitation to a friend's house. The girl's mother, whose parents emigrated from Northern Europe before she was born, offers to pick them up from school for the play date. Not knowing them, I ask that we meet first.

The request turns into an invitation to the house for tea, which blossoms into ever more friendships— between us moms, between Titi and her friend's two older siblings. While they play, the girl's mother asks me about our story. After I tell it, she says if there's a way she and her husband can help to just let them know. "Anything," she repeats, before rattling off a list of suggestions. For having been a complete stranger before today, her generosity touches me deeply. She owes us nothing, yet offers everything.

It's always been an important part of Eritrean culture to help others less fortunate than ourselves. We teach this behavior to our children, and they pass it along to theirs. I admit I hadn't expected to experience this kind of generosity here in America, partially because it's a part of our culture I'd always considered to be uniquely our own. But I'd also been led to believe that everyone here resented immigrants. In my experience, that's actually the exception rather than the norm.

My new friends know we're still dependent on others for transportation, so they offer to drive us places— to the park for picnics, to the lake, into the city. They extend more invitations to us for dinner at their house. The girls get along very well and always enjoy these times together. And while I'm truly grateful for such hospitality, I just can't get used to being so dependent on other people all the time. I don't *want* to.

Which is another reason why I've been working so hard and saving every penny I can, so I can buy myself a car to drive ourselves around. But hard work and desire can only take one so far. My savings is too small to pay cash, and I have no credit history to qualify for a loan. When I mention this to my friend at Catholic Charities USA during one of our checkups, she tells me about a program through a group called the International Rescue Committee, which matches savings dollar-for-dollar to encourage immigrants to develop good money management skills. The match can then be used to pay for such necessities as educational courses, computers, and automobiles. I contact the IRC right away, but I'm told the program I'm interested in will soon be shutting down for lack of funding support. Undaunted, I press her until she agrees to enroll me, despite her qualms. "You won't have enough time to meet the minimum savings amount before the deadline," she predicts.

I prove her wrong. I work extra jobs, shop even more carefully than I have been, eat more frugally. It's hard for both Titi and me not to splurge occasionally or have a special treat now and then, but we both accept that our situation will be so much better once we have our own car. Besides, how can we not try as hard as we possibly can, when such an incredible opportunity is given to us?

The day the IRC caseworker signs the check over to me with the matching funds, she confesses how surprised she is, not to mention impressed. "You were the very last person we enrolled in the program, and this is the very last check we'll issue. Next week, our doors will shut for good."

As hard as it was to save for the car, it turns out to be much easier buying one than qualifying to drive it, at least for me. Despite already knowing how to drive, I repeatedly fail the licensing test. I know it's just my nerves getting the better of me. I've been working so hard for so long just for the privilege that I end up turning myself into a nervous wreck every time I try. Finally, on the fourth attempt, the tester, a kindhearted Asian woman with a round face and puffy red cheeks, tells me to just relax. She's very patient with me. When I finally receive the paper with my temporary license, my relief is too great. I spend the first half hour as a licensed driver in my car — *my very own car!* — doing nothing but sitting in the parking lot of the DMV and sobbing with joy.

BUREAUCRACIES (III)

The studio apartment where we have been living was never meant to be permanent, or even long term. It's a blessing for someone just starting out, but we quickly outgrew the small space after obtaining just a few modest household items, mainly purchased from thrift stores and yard sales, but also donated by generous friends, so it's time to look for another place. Besides, there's always a waiting list of people hoping to get in, people with dreams of setting out on their own, people in as much need as we were when we first arrived, whose lives are filled with much less stability and certainty than we have now. So, I have begun looking for a new place to live. It'll be nice having our own space again, including our own bathroom, kitchen, and yard. When multiple families share these areas, they inevitably form close bonds with each other by being part of a community of individuals who are dependent upon one another, and I'll miss having this. But shared community doesn't always translate to shared responsibility and mutual respect. Some residents aren't as diligent as others when it comes to cleaning and other chores.

I've had my sights set on a nearby apartment complex for a while. The buildings appear to be relatively new and the grounds are well maintained. There's a lot of shade and areas for the children to play in. But I could never afford the rental fees on my small income. Still, on a whim, I decide to pay the leasing office a visit one day. It doesn't cost anything to talk, and it'll give me a better idea of what I need to do to prepare. Or to rule it out as completely beyond my reach.

The manager of the complex is happy to show me around, and she takes me directly to one of the empty apartments. It's so spacious that it seems palatial. But when I tell her my situation, she isn't put off right away. Instead, she confides that they have a few dedicated units for low income families. "However," she warns, "the waiting list is miles long, and we give priority to tenants already renting here at the full price. You could do that and get your foot in the door."

"It would be impossible," I reply. "But I would like to add my name to the list anyway."

I continue to search the surrounding neighborhoods and refuse to be discouraged. As part of my routine, I return regularly to the apartment complex to ask if one of the low income units has become available. One day I'm surprised when the rental manager tells me she has one. "But I wouldn't hold my breath," she warns, and reiterates what the complex manager already told me about how existing renters are automatically given first choice.

I ask her to make a note that I'm interested.

Several days later, after returning home from an outing with a friend, yet another recent Eritrean transplant to America, I find a message on my answering machine. It's the leasing agent calling to tell me about the vacancy, and asking if I'm still interested. I immediately start jumping up and down and dancing. I'm sure if Titi were home, she'd be mortified by my behavior, but I'm too happy to care. My friend and I rush right over to the leasing office, only to discover that I'm not the only one who was notified. Another person is already waiting for the manager to return from lunch.

"There's a one hundred dollar deposit to secure the spot," the manager tells the three of us. My friend and I run back to my apartment to get the money, hoping we haven't lost our chance by coming unprepared. When we return, the agent says she can't accept cash. So, out we go again to get a money order. I feel guilty about trying to outdo the other woman, but we were both told it's first-come, first-served. In the end, however, she never returns, and we realize she didn't have the money for the deposit. If Titi and I hadn't made the sacrifices we did, we wouldn't have been ready to jump on an opportunity such as this one. I let out a huge exhale of relief when the manager accepts the deposit this time.

Unfortunately, it's only the first hurdle to overcome before we can move in. Next, there's the rental application, and where it asks for marital status, I check "MARRIED," which prompts the manager to ask for Yikealo's details, including his address, job, and income.

"But he lives in another country," I explain.

"We still need his income data to determine whether or not you qualify for the subsidized rate."

"But he makes very little money," I argue. Even though he's working on a project for a different company now, he's still in the National Service, and his pay is no better than it was before. "He doesn't support us at all."

"We still need the numbers. I'm sorry, but the government requires that information to determine your financial eligibility." She hands me a form that Yikealo will need to fill out and have his employer sign.

At this point, I realize the document could upend any progress we've made thus far on getting him and my other daughter here. We have tried to be as discreet as we can as it regards our continued stay here in America, so that people in the government won't hassle him. But by complying with this new request, we're not only announcing that we've remained out of the country far longer than originally intended, but we've taken steps to settle down here permanently. I try to explain this situation to the manager, about how the Eritrean government has taken to persecuting family members of those who have emigrated. I tell her we've been quietly working to bring my husband and daughter over, and this could complicate the matter tremendously. But all she can do is apologize. "I'm sorry, but my hands are tied."

I have no choice. At some point, our plans will become widely known. I simply have to trust in God that I'm making the right decision. I send the form to Yikealo, and I do what the rental manager advised me not to do when I first inquired about the apartment: I hold my breath. After a few days, the paperwork is returned. I don't know what exactly my husband tells his boss, but the form is completely filled out and signed. The apartment manager checks the numbers, adding my husband's income figure directly to my own without first adjusting for the exchange rate.

"This is in *nakfa*," I note, pointing out the error, and provide her the converted figure. The new total barely nudges the figure any higher than my income alone.

In disbelief, she says she'll personally need to speak with Yikealo over the phone. I can tell she can't comprehend how someone could make so little money. She doesn't understand that the average person in Eritrea makes less than a couple hundred US dollars per year.

The entire application process has become so onerous that I feel like I should be buying a house instead of renting an apartment. I want to plead with the agent to just accept the figures as truth, because they are. I'm afraid any further delays will cause me to lose this chance. "You have to understand," I tell her. "He lives in a totally different time zone. Daytime here is nighttime there. It's not easy to get a hold of people there when it's daytime here."

But she's nothing if not committed to following the rules. "I'll get in big trouble if I'm caught putting the wrong information down on your application." She tells me to come back to the office later that night so we can make the call.

I'm so distraught by this point that I call my friend from the Catholic Charities USA for advice. "Why is everything always so hard?" I ask. She tells me that this is just the way things are for everybody. "The rules are in place to ensure fairness to everyone." Then she advises me to be patient and offers to email the leasing office explaining my situation. Eventually, the manager decides to start the entire process all over again from scratch.

But it still doesn't solve my problems. This time, there's a question of why Titi's father isn't paying child support. Once again, I patiently explain our situation and point to the disparity in our incomes. And once more, statements are written and included in the application. Finally, it's ready to be submitted. I'm on pins and needles while we wait for the appropriate government agencies to review it.

The day she hands me the keys, she includes this stipulation: "Based on the information we provided, you need to understand that your husband can't live with you in this apartment after he arrives. You'll have to move or submit a new application so your subsidy can be recalculated."

I happily agree. I don't care about any of that at this point. I'm just thrilled to be able to move into a larger place, one with our own kitchen and living room and refrigerator and bathroom. I'll agree to just about anything by now. Besides, it's starting to look like my family coming over won't be an issue anytime soon. Last we heard, the government of Eritrea has blocked anyone from leaving.

CHASING THE DREAM

The town we live in is small and quiet. It's tucked into a valley between a pair of larger cities to the north and south, respectively. The hills to the east and west offer a variety of hiking trails. In the winter, the slopes are covered in snow; in the summer, they're green. The community is close knit. There are festivals, weekly summer events, and celebrations for all of the major holidays and some of the minor ones. Participating in them makes me feel like I'm back in Asmara again, when friends and neighbors would take to the streets to commemorate one religious holiday or another.

Eritrea doesn't celebrate Halloween. I only learned about this event after Titi came home one day and asked about making a costume so she could go trick-or-treating. It seems like a strange thing, but here the townspeople really get into it. All of the business owners on the main street through the center of town invite revelers to come and listen to music. They hand out treats along with business cards and pamphlets advertising their businesses. The sidewalk cafés fill up with partygoers early in the evening. The roads are blocked off at five o'clock and almost immediately clog up with people on foot, both young and old, who wander about and enjoy the festive atmosphere. It's a small enough town that many people know each other.

The run up to Christmas sees the businesses decorated with lights and oversized ribbons and bows. Giant gift-wrapped props adorn the center median of the main street that runs through town. Despite the cold, there's an evening parade, as well as other events, when the colorful lights add to the wonder. In the summer, musical groups come and give outdoor concerts. There's a playhouse, where amateur actors from the community put on shows. One of the biggest summer events is the celebration of American Independence from British colonial rule. People line both sides of the street for miles along the parade route to see the dozens of floats, marching bands, fire trucks, veterans, and high school athletes. The parade also has a distinct multinational flare, with Chinese dragons, horseback riding mariachi singers, and Indian dancers in their colorful saris. To see such patriotism and multiculturalism intermingled in one place makes me realize how special this country is. In the evening, the town puts on a spectacular fireworks display that draws people from miles around.

Eritrea celebrates its Independence Day in May. It, too, includes a parade and fireworks in the capital city. In the past, Yikealo and I would go to watch it at the stadium and cheer with all the other people. But now I realize how much of it was carefully choreographed pageantry meant more to impress its citizens with the country's military might than to instill a sense of exuberance, pride, and optimism. It's meant to remind us of the president's strength and vision, except now I see that it's another example of his iron grip over the nation. Reflecting back on those experiences, I now understand how much of what I watched was an illusion, a poor facsimile of what the celebrations were actually supposed to be about— remembering the martyrs who gave their lives, and the oppression they freed us from. The charade is an affront to the hopefulness every Eritrean held in the early days of our liberation.

Sometimes it's hard to wake up and know it was nothing but a dream. We were led astray, and any hope I have that we'll find our way back dwindles by the day. I often worry that my newfound dream of settling down in my adopted home in America may be just another illusion. I'm aware of its history; I'm not blind to its ongoing struggles with racism, immigration, and economic disparity. As much as I appreciate all I have been given since arriving here, there are times when I feel a familiar sense of uneasiness in my belly. All I can do is stay focused, have faith, and push as hard as I can toward my goal while I can.

One day, a financial planner from the school district comes to talk to me about retirement plans. I'm working mainly as a substitute teacher by then and looking for a second job to supplement my income. I had worked for a while as an assistant at an after-school tutoring service, which helped a lot with the expenses, but the job ended. Now, on top of my substitute teaching job and being the sole care provider for my daughter, I'm juggling classes to get my teaching credential. It's not easy to find time for another job, but we need the money. I've always hated living paycheck to paycheck, especially since there are mounting expenses associated with our ongoing attempts to bring Natsanet and Yikealo here. The old bribery system is alive and well in Eritrea, especially now, and some of the "opportunities" we seek run into the thousands of American dollars.

"This is all of your income?" the advisor asks, when I show her my pay stubs. "Where's the rest?"

"That's all of them." I tell her about the small subsidy I'm receiving for my rent, but otherwise, it's all I have coming in.

"Don't you have children?"

"I have one living with me right now. My younger daughter still lives with her father in Eritrea. I'm working on bringing them here."

The woman gives me a puzzled frown, then gathers her papers. Apparently the meeting's over, because there's no reason to discuss a hypothetical retirement plan and funding it with nonexistent savings.

"I'm still interested in my options," I say. "I like to be informed, just in case."

"Just in case of what? With your income and expenses, there's no way we could set up a savings plan."

"But I'm always looking for other jobs."

"When you find one, let's talk." She gives me her card with her phone number and email address on it.

At this point, I'm thinking this is the last I'll see of her, but she finds me again later in the day as I make my way to my classroom. "Do you and your daughter eat?" she asks, looking concerned.

"Yes, of course," I reply. The question feels judgmental. It reminds me of the time Titi's cardiologist suggested I was neglecting Natsanet. I can't help feeling that she's implying the same thing, that I'm not a good mother simply because I don't have very much.

"It's just . . . ," she says, before realizing how this must look to me. Her face reddens, and she apologizes. "I mean, how can you afford to live on your own and pay for food with so little income? I'm not trying to pry, but I'd really like to understand. Between my income and my husband's, we still never seem to have enough money."

I stop and turn to face her. "It's easier if you have a plan and stick to it," I say. "For example, I pay the rent on the first day of the month because I need to be sure we have a place to live. Then I make sure I have enough gas in the car and pay the insurance so I can drive to work and to the store. Then I pay the utilities, because without them I can't cook or talk to my husband on the telephone. Nearly everything else goes for food. Sometimes we have a little extra, which we save or spend on other things we might need."

"Do you receive food stamps?"

"I used to, but not now."

She still looks puzzled.

"We don't go to restaurants," I explain. "I prepare all our meals. We don't go to the movies. Instead, we go to the park or the beach. There are lots of free activities."

"And clothes?"

"I look for sales. I shop at thrift stores. We buy second-hand." I smile and shrug. "The Dollar Store people and the Goodwill people know me very well. We're making sacrifices now in order to live more comfortably later. Isn't that how one is supposed to save for retirement?"

She shakes her head in disbelief. "I still don't understand how you do it, but I really admire the way you're handling your life. You're a much stronger person than I could ever be."

It's nice to be told this, but the truth is, I'm no stronger than any of the dozens of other immigrants I have met along the way— the Afghani gentleman and his family, the woman cleaning tables at the mall in Raleigh, the couple who immigrated from Ethiopia. Or the thousands of others, strangers who come here every year, some from far worse circumstances than mine. We all share the same universal desire: to make a better life for ourselves and our families. It may be hard work— No, it is *absolutely* hard. Sometimes, it feels like the so-called American Dream is just within reach. Other times it seems impossibly distant. But nobody ever promised us it wouldn't take effort. In fact, now that I've been here a while, I know it's not even a guarantee. But it is achievable. I know it is. After all, I see other people live it all around me every day.

* * *

I love teaching, but it's not all I enjoy. When I was living in Eritrea, I took correspondence courses in the field of insurance and management. I even worked at various times as an insurance agent, administrator, and a Human Resources professional. I love working with people and hope to eventually find a position where I can advise others how to improve their lives.

One day, a position at the local Workers Compensation Office is posted in the newspaper. I decide to apply, even though I lack the proper certification. I'm thrilled when they call me in for a written examination. On the day of the test, I walk in to find the room filled with hundreds of other applicants, and my heart sinks. Is this how competitive the field is? How could I possibly expect to do well when there are already so many others, most of whom were born and educated here?

A few days later, I receive a call asking me to come in for an interview. My score on the exam placed me tenth — not in the tenth percentile, but tenth overall — and qualifies me for three different positions. Knowing that I won't be offered a job without the proper certification, I decline. I think some people would look at this entire exercise and say I wasted my time, but I had seen it as a personal challenge, a way to gauge my competitiveness. Now that I know I am just as good, my confidence soars. It encourages me to get my license to practice as an insurance agent.

The licensing process requires me to take a week of intensive coursework, including eight hours in a classroom each day and several hours of review and homework each night. On top of this, there are study sessions in the evening.

As it's the week before Titi's school starts, we decide to stay at my sister's house outside Springfield, so my daughter won't have to be left home alone. It also helps me avoid the long, slow commute into and out of the city. By the end of the week, I'm so exhausted I don't want to do anything but sleep. But the test is on the following Monday, so I force myself to study.

And I pass.

Over the course of the next year, I take two additional courses on life insurance policy writing to enhance my employability. Thankfully, I'm able to take these online. Then, armed with both licenses, I begin to apply for jobs and accept an offer to join a major life insurance provider. I know sales is not my strength, but I remind myself of the advice I was once given: Don't be picky. It's always worked for me in the past.

This time, however, it works against me. I hadn't expected such long and strange hours. Most sales are made in the evenings and on weekends, when customers are away from their regular jobs. The work eats into my time with Titi. We drift apart. Still, I feel obligated to stick with it. I've already invested so much time and money into getting myself to this point.

Then comes the news from Eritrea. It's both good and bad. First, the government has finally granted Natsanet another exit visa. She'll still need an entry visa to come to America, the same one she'd been denied before, but permission to leave at all is a huge achievement.

Yikealo's request, on the other hand, has been denied.

PART THREE
COMING HOME

RANSOM MONEY

It took US Immigration Services more than six months from the day we received our residency permits in 2004, to actually clear Natsanet and Yikealo to come to America. Even though they were automatically given residency status along with us, their cases still needed to go through the security clearance process. I remember receiving the letter as if it were yesterday. I collapsed to my knees and kissed the floor. I shook so hard I couldn't stand up, and instead just lay there weeping with relief and thanking the good Lord for granting me this miracle. At the time, our family had already been separated for nearly a year and a half, and I missed them both so terribly much that even another month seemed unbearable. That letter gave me the hope and strength to carry on.

On that very same day, Yikealo started the process of securing another exit visa for Natsanet from the Eritrean government. We would need it before applying for an entry visa from the American consulate in Asmara. We were familiar with the processes by then and so we had focused all of our efforts on our daughter's paperwork. We knew we'd encounter considerable resistance getting Yikealo here, so we agreed not to let that delay Natsanet's case. After she was here, we could then devote all of our time and attention to bringing the last member of the family to America.

But that was now fully two years ago. Somehow, that one extra unbearable month turned to two. Then six. Then that doubled twice more. It has taken more than two years of nearly daily phone calls and emails. Two years of hoping and praying for positive updates. Two years of setbacks and recoveries. Two full years fighting two different governments, one that, in a post-9/11 world, very carefully scrutinizes every single person who applies for entry, and another that, post-independence, cares only about keeping its citizens as prisoners.

Yikealo fought as hard as he could while trying not to rile people up to challenge his efforts. It was a delicate balancing act. He made appointment after appointment at the local Immigration Office in Asmara. They gave him the expected runaround. Sometimes they'd ask him to bring in some new document he'd never heard of before. Other times he'd have to submit to another interview in what seemed an endless line of them meant only to delay and frustrate. First thing every morning I'd get out of bed and power up the computer to check my email account. The last thing I'd do in the evening before going to bed was recheck it. Some days it felt like we'd taken one tiny step forward; other days, we couldn't seem to stop sliding backwards. Slowly but surely, however, we made progress. That bridge my friend Aysha had dreamed about? We were building it, slowly, one small brick at a time. Natsanet was inching closer to joining us here in the US.

Until the entire structure threatened to come crashing down.

One day, about a year after receiving that letter from the Eritrean consulate in Washington, DC, Yikealo emailed me with bad news. The new application for Natsanet's exit had been rejected by our own people in Asmara. Suddenly, the fruits of our carefully laid plans over the past few years seemed to simply evaporate into thin air. All the pain and sorrow I'd been suppressing returned in a rush, sapping me of my last ounce of strength. I was so upset I could barely find the breath to ask him why they would make this decision, especially since they had already granted it years before. He replied that they couldn't move forward until I could present myself in person to argue our case. We both instinctively understood that this was a lie. They only wanted to trick me into returning to Eritrea. And of course I would bring Titi with me when I did, since no mother would leave their young child alone when there was a risk she'd never see her again. And it wasn't just a risk, but a certainty. If I ever did go back, the Eritrean government would never allow me to leave again.

When that didn't work, they argued that since Titi and I had left the country on medical tourist visas, not immigration visas, we didn't have permission to remain out of the country indefinitely. As such, I had no legal basis for inviting my family to join us in the US. They didn't care that we'd already won resident status, the first step allowing Yikealo and Natsanet to immigrate.

"What legal basis have they to hold my daughter prisoner?" I cried out in frustration.

Instead of caving in to their demands, Yikealo offered to provide documentation in support of our prolonged stay in America. Titi's medical condition was still being monitored, and there was a risk — much smaller by now, true, but a risk nonetheless — that she would suffer by returning. He was asked to get the statement authenticated by the Eritrean Consulate here in America before they would accept the reason as valid.

I explained the situation to Titi's current cardiologist, who was more than happy to help. She wrote a letter that same day, which I presented to the consular's office in Chicago. The agent I spoke with seemed sympathetic, although he did offer what I interpreted at the time as a cautionary note, as if to temper my expectations. "I know there are many legitimate reasons for families to be here," he said. I expected him to deny my request right there and then, but he authenticated the letter and faxed it directly to Asmara. I still don't know what he was thinking. Maybe he was just trying to let me know we weren't alone in our struggle. Or maybe it was all the sympathy he was able to express in his official capacity. Eritrea's poor treatment of its citizens was not a secret, even if the scale and scope of the problem was barely understood by most people outside of the country.

Once more, we waited as Yikealo collected the facsimile from the State Department in Eritrea and hand carried it to the Immigration Office in Asmara. Once more, we felt our hopes rise. After all, it was they who had implied it would suffice in the first place. Their own consulate here in America had verified it.

But the statement was rejected. "It's a fake," they told Yikealo. "Anyone can buy such papers from any place in the US. You can even make the letter yourself and buy a stamp. It's forged."

My friend from the Catholic Charities USA tried to console me. She, too, couldn't understand how any government — or any individual, for that matter — could be so cruel as to deny a child, a six-year-old by now, the right to reunite with their mother after more than two years apart. It was obvious, even to her, that their intention was to hold Natsanet hostage until Titi and I returned.

Having exhausted every legal and diplomatic option we could think of to obtain the visas, Yikealo and I began considering ones outside of the official channels, namely bribes. In Eritrea, taking or offering such a payment is a crime. In fact, the government works very hard to give the impression of not tolerating corruption. In reality, however, it has infected nearly every level of politics and business to such a degree that it's become a totally parallel economy altogether. The difference is that everything is done indirectly, through middlemen, so one rarely ever knows who is offering the bribe and who is taking it. In addition to inflating costs, this system introduces uncertainty that invites its own abuses. All too often a bribe is paid and the money disappears without the service ever being rendered. I remembered this from my own experience trying to get exit visas for me and Titi. If we were to attempt it, Yikealo would first have to find someone he could trust as a go-between, and that was not such an easy thing to do. Asking the wrong person could easily get you arrested.

We knew it might take him a long time to find the right people to do the job, and we were correct. We lost thousands of dollars to thieves in the process. Each failure ratcheted up the pain and our sense of helplessness tenfold. I didn't care so much about the money, although it's always painful to pay and get nothing out of it. That lost money meant we'd have less to spend for food or clothing or rent. Rather, the worst part of being robbed was the reminder that the real victim unnecessarily caught in the middle was a little girl who just wanted to see her mother. I worried that each setback tore a little more of her away from me. I feared she would simply disappear before I could save her. That's how desperate I felt.

The photographs Yikealo sent of her from home only fed my concerns. While I longed for the images and treasured them, it was painfully clear to me that Natsanet continued to suffer from the same nutritional challenges that had plagued us before I left. Already small for her age when I came to America, despite growing taller in the years since, she continued to appear physically skinny and fragile. Each time I received a new picture of her I would long to reach into the photograph itself and pull her out so I could hold her, feed her, bathe her, brush her hair. I knew her father and our other relatives were doing everything they could to keep her healthy, but it seemed like nobody had been able to figure out how to get her to put on weight. She simply wouldn't eat more than a few small bites at a sitting. Unless it was sweets. That was her weakness. She had no problem eating them, and so it was always tempting to feed her nothing but candy, just so she wouldn't look so scrawny. But we all knew she wouldn't stay healthy on such a diet.

The holidays were the worst for me. Missing her fourth birthday was painful. It only got worse when I missed her fifth and sixth. And then came her seventh, and I was a complete wreck for that one. Her eighth was just a few months away, and we still hadn't figured out a way to get her visas stamped into her passport. Talking to her on the telephone was agonizing. She would always ask if I had good news for her, and I could never say yes with any conviction. How could I explain to her why she was unable to come? It wasn't because I didn't want her to, but because the people in the government didn't want us to be together— unless it was together in Eritrea. It was just like that couple who had no choice but to leave their little boy behind after coming here. I'd have to deal with all that same bitterness when Natsanet finally arrived.

Christmases were especially hard. In general, any holiday we would normally spend together as a family felt lonelier than usual.

I know it was just as tough on Titi, although she did a better job of hiding it. Or maybe it was because she was younger and her memories of her father and sister were fading faster than my own, so she didn't wear her disappointment so close to the surface as I did. Either way, it still broke my heart.

As the months turned into years, more and more people I shared my story with would tell me it was time to arrange for Natsanet to leave the country illegally. But how could I risk such a thing, when there was even the slightest chance she could be caught? If that were to happen, I would never see her again. *Never.* They would put Yikealo in jail, torture him, maybe even kill him. They would send Natsanet somewhere and I would never find her. She would end up an orphan, where she'd almost certainly be abused. Or worse, a victim of human trafficking. And if she managed somehow to avoid all that, she'd still have the harsh training of Sawa to look forward to as a teenager. I had no doubt anymore that that particular situation was never going to improve.

If Yikealo was able to avoid capture while attempting to take her across the border into Sudan, the brutal environment offered its own terrifying challenges. It was too painful for me to consider how much she'd suffer physically. And then, what next? Fleeing Eritrea was only the first step. Navigating the refugee process was equally as difficult and just as riddled with corruption, abuse, and bureaucracy. I didn't want to imagine my daughter and her father stuck in a refugee camp for months or years, sharing too little food and too few facilities with so many thousands of others.

Every night I would pray before going to bed: "God Almighty, if you're able, please find a safe path for them to come here. I know you'll make it happen, if it is your will."

My sleep was haunted by terrible visions. In one, I'd be holding my daughter in my arms, hugging and kissing her, playing with her, and I couldn't be happier. But then I'd wake up and know it was an illusion. Reality would sink in, leaving me despondent, spoiling my mood for the rest of the day. Other times, my dreams would be filled with vague and troubling images, as if to warn me her life was already in danger, and on these days I would feel desperate and helpless to do anything.

When we received the second rejection, I didn't know what to do for a long time. Eventually, I decided we couldn't give up. We needed to keep pushing. Defeat is self-fulfilling. You fail because you quit. You succeed only because you resolve to move past each of your failures. It was the holidays, and I knew that the consular services in both countries would be shutting down most activities until after the first of the year. I told Yikealo to take a break, then restart the whole process over again in January. For some reason, I felt optimistic the new year would bring a fresh dose of luck.

"What good will that do?" he replied. It was easy to hear the resignation in his voice. We were all feeling beaten down. "I've been there so many times and they've told me in clear terms that they aren't going to give it to her. I'm tired of them. I just need to find the right person to connect us to the people who can make it happen."

"Yes, do that as well, but don't shut the door on the other way just yet. Go back and tell them that we'll be happy to put down some money as collateral. Tell them it's not a bribe. They might give her the visa if they can see that we're willing to pay for it in advance. Who knows, maybe you'll get someone different this time. Just please try once more for me."

"Okay, Wudasie. I will go there and try again. But I'm not hopeful."

The next time we spoke on the phone, I heard something different in his voice, something I hadn't heard in a long while— the faintest glimmer of hope. "They're asking if we're willing to put down some money, just as you said, as collateral."

"How much?"

"Ten thousand."

At the time, ten thousand *nakfa*s was roughly equivalent to six hundred and fifty American dollars. "That's not so much," I said, surprised at the relatively modest sum.

"Ten thousand *American*. I told them it's too much. How can we give them that much money? No, now that we know it's possible, I'm looking for someone willing to do it for less."

"No, please," I told him. "We don't have any choice. I think you already know this."

"But it's so much, and we have already lost so much. And even if we do pay it, there's still no guarantee it will work. Maybe I can bargain with them to reduce the amount. They won't refuse less money once they have gone through the process."

"That's true, but you still need the whole amount in hand," I said. "What if they demand the full payment at the beginning? No, I can't wait any longer. I need to have my daughter with me. I don't care about the cost anymore. I'll find the money from somewhere, even if I have to work my fingertips off."

It still took months to make it happen. And in the end, Yikealo was able to negotiate the amount down to half, just as he'd said was possible. Somehow, I found enough work to pay it all, even though it meant Titi and I had to sacrifice even more than we already had. Five thousand dollars was a small ransom to pay to get my daughter back.

But I would have paid five thousand times as much.

EXIT YES; ENTRY ... MAYBE

Natsanet's exit visa is only good for a month, and we still need an entry visa stamp in her passport from an American consulate. Unfortunately, the office in Asmara is understaffed as a result of the breakdown in diplomatic relations, and all requests for travel to America have been referred to other consulates in the region. The situation is mainly due to rising political tensions between Eritrea and the rest of the world, but especially with the US government, which through the United Nations has accused Eritrea's president of human rights abuses. Isaias Afewerki's response to this condemnation has been to further isolate my homeland. In northeastern Africa, the consulates in Egypt or Kenya are the most friendly to America, so they're our best options for Natsanet.

She'll need an adult to accompany her and present her case, but Yikealo is still unable to get an exit visa to leave the country for any reason. The only citizens allowed to travel are the very young, very old, or very well connected, which gives us few options. My mother, who speaks only Tigrinya, volunteers, but how can she help if she can't even communicate with the consular officers? Yikealo starts looking for friends and relatives in those countries who might be able to assist. I also email my uncle who lives in the United Arab Emirates, and I call the US consulate in Dubai directly for advice. The consulate insists it can't help, as it has no jurisdiction over our case, but I'm not yet ready to give up on them. I won't close any doors just yet. With so much going on all at once, I feel like I'm running on top of the water. If I stop for even a moment, I'll fall through the surface and drown. Sometimes it's better to just keep moving, even if all I'm doing is running in place.

I press Yikealo to keep trying at the American consulate in Asmara on the off chance they'll make an exception. "Tell them everything we've tried so far," I say, "and ask them if there's anything else we can do within the limited time we have."

"They won't issue visas here," he says. "I have been there so many times and asked that I can say for certain there's no chance. They're referring people to neighboring countries instead."

"But if we can't even *leave* the country—"

"I think that's the point. They simply don't care."

"I don't think that's true. Go back and try again. It worked for the exit visa, so keep pushing. They might have a new idea. At this point, they must be facing this kind of situation all the time. It's better to try again and again."

Yikealo has a difficult time breaking the rules. He's more inclined to obey whenever someone in a position of authority tells him something. He's always been like this, willing to believe in the system or in another's good faith. But ever since he was conscripted into the army, which forced him to follow orders and regulations to avoid being punished for defiance, he's become even more so. Discipline and respect for authority was beaten into him, whereas thinking independently was beaten out. Even now, after so many years since his training in Kiloma, it still manifests its effects on him as clearly as the scars on his skin. He's much more cautious, more analytical, than he ever was before. He's prone to bouts of excessive patience. He likes to know his chances of a particular outcome before he makes a decision to act.

I am different. Most of the time I abide rules and regulations, but I'm more willing to consider exceptions and push boundaries. I know I can be more impulsive, depending on my emotions at any given moment. I have learned to control this impulse, to channel it, especially when doing so can help me find the best path forward. And there are almost always different paths, if not better ones. As I have come to learn, every office has two doors. The door in front is the proper one that everyone uses, where you follow procedure and file your paperwork and dutifully wait for a response. The door in back is where you go if all else fails, where you appeal to sympathies, use leverage, pay the secret fees. There is almost always this alternative option, because there are always those willing and able to pay it, and someone greedy enough to accept it. I know that every process is governed by rules, and I try to give them fair consideration at first. But I also know that decisions are made by people, and people have emotions and egos and their own personal agendas. And in a place like Eritrea, money and power go hand-in-hand.

So Yikealo goes back to the US consulate in Asmara, and this time when he tells our story, the officer is moved enough to take on Natsanet's case. The deeper he digs, the more surprised he becomes, first that our government fought so hard to deny her exit visa given the circumstances of our separation, and second that someone actually granted it in the end. Yikealo doesn't tell him we paid dearly for it. That's not something you talk about. Besides, the officer probably already suspects how it was obtained. "Well, having the exit visa already does make things a lot easier," the man admits. "I'll make no promises, but I'll see what I can do. Bring your daughter and her passport here, along with money for the processing fee."

Yikealo hesitates. "How much money?"

The officer slides over the form listing the standard fees. He doesn't ask for a bribe.

"There's only two weeks before her exit visa expires," Yikealo notes.

"Then bring her here first thing tomorrow morning."

When the officer meets with Natsanet, he asks her a simple question, "Do you want to go see your mom in America?"

"Yes!" Natsanet tells him without hesitation. "Yes, very much!"

"Very well. I'll try my best. And who will travel with you on the airplane?"

"We have no choice," Yikealo tells him. "She has to go alone, since I can't leave. The government won't issue me an exit visa."

"I understand, but I can't in good faith allow a child so young to fly by herself halfway around the world. You must find someone to go with her, an adult who can be responsible for making sure she's safe and will hand her off to her mother when she arrives in Illinois."

A few days before, Yikealo happened to run into an old colleague of his whose sister was visiting from the US and was due to return soon. After the meeting at the American consulate, he hurries over to ask about her plans and where she'll be flying to.

"I'm going back next week," she tells him. "To Chicago."

"My wife, Wudasie, lives near there with our oldest child. I'm trying to send our second daughter to be with her and her sister."

"Yes, in fact I know about them. Your wife is part of our regional support group. Let me give you my schedule while I'm here. If you can arrange for your daughter to be on the same flight, I'll be more than happy to take her with me and hand her over to her mother. In fact, I have one boy and two girls traveling with me, so she'll even have someone her own age to keep her company."

When Yikealo tells me this, I can't believe our luck. What are the chances of this happening? I know it's a miracle, and I don't dare question it. If ever I needed proof of God's hand at work, I have finally received it. How else could one explain such a coincidence? "It's still not guaranteed," Yikealo warns me. "We still don't have the entry stamp."

Nevertheless, armed with this new information, Yikealo returns to the American consulate, where the officer advises him to go ahead and purchase the ticket. Yikealo wants to wait until we have all the proper travel documents in hand, but I don't. I call the airline directly and request a seat near my friend on the same flight. "I can book it, Ma'am," the agent warns me, "but the cost will be more than three thousand dollars. If you go directly to the website yourself, you might save yourself some money."

I don't care. I just want to be absolutely certain there are no mistakes whatsoever, not when we've come so close to finally making it happen. And I don't trust the online process or myself. I could make a silly mistake in my haste, and I'd never be able to forgive myself if Natsanet couldn't come because of it.

Within minutes, the ticket is purchased. My daughter, who is now almost eight years old, is scheduled to fly to America on Saturday. Not a Saturday in a couple weeks, but in only a few days. I can't believe I'll get to see her again for the first time in three and a half years.

But when Yikealo goes back to the consulate the next day with the ticket information, his greatest fears are realized. He is told the exit visa request has not — and cannot — be processed. "I'm sorry," the consulate officer tells him, "but the computer systems are all down. I've been unable to clear the request with Washington."

"When will it be up again?"

"I honestly don't know. Hopefully soon."

Another day goes by.

Then another.

At 5PM on Friday, just hours before Natsanet is scheduled to leave, the officer hands Yikealo her passport. The entry visa had been stamped into it just moments before.

A BITTERSWEET REUNION

It's late Friday night, and I can barely sleep thinking about Natsanet flying all the way here without me or her father by her side. I remember how long it took me and Titi all those years ago, how lost and overwhelmed I felt. How exhausted we were when we arrived. And how I didn't know what to expect afterward.

I rise very early on Saturday morning and wake Titi. It takes her a moment to remember today's significance, but when she does, she jumps out of bed to get ready. She's been so excited to see her little sister again that I didn't think she'd get any sleep at all. After we've eaten, we drive over to my sister's house, where we pick up a few more people.

The plane isn't scheduled to arrive for another three hours, but we end up waiting far longer than that because we'd underestimated the amount of time it would take for Natsanet to get through all the security and immigration checks before she can be legally allowed to enter the United States. I don't know who's more nervous, me or my sister. Titi sleeps with her head on my lap while we sit on the airport's hard plastic seats and wait. I have a difficult time keeping my own eyes open, despite my anxiety. School has just ended for the year, and the combination of work, worry, and days of sleeplessness has drained me both physically and emotionally.

I had called Eritrea the day before to speak with Natsanet. I wanted to assure her that everything would be okay. It was already Saturday morning there, and Yikealo was just about to take her to the airport. I only had a few minutes, so I told her we were all very excited about her coming, and that we couldn't wait to see her.

"Are you excited, too, honey?"

"Yes."

"Did someone help you braid your hair?"

"Yes."

"Are you ready to come? All packed?"

"Yeah."

She didn't sound excited at all. In fact, she sounded fearful. I tried to reassure her that she'd be completely safe, but even at her young age she instinctively understood I couldn't guarantee that. Yes, I knew the person she'd be traveling with, and I trusted her, but Natsanet didn't know her at all. She'd be traveling with a complete stranger. She'd feel totally alone, and it reminded me again of how badly I had betrayed her trust all those years ago when we slipped away in the night, just me and Titi, without telling her a word. It's a decision I've regretted every day since.

Now it's been twenty-four hours since we spoke, and I long to hear her voice again. I check the clock for the hundredth time. Each of the ninety-nine times before, I'd pictured exactly where she was at that given moment: *Now she's in the airport in Asmara. Now she's left the country. She's in Europe now, waiting for her layover. Now she's flying over the ocean. Now she's somewhere over the US.*

And then, suddenly people are streaming in through the security gate and there she is, stepping through, her eyes wide and her face pale. She's so much taller than I remember her, yet so much tinier than I'd hoped. She's so small in that crowd of grownups, so lost and helpless. I jump to my feet. "Oh my God," I gasp. "My baby!" No longer able to control my emotions, I scream her name. But I don't care who might see and hear the spectacle I make of myself. "She's here! My baby girl is here at last!"

I call out her name again and expect her to come running. But when she sees me, she only gives me a wary glance. She drops her backpack to the floor beside her. She looks like she's ready to run away if I make any attempt to come closer. "Sweetie?" I say, stepping cautiously toward her. I drop to my knees when I reach her side. The passengers swirl past us, heading to their own reunions and business meetings and vacations. I don't care that we're right in the middle of the floor, blocking the way. And still Natsanet doesn't make a move. She looks confused. There's no recognition in her eyes. "Honey? It's me," I say. "Your mother."

A pair of young girls pass us, bright colorful jackets and youthful giggles. Natsanet's eyes flick toward them, then back at me. I dimly hear the girls squeal when they see their waiting father. Without warning, my daughter breaks away from me and rushes over to them, and I realize that these are the little girls she's been traveling with. Their brother is with them, too, forming a ring around their father's legs.

"Natsanet!" they say, when they see her standing beside them, and their clasped hands open up to invite her in.

She's more afraid of losing sight of her new friends than of being with me. I'm her mother, yet I'm a stranger to her. The people she didn't know a day ago give her more comfort than I do.

My brother-in-law brings the car around from the parking garage to pick us up. Natsanet's new friends have already gone home. She's still not sure about me or Titi.

I try to hug her, but she resists my embrace. I can't believe how skinny she is. She looks like she's been starving to death.

"Don't you remember me?" I ask.

She hesitates, then shakes her head. She keeps glancing around, as if she expects her friends to come and rescue her. A terrible feeling rises up inside of me that she might actually try to run away, and I'll never see her again.

But she doesn't. She finally seems to accept that I am who I say I am. But this knowledge doesn't bring us any closer together. Instead, she hides her discomfort with indifference and turns her attention through the car window to the scene outside, as if she hopes I'll forget she's there. When I ask if she's hungry or wants anything, she ignores the question and instead wonders aloud, "Why are they driving in circles? Why are there so many people? Where do they all live?"

On the drive home, I'm beside myself with emotion. I don't know what to do. I want to hold her, to protect her. I'm afraid of what she'll do if I try. I don't want her to reject me. So I sit where I am without moving, and she sits just a couple feet away beside me and stares out the window, her hands resting on her lap, her tiny fists clenched tightly. I could reach out and touch her, and yet she's miles away from me.

My brother-in-law tries to console me from the front seat. "She'll be fine. She's just overwhelmed. Give her some time. She's here now after all your hard work, so you can be grateful for that. It's a miracle you succeeded."

I know he's right, but it's still hard to ignore the crushing emptiness I feel. I fear the gap between us, the gap I created, will never be filled. All I want to do is take Natsanet's pain away from her, but I can't even get her to acknowledge me.

That evening, after I get her home and bathed, I give her some food that I think she might like. But she barely eats a thing. "Please," I beg her. "For Mom."

"You don't look like my mother."

"What do you mean?"

"You look . . . different."

I remind myself that she was still very young when I left home. She'll have lost my image in her mind. But she's also right that I have changed. I've aged. I've gained weight. I wear different clothes.

"It's still me," I tell her. "And this is Titi, your sister. You remember her, don't you? You two used to play together. Aren't you happy to see us?"

She looks at her older sister with distrust. And for the first time, I see Titi with fresh eyes. I see how much she's grown since the day we left Asmara. She was Natsanet's current age then. Now she's almost eleven years old. She's done a lot of growing in the last three and a half years. She would have changed even more than me.

I tuck Natsanet into bed. She falls asleep right away without saying a word.

The next day, my sister, her husband, and several of our friends come over. It's Father's Day, and they've all decided to forego their own private celebrations to be with us. The fact that this is a special day for fathers here in America only adds to my pain, since neither of my children has theirs.

We all try to engage Natsanet, to help her see that she's both welcomed and loved, but there is no sign of the joy I had so hoped for. She plays with the other children, but it's tentative and feels like she's just doing it because that's what we expect of her. I know it's not simply because she's tired or overwhelmed. She watches the other children and the adults with keen attention. Every time I get up to leave the room, she gets agitated.

When she goes to use the bathroom, she leaves the door open.

"You have to shut it," I tell her. "You need privacy."

But she refuses to do it. "What if you and Titi disappear again?" she asks.

I did this, I tell myself. I did this by leaving her when she was barely still a baby. I let too much time pass, and now she doesn't remember who I am, only what I did to her. Even worse, I've done it again, taken her away from her father, the only parent she remembers. I've taken away her grandparents and replaced them with a new aunt and uncle she has never known. How could she trust me? She can't, not when she expects me to leave her again at any moment. Or take her someplace else again where she knows nobody. *She's afraid of me.*

Oh! This breaks my heart all over again.

She asks for her father, so I call him on the telephone so she can speak with him. After she hangs up, she's inconsolable. I try to assure her that he'll be following along soon enough. It's like tearing open an old wound, lying to her like this. I try to reason to myself that I'm really not lying, that I'm praying for a certain outcome instead. But I know I might as well ask for the moon, too, while I'm at it. Because however hard the obstacles might have been bringing her here, no matter how high the cost, they will be a hundred times worse with Yikealo.

ONE SETBACK AFTER ANOTHER

Natsanet's arrival coincides with the first week of break from school, so we have the entire summer to rebuild the relationship we once shared. The progress is frustratingly slow, but I'm encouraged we're making any at all. Day by day, she opens up a little more, like a turtle slowly sticking its head out of its shell, or a flower opening up in the morning sunlight one petal at a time. She starts to gain weight— not a lot, but enough so that she doesn't look so frightfully skinny anymore. I feed her as much as she is willing to tolerate. She continues to be the same picky eater I remember back home, but here we have a much larger variety of choices to try than we had in Eritrea, so it's easier to find something that's both nutritious and acceptable. I resign myself to the fact that this will probably never change about her.

Having time off from my job at the school is a mixed blessing. My days are now free to spend in their entirety with my daughters. But living without that income means we have to draw money out of our modest savings. I try to work for an insurance company for a little while, as the hours are flexible, but it doesn't take long before I realize it's just not worth the sacrifice. I can either have money and no time with my family, or time and no money. I choose the latter. It isn't easy, especially when there are so many things I want to do with my girls, so many new experiences I want Natsanet to have, and so many places I want her to see. Instead, we compromise and revisit many of the same places I once took Titi when we were still new to America— the lake, parks, anywhere free. The big difference this time is that I don't have to depend on someone else to drive us. We can just pack up and go whenever and wherever we want.

The connection between the two sisters grows noticeably stronger by the day. Titi helps Natsanet daily with her English, and I'm pleased to see how quickly she picks it up— much more quickly than Titi did, in fact. I'm glad to see the bond between them has remained strong. By the following fall, Natsanet has settled in enough and become confident enough in her communication skills that she's eager to begin school. Her transition goes very well. In fact, everything goes a lot smoother this time around. The teachers, who already know a lot about her from a family poster Titi created the previous year, as well as from the stories I shared in conversations, give her the warmest welcome imaginable. It doesn't take long before Natsanet is making new friends and coming home to tell me how much she likes her teacher.

Within a few weeks of the start of school, she completes her English Learner's program and is placed into a regular classroom, which delights her even more. I'm constantly surprised by how hard she works. She's so eager to learn. She's nothing like the terrified little girl I saw in the airport just a few short months before.

Slowly, my anxieties about her begin to fade. For the first time I can imagine us being the way we used to be, only better because of the new opportunities Yikealo and I could only have dreamed of before.

Then, just as everything seems to be getting better, there is an accident at work, and I'm injured. While helping a fellow teacher move a heavy filing cabinet, the dolly we're using breaks, and a corner of the unit lands on my foot, crushing it. The pain is immediate and excruciating.

I remember being put on a stretcher and riding in the ambulance to the hospital. And all I could think the whole way there was that I won't be able to work for a very long time. From my experience as an insurance adjuster, I knew immediately I'd suffered the type of injury that will take many weeks to heal.

The x-ray proves me right. It shows several broken bones in my left foot. After applying a thick bandage, the emergency room physician refers me to a specialist. Then I'm released with a pair of crutches.

Life at home becomes a series of daily challenges. Even the simplest of tasks suddenly become nearly insur-mountable chores. I have two young children to take care of, to feed and dress, to get to school and back. They bravely try to help. My sister and brother-in-law come over to assist. My friends, too. One tells me, "I'll drive the kids to and from school." Another tells me not to worry about all the rest. "Anything you need, just tell me." I'm blessed to be among such good people, but I'm not very good as an invalid. While I have worked many jobs where I have been responsible for matching assistance with those in need, I've never been comfortable being on the receiving end of charity. And despite how much of it I've received here over the years, I've never been able to get used to it. All the help in the world, welcome or not, could never replace my need to do it on my own.

After a couple of weeks, the specialist advises me to put aside the crutches and walk on my foot as much as I can. "It will be painful, but we don't want your muscles and tendons to get weak."

I do as he asks, and although it's agonizing at first, the healing does seem to progress more quickly. Nevertheless, the injury is so severe that it keeps me out on disability for several weeks longer than I'd expected. Unable to work, my days become as empty as the apartment is in the middle of the day when the girls are off at school. Knowing that inactivity can lead to depression, I do my best to fill the time productively. I read. I clean. I work on Yikealo's case, hoping to appeal to the people here in America to try harder to get him out of Eritrea. But there is only so much reading and cleaning and phone calling one can do, especially when so little of it ever seems to lead anywhere, or makes a lasting impact. Plus, I'm so easily distracted. I'll read a book or a magazine article, and the passages will slip immediately from my memory because I can't put Yikealo's situation out of my mind. I admit that there are times I think I might go crazy from the stress, the helplessness, and the boredom. If not for my daily escapes into TV Land with Ellen in the morning and Oprah in the afternoon, if not for their overwhelmingly positive messages of self empowerment, I probably would.

One day, I wake up to find black spots swimming before my eyes. I had recently been testing contact lenses to replace the glasses I've worn since I was six years old. There had been some initial discomfort, which the optometrist said was expected, so I assumed this was all part of the breaking-in period. But the spots continue to bother me all day until, on the verge of panic, I finally call the optometrist's office. When I describe what's happening to me, she orders me to come in immediately.

"It looks like you've suffered some kind of stroke in your left eye," she tells me, after a quick examination.

"What?" I exclaim, terrified by the word. Yikealo's father suffered from a stroke many years ago and as a result has been partially paralyzed and bedridden ever since.

"There appears to be some bleeding behind your retina."

"But what caused it? Could it be due to the contact lenses?"

"Not the lenses. But I'm not a medical doctor, so I can't give you a proper diagnosis. I can say, however, that it's not all that unusual. I've seen it happen to people after strenuous exertion. The blood vessels behind the eyes are very delicate and can burst. Sometimes it's because of high blood pressure. I would strongly recommend that you get your doctor to check it. For now, I'm going to refer you to a retina specialist."

The specialist takes several pictures and shows me the affected areas. "It looks like macular degeneration," he says. "It happens to a lot of people as they get older. It's caused by abnormal blood vessels leaking into the part of the retina called the macula. Unfortunately, there's no treatment for this condition. We can only try and slow it down, not reverse the damage that's already been done." He writes me a prescription for a mild painkiller and tells me to come back in a week.

I don't like driving around with my vision impaired, but I have no choice. Until my next appointment, I'm too scared to take the girls anywhere unless we absolutely must go.

On my next visit, the doctor is surprised to see the bleeding has diminished. And over the next couple of weeks, the affected patch grows smaller still. "You're lucky," he says. "It's very rare for patients with macular degeneration to show regression of their symptoms. What are you doing?"

"Drinking a lot of vegetable juice," I tell him, sincerely. I had heard it can help with eye health.

He laughs. "Well, whatever it is, keep it up. It's obviously working for you."

I'm eventually cleared to return to work, even though I still have a lot of pain in my foot and, secondarily, in my back. I'm told that in all likelihood I will always have some discomfort, and the foot will never be as strong as it was before the accident. And while my vision has cleared a lot since that incident, I still experience some occasional visual impairment.

But it's not the end of my medical woes. While receiving a root canal on a problem tooth, the dentist informs me that a specialist will have to extract a tiny piece of instrument that broke off inside. Although the dentist seems unworried about this, the unexpected development only adds to my anxieties.

Growing up we had limited exposure to proper dental care. I can remember hearing stories about people suffering greatly at the hands of the local practitioners. One of our neighbors suffered terribly from a procedure that went bad. The pain he was forced to endure was so great that he screamed for hours until he passed out. In my mind, I can still hear the echoes off the walls of the compound. He died in the middle of the night. I remember seeing the body when he was brought out. The infection caused his face to swell up like a balloon. I keep waiting for my face to do the same.

The procedure to extract the metal bit from inside my tooth is quite painful, but it's nowhere near as painful as the bill I receive a couple weeks later. After the initial shock wears off, I realize there must be some kind of mistake. Surely it must be covered by my insurance, especially since it happened as a consequence of another covered dental procedure. But when I call to inquire about it, I'm told that I am financially responsible for the entire amount. How am I going to pay for it? I don't have thousands of dollars just sitting around!

Between the stress of our expenses, caring for two young children alone, and trying to figure out a diplomatic solution to getting my husband out of Eritrea and over to America, it seems that my run of medical issues is my body's way of sending me warning signals to slow down and take better care of myself. But I don't. I tell myself I can't afford the luxury of heeding the warnings, not while my husband still suffers from the ever-worsening conditions in Eritrea.

Until my body finally offers up a signal I simply can't ignore.

One day, after an especially frustrating conversation with the billing people at the orthodontist's office, my heart begins to race uncontrollably. I try to calm myself down by sitting in my darkened living room and closing my eyes and focusing on a positive thought, but the pounding in my chest doesn't lessen at all. Terrified, I begin to imagine the worst. An image of my children left alone in America flashes before my eyes. Who will care for them should I die?

After several minutes, the heavy beating subsides, but the episode leaves me shaken. I half expect it to return and promise myself that when it does, I'll go directly to the hospital. But it doesn't come back the rest of the day.

The next time it happens, a few days later, the pressure in my chest wakes me up from a dead sleep. There's no pain, just that feeling of being unable to catch my breath. Eventually, it too fades away. It's easy to make the connection between my sudden heart problems and Titi's condition. I spend the rest of that night on the internet searching for clues as to whether it's possible for an adult heart to suddenly form holes. I find nothing of the sort, but the information I do come across terrifies me anyway. There are so many different explanations for what might be causing my symptoms, ranging from the harmless to the deadly, and I'm convinced I'm closer to the bad end of the scale. Am I suffering from some kind of heart attack? Is my heart beginning to fail for some reason? I learn that heart disease is a bigger problem for women than men, more so for African women, and it gets worse as we age. The more I read, the more convinced I become that my time is limited.

My first concern is, again, for my girls. I worry about leaving them alone in a land that's still more foreign to them than familiar. But even more worrisome for me is the thought that they'd be forced to return to Eritrea if I were to die, since that is where their father is.

Funny how we can so easily rationalize away our own personal issues, especially when they slip away as quietly and completely as they arrive. In the morning, as the first traces of sunlight begin to filter in through the curtains, I wake to the alarm feeling physically fine. There's no lingering trace of the heart palpitations or shortness of breath. And so, with much to do before the day officially begins, I again foolishly put my worries aside to prepare the girls' school lunches.

The third time it happens, I call for an ambulance right away. The pounding is so bad this time I swear my heart is going to explode out of my chest. With my phone in hand, I stumble out to the curb to await the arrival of the medics, and manage to connect with a friend, who promises to come right over to look after the girls. This is the first time my daughters have witnessed me having one of these episodes, and they're clearly just as scared as I am. I tell them to go back inside the house to wait, but they ignore me. Thankfully, my friend arrives soon, followed shortly by the EMTs.

Everything's a blur. They lay me down on a stretcher, put cold pads on my chest for an EKG, take my blood pressure and pulse. I want to sit up to catch my breath, but the medic tells me to remain lying down. I want to see my girls, but my friend has pulled them to the side away from view.

Ma'am, what's your age?

Describe your symptoms. Is this the first time?

What medications are you taking?

Do you have other adult family members here? Are you married? Where is your husband?

They take me straight to the emergency room, where another EKG is recorded. A nurse comes to draw my blood, and take my temperature, blood pressure, and pulse. Some sort of device is clamped onto my finger and left there. I get an IV. The doctor on duty asks me more questions. He shows me the EKG and explains that there's no heart disease. He tells me that what I'm experiencing is not all that uncommon. Or dangerous. He doesn't try to tell me it's not frightening. He can see how scared I am.

"No heart disease?" I ask, only partially relieved. And yet I know that something must be wrong, because normal people don't feel like this. "What could be causing it?"

He shrugs. "Lots of different things can trigger palpitations of this sort— fatigue, caffeine, stress, exercise, hormones . . . ." Another shrug. "Have you experienced any especially stressful events in your life recently?"

Have I, I think. *Where do I even begin to explain how my life is one stressful event after another lately?*

I'm discharged after a couple of hours, and my friend insists we all stay with her and her husband overnight, just in case I experience another episode.

Several times over the next few weeks, my cardiologist checks my heart again. Then he has me submit to a stress test. The episodes keep coming, hitting me at random moments, completely unannounced, then departing again without reason. In the end, the doctors are completely convinced I have nothing wrong with my heart. They tell me again and again to eliminate caffeine and stress, get lots of rest and exercise, drink lots of water.

I ask what if it happens when I'm driving. "Pull over," the doctor tells me.

It's terribly frustrating when you have so little control over anything, especially your own body. Eventually, I learn techniques for managing my stress. And I get used to the palpitations. They still come, although with less frequency and severity, and they don't worry me as much as they once did. I still don't like them. They're reminders that my life is far from stress-free.

And as for that dentist bill. It took dozens of phone calls to the orthodontist's office, several visits in person, and a lot more patience than I ever knew I possessed, but the matter is finally resolved. Maybe they got tired of arguing with me. Or maybe they finally accepted the fact that I shouldn't be financially responsible for something I didn't do. It's just as well. I would never have been able to pay the thousands of dollars they were asking for, especially since I'm spending thousands to get Yikealo out of Eritrea.

TURNING ILLEGAL

Four and a half years after I left Eritrea, Yikealo's case is finally approved by US Immigration Services, meaning we can apply for an immigrant visa. It's mid-2008, and the news lifts our spirits just when we need it the most. Natsanet has missed her father terribly in the year since she came over. Even twelve-year-old Titi, who hasn't seen him since she was seven, talks eagerly about him coming home.

Everybody wants to know how long we expect the process to take. My best guess is that the application for an immigrant visa will require at least six months to be approved, so the earliest he'll be here is near the end of the year. At this point, we can see no reason for it being denied, since he's already been vetted and qualified for permanent resident status, the rest of his family is already here, and we're stable enough financially that we can support him.

The months pass with excruciating slowness. Each time I inquire, I'm told the application is still being considered. But near the end of the year, when we expect the evaluation to be completed, we receive word that the immigration visa "cannot be issued at this time, however we will let you know as soon as it is."

I have to keep a positive outlook for the children's sake. I try to be optimistic and suggest to them the delay is because of the holidays. "They'll have more openings in the new year," I say. But they take the news hard and direct their anger toward me. "You always tell us he's coming soon, but then it doesn't happen!" I try to explain that it's just a minor setback. "There's only a certain number of visas they're allowed per year. Maybe they ran out. Dad will be at the front of the line now. Another few months, okay?"

At least we know the process hasn't stopped. We're told that Yikealo must be interviewed by a consulate officer. Unfortunately, this puts us right back where we were with Natsanet a year and a half before, when she needed to be interviewed. The difference this time is that the US consulate in Eritrea has shut down all travel operations and is taking absolutely no new cases at all. No exceptions. This leaves places like Cairo and Nairobi as our only choices. And this is where it gets even trickier than before, as we learn that Eritrea has completely stopped granting exit visas to anyone under the age of fifty-five to anywhere in the world for any reason.

All the bribes in the world won't work for Yikealo. Only a miracle could make it possible for him to legitimately leave our homeland, and we're just not sure we can wait for another one. After coming to this conclusion, we have our first serious discussion about sneaking him across the border into Sudan and becoming a refugee.

It's been nearly two decades since Eritrea cast off the cloak of foreign oppression, and yet our citizens are no more free today than they were during the worst of times under Ethiopian or Italian rule. Now, thousands of Eritreans leave their homeland every month to escape the mounting tyranny, the constant threat of war, the unending conscription into the National Service, the poverty, sickness, and lack of modern medicine and technologies. Every resource is funneled into so-called national security. The government is starving its own citizens while claiming it's protecting them. Eritrea has become a full-blown totalitarian regime, with Isaias Afewerki as its unchallenged dictator.

Naturally, such a government doesn't want its citizens departing, and it has become fairly efficient at preventing it. They employ their grossly oversized military to patrol the border, where they impose order with unrestrained violence. They do not tolerate any dissent at all. Fortunately for people like my husband, who are committed to leaving it all behind, there are well-developed networks in place to facilitate illegal crossings, and they've only grown in sophistication over the years. We just need to figure them out and use them discreetly.

The consequences of being caught planning or attempting an illegal border crossing are terrifying to even contemplate. One slip of the tongue or misplaced word into the ear of one wrong person and Yikealo could be detained and interrogated. Soldiers have been known to harass family members on the merest of suspicions. If a crosser is stopped at the border, they might be executed on the spot. And that's not the worst of the possible outcomes. If taken alive, he could very likely be sent straight to jail without benefit of a trial, where he would be tortured using techniques taught to us by our former oppressors. We personally know too many friends who have ended up in prison this way, either by trying to escape themselves, or simply by association with someone who did. If they survive their "interrogation," those kept in prison are subjected to hard labor for months or years. Some succumb to disease and malnutrition. Many die.

Aside from those risks, there are dangers just in making the crossing. The land between Eritrea and Sudan is open, barren desert with little protection from the sun. Many people attempting the crossing die from injuries, illness, or dehydration. Some are attacked by wild animals.

Then, if successful, the crosser must navigate the logistical maze that is the overburdened refugee system in Sudan.

Making such a choice is never easy. Nobody becomes a refugee unless they've exhausted all of their other options first. Those who flee their homeland aren't lazy or simple-minded. Stepping away from one's home with no promise of ever finding a new one, and no chance of ever being able to return, is one of the most desperate of human acts. But it's now been two years since Yikealo sent Natsanet away, and Eritrea has slipped so deep into a darkness we thought we'd permanently abolished, that it no longer resembles the vision we once had dreamed it would be. Our homeland has become a place that will never allow him the freedom of choice we were once promised. Nothing there is changing for the better, and there is no indication it ever will. The time has come for my husband to rejoin his family, by any means possible.

I don't tell the children of our plans. I don't want to worry them unnecessarily. I don't know what I'll tell them if something bad happens to their father along the way. I'm sure they'll blame me if it does and they're faced with a future without him. I'll cross that bridge if and when I have to, but not before.

I pray I never will.

With the help of trusted friends and relatives, Yikealo carefully plans his escape. I don't know when it'll happen, since the arrangements are made in secret. Neither does he. He's given no details until the day it happens. And when it does happen, I only find out afterward that he has failed.

"I waited at the border," he tells me on the phone after returning to Asmara, "but my contact never showed up. There were soldiers everywhere. And I had to come back or else my employer would know something was wrong when I didn't show up at work today."

I'm greatly relieved to hear he wasn't caught, but I also fear the failure will discourage him from trying again. A second attempt only multiplies the risks.

A week later, I'm unable to reach him. His phone at home rings without being answered. I call my mother. I call his parents. No one seems to know where he's gone. He's simply vanished. I have to assume he tried again, but if he has, I don't know whether he's succeeded or been caught and taken to prison. And if I don't hear from him soon, I'll have to assume it was the latter.

REFUGEE

The harsh jangling sound of my telephone ringing snatches me out of my sleep. Blinded by darkness and clumsy with exhaustion, I accidentally knock it off my bedside table and onto the floor. It's the first night in more than two weeks that I've been able to fall asleep before midnight. When I realize how late the hour is, I know the call is coming from halfway around the world. But who is it? And is it good news or bad? For more than a week, I've known from my mother-in-law that Yikealo did, in fact, try again to cross the border. But nobody has heard from him since. Nobody knows if he's still in Eritrea.

At last I find the phone. My fingers are numb as I try to answer. My heart races as if it wants to jump straight out of my chest. "Hello?"

"It's me."

I don't know what words come pouring out of my mouth the moment I hear his voice. I'm babbling with relief that he's still alive, yet suddenly certain that he's calling from prison.

"Stop!" he tells me. "Just stop and listen."

"Where are you?" I demand. "What's happening? Are you okay?"

"I just arrived at a border town inside Sudan."

"Inside Sudan? Does that mean—"

"I'm fine. I crossed over safely earlier today. I'm staying with some good people for now. You don't have to worry."

"You crossed the border? You're already in Sudan?" I know that this is what he just said, but my mind refuses to accept it. I need to hear him say it again.

"Yes, I'm here."

"And you're okay? You aren't hurt?"

"I'm okay, praise God! Now, I must go. There's still a long way to go and a lot to do before I'm safe."

He spends a week hiding in Kassala, a town just a few miles from the border, while he waits to move on. He's still vulnerable. Not until he reaches a refugee camp and registers with the United Nations High Commissioner for Refugees will he be able to relax a little. Each day, I fear hearing news that the Sudanese military or police have caught him and taken him back to the border, where he'll be handed over to Eritrean soldiers. Each night I settle in with worries that those same soldiers will sneak over the border and snatch him while he sleeps.

On August 22, 2009, he's received by UNHCR officials at a small United Nations-run refugee processing center near the town of Showak. He spends two nights there before being transferred to the Shagarab Refugee Camp, filled to bursting with tens of thousands of Eritrean escapees, some of whom have been there for years and now call it their permanent home. There, he must register with Sudan's National Security Service, which exposes him to yet another opportunity for deportation. Many officers in the NSS are corrupt and demand money, knowing that few refugees leave their home country without their life's savings in their pockets. Some refugees are falsely accused of crimes and threatened with deportation if they don't pay off the bribes. Even the camp itself isn't a totally safe place. People are regularly abducted for the human trafficking trade. Women are raped. Children are taken and held for ransom or sold off for unimaginably horrific purposes. The UN personnel can't offer complete protection. Some of the aid workers themselves are guilty of taking bribes.

After registering, Yikealo and the other new arrivals to the camp are provided a single meal. After that they're on their own and must find their own food. The camp is like a small city, complete with established vendors and cafés offering a surprisingly wide range of supplies and services. Naturally, everything costs money, and Yikealo has a very limited amount with him that he can't spend too quickly or lose to thieves. We've already paid off thousands of dollars to helpers just to get him to this point, and he still has a long way to go before he can get to Cairo for an interview.

The process of obtaining refugee status can take months. He has to apply for permits from both the Commission for Refugees and the UNHCR. Then he needs to request permission to leave the camp so he can go to Khartoum, the capital, for travel out of the country. Without these documents, he'll be restricted to Shagarab. If he's caught anywhere else in the country without them, he could be detained, harassed, and deported. But with so many new arrivals each day, the process is overworked and slow. While he waits, he rents a small shelter and bed to protect him from the weather.

After nearly a month, he finally receives his UNHCR papers and heads to the regional office of the Commission for Refugees at Khashm el-Girba to get his photo ID, which will allow him to travel throughout the country. The ID won't protect him from harassment by the NSS, but at least he won't be sent back to Eritrea, not unless he does something very wrong. Or is accused of doing something very wrong.

The next day, he's on a bus to Khartoum to apply for his travel visas. It's mid-September, 2009, ten years since he trained for the ENS in Kiloma. Nearly ten years since Natsanet was born. Today, he's an illegal escapee from the country he once served, an illegal visitor in a land full of people just like him. He technically has no permission to be there, and no legal means of leaving.

For the first time, I worry that going to Sudan might have been an error in strategy. I fear he could be stuck there forever. He assures me it won't happen, but I can't help doubting him, myself, the system, and even God.

After a long bus ride interrupted multiple times by security checkpoints manned by NSS guards, many of whom demand bribes to pass through, Yikealo finally arrives in Khartoum. Two friends formerly from the Shagarab camp take him in. He stays with them for a while before moving into a larger house with eight roommates. As soon as he's settled in there, I begin working to get Yikealo scheduled for an interview with the US Consulate in Cairo. It's a long, complicated process, so I try first to get his application reviewed by the US Consular Office in Khartoum. Ideally, we'd avoid Egypt altogether, but I have little hope of getting what we need in Sudan.

After dozens of calls and just as many excuses for why it's taking so long, we're no closer to getting my husband to America than before he left Eritrea. In January of 2010, Yikealo moves to a different house in one of the districts of the city where there are a lot of Eritrean migrants. With no resolution in sight, he starts searching for a job. Life in the capital is expensive. On top of the costs associated with his immigration case, I have to send him money just so he can survive. While it would be a great help for him to earn money, I secretly fear what having a job could do to him psychologically. I don't like the idea of him settling down and insinuating himself into the community.

In the end, it doesn't matter what I think or want. Jobs are nearly impossible to find. Even the illegal work has all been taken.

One afternoon, while chatting with my fellow parishioners at my church, the pastor asks about the status of my husband's case. When he hears about all the frustrations I've been experiencing, he offers to write a letter to our district's representative to the US Congress requesting their assistance in bringing Yikealo here to reunite with his family. Within days, the US Immigration Office notifies me that they've referred the case to Egypt. Unfortunately, this only complicates my request for Khartoum to handle it.

I file an appeal explaining the difficulties of refugees securing visas, but I'm told there's an official process and there's nothing else they can do about it. I'm told unequivocally that the case must be considered in Cairo. So Yikealo applies for an entry visa at the Egyptian consulate in Sudan and is told to wait for their call for an interview.

At the same time, some friends who have already been through the same process as Yikealo warn him not to expect to make any progress with the Egyptian consulate in Khartoum. After years of social, political, and religious turmoil in the region, they've begun delaying issuing some travel visas to Egypt and denying others outright.

In the spring of 2010, long simmering tensions between the Muslim part of Sudan and the Christian south come to boil in the weeks before the presidential election. For nearly twenty years, the southern half of the country fought for independence. In 2005, President Omar al-Bashir granted Southern Sudan autonomy for six years, at which point the issue of independence would be put to referendum. With his

LAST RESORT

We decide to transfer the case to the US Embassy in Nairobi, despite knowing it's outside of the proper channels. We're also advised to file a formal request with the Nairobi office to consider the case, as they have no jurisdiction over immigrant visas for Eritrean citizens. Surprisingly, the process goes fairly smoothly, and despite having been told it's out of the question, Nairobi is officially assigned the case in late June.

Now, Yikealo must figure out how to get an exit visa from Sudan and an entry visa to Kenya. On top of all that, Yikealo's passport has since expired. We had hoped he'd be in America by now, but with so many delays, it didn't happen as planned. So now, before anything else can happen, he has to go back to the Eritrean Embassy in Khartoum. Another delay in a complex process where a thousand different pieces need to be moving all at once, and each of them is headed in its own separate direction at its own speed.

The passport is finally renewed, although not without its own difficulties. With it in hand, Yikealo applies for his exit visa from Sudan. Once more the process requires working outside of the official channels. This time, it's a retired police officer who executes the transaction. The cost is a fraction of some of the "fees" we've been forced to pay previously — barely a pittance — and yet it's surprisingly efficient. Less than a day later, Yikealo has his exit stamp. Now, all he needs is to get the entry stamp into Kenya.

But when he inquires at the Kenyan Embassy in Khartoum, he's told he actually doesn't need an entry visa, since Eritrea and Kenya are members of the East African Intergovernmental Authority on Development. The agreement grants citizens the ability to travel between member states without a visa. Sudan is also a member, but visa-free travel is restricted to only between one's home country and a member state. In order for Yikealo to travel to Kenya, he would first need to return to Eritrea.

"I can try to go straight there anyway," Yikealo tells me, "but there's a chance I could be denied entry upon arriving at the airport."

Once more, it seems as if every time we make progress, another obstacle gets thrown in our path.

"I'm going to try it," he tells me. "A friend has agreed to arrange for me to connect with a person who lives in Nairobi and deals with these types of situations. He'll receive me at the airport and facilitate my entry."

"How much will it cost?" I ask.

"Two hundred American dollars," he says.

I don't hesitate. "Buy the plane ticket," I say.

On the last day of July 2010, a year after slipping out of Eritrea, Yikealo departs Khartoum for Jomo Kenyatta Airport in Nairobi. He promises to call me as soon as he clears all the security checkpoints and is safely and securely inside Kenya. I pray every minute of every hour that he doesn't get stuck. If Kenya refuses to allow him entry, he won't be able to return to Sudan. There is only one place he could go from there, and in that place he'll be considered a traitor.

"No problem," he tells me, when he finally calls a few hours later. "I'm here. We're going to a hotel now."

280

I let out a huge sigh of relief. I feel like I've been holding my breath the whole time. The moment he's off the phone, I start calling to arrange for an interview at the US Embassy.

Yikealo stays with a friend and his family for a month. Like him, they're Eritrean émigrés waiting to make their way somewhere else. Then, after a different friend and former coworker from Asmara arrives from Sudan, they rent a room together in a different neighborhood. This other friend has been lucky enough to win entry into the US through the Diversity Visa lottery, the same one my sister Aster was awarded years before. But because of quota limitations, the friend will have to wait until 2011 to come to America. Both Yikealo and I hope it doesn't take that long for us to be reunited. It's been almost seven years since we last saw each other. But if it does, we can wait.

We had asked for his paperwork to be sent to Nairobi in mid-June, but by mid-August it still hasn't been received. When I call the state department, I'm told that it's being sent by diplomatic courier, but because it must be routed through Washington, DC, it can take eight weeks or more to reach its final destination. It seems incredible that in this day and age, when so much information is sent instantly by email, that we are forced to wait for someone to hand carry the papers. But there's nothing we can do about it.

The file finally arrives in September, three months after the transfer request was submitted. Then things start moving again. Yikealo's first requirement is to submit to a medical checkup at the International Organization for Migrants in Nairobi. After that, he's scheduled to meet with a consular officer.

"Are you nervous?" I ask him on the morning of the interview.

"Yes."

"You don't need to be. Just be honest in your answers."

"That's easy for you to say," he teases.

The next time we talk, I expect him to tell me he worried for nothing. Instead, when I answer the phone a few hours later, he tells me about yet another holdup. "There's a form you need to submit showing you have enough income to support me."

"A form? That's it?" I ask, both immensely relieved and mildly frustrated. After the tens of thousands of dollars and the tens of thousands of hours working on our reunion, it seems like the most trivial of requests.

I receive the form the next day. Then, with my signature and income verification attached and my brother-in-law as co-sponsor, I send it back. Within a day it's accepted.

In October 2010, Yikealo secures his entry visa to come and live in the United States. It's been seven years since Titi and I told him goodbye, more than three years for Natsanet. Those lost years are filled with a lifetime's worth of heartache and hope, frustrations and miracles. We've spent so much more money on leaving Eritrea than we ever could have dreamed of making had we stayed. And I can say without reservation that it's all been worth it. Every single *nakfa* and dollar.

Because soon I'll have my family back together again. It's all I've ever wanted. It's everything I've fought to achieve.

So now, I guess it's time to look for another apartment.

AFTERWORD

"Natsanet Yikealo!" the speakers blare, and I cheer as loudly at the top of my lungs when my daughter mounts the steps and crosses the stage. In this moment, the culmination of so much hard work and pain, the only thing that matters is how proud I am as her mother.

The litany of names being called takes me back to a century-old Spanish Mission-style building where another stage awaited. I'd woken early that morning and put on a summer dress I purchased just for the occasion. Yikealo drove us, complaining good-naturedly that we were going to arrive too early and be forced to just stand around and wait. He was right, of course. But no one minded. It was too beautiful of a day to be anything but thankful for the blessings we'd received.

The others came, arriving by the carload from different towns in the region. The crowd outside the doors swelled until we blanketed the carefully manicured lawn in front. The grass had been freshly mown the day before, but now it was trampled flat by the hundreds of feet. Bits of it stuck to our shoes with morning dew. Soon there were more than five hundred of us standing about. We were all abuzz with pent-up emotion— happiness, tears, laughter, relief.

And anticipation. We'd all waited for this moment for so long, endured such trials, suffered such pain to get here.

Looking around at them, it was impossible not to be struck by our diversity, and that was the whole point. We were a community of many colors and cultures. Men and women, young and old, children and the elderly. Yet all unified with a singular purpose.

Snippets of conversation drifted over from every direction. I picked out at least a dozen different languages, heard hundreds of accents. Names as varied as their stories. I knew some of them already and learned more that day. In such company, I realized that my own story was no more or less remarkable than theirs. We shared the same hopes and dreams. We'd experienced similar challenges. Some considered this the beginning of their journeys; others the destination. We all followed our own distinct path, but we'd all arrived at the same place: home. Stories like ours are nothing if not universal.

The sun rose higher into the sky and the air heated up. We took shelter in the shade, waiting to go inside. We didn't mind the temperature. It paled in comparison to the extremes we'd already endured. It was a blessing, in fact, to be given such fine weather.

At last, the doors were unlocked and we were let in.

The din crescendoed, echoing off the walls and ceiling high above us. Something big was about to happen. The very air seemed to vibrate with expectancy. I wanted to scream. I wanted to jump for joy. I could hardly breathe from being so excited. But I was also scared. I told myself to keep calm. *Breathe, Wudasie, breathe.* The exercise helped me focus.

I remembered my friend's words from so long ago, a completely different lifetime it seems: "God's calendar is different from ours." *Indeed it is*, I thought, and chuckled in amusement. Aysha had been right after all. She'd always been right. Her faith had never wavered. It inspired me.

A side door opened, and a hush settled over us. The officials had finally arrived. They told us to form two lines. I went to one; Yikealo joined the other. His time would come soon enough.

Everyone sat, and the rumble of voices dipped while we waited expectantly.

There was a delay while the officials got themselves organized. Again, we didn't mind. What was a few more minutes after so many years?

I received a text on my phone. It was from my friend, the one who came with me when we picked Yikealo up from the airport just last year. I remember my husband looked younger than I had been expecting, as if a great weight had been lifted away from him. He had changed, of course. He was older and thinner, and yet he seemed more full of life than ever. "I see where you're seated," the message read, and tears flooded my eyes, obscuring my vision as I tried in vain to locate her in the crowd of witnesses.

I texted back: "You came."

Her reply: "Of course I did."

I knew how lucky I was to be there, to know such good people and be surrounded by them. There were times I was sad for the sacrifices I had to make to get to that point, of everything I'd had to leave behind. I thought about how hard it was— not just for me, but for every single one of us on this incredible journey. How hard it will continue to be for us. And for others yet to follow. But then I remembered how much I'd gained, and I was hopeful again. And proud. I hadn't given up. I'd persisted. And I'd won. I had my family all back together again.

I recently had another one of those dreams, the kind Aysha would be sure was prophetic. I was flying like a bird, flapping my wings as hard as I could, struggling to climb ever higher. Before me rose a massive edifice. After some effort, I managed to make it to the top, where I landed and looked down. Far below me a crowd of people had gathered. They were waiting in front of the doors to be let inside. Somehow, I knew that it was up to me to help them in. But how?

This was the question that confronted me that day, as the loudspeakers crackled and someone finally stepped up to the microphone to address us. There were speeches, but the one remark I will always remember was about how each of us had our own unique story to tell. "Each of those stories," the speaker went on, "is a thread now sewn into the great fabric of this country."

Next came the oath, which we dutifully repeated, words that seared themselves into our hearts and minds. Many of us cried tears of joy. Then, finally, the words we'd all been waiting to hear: "Congratulations, newest citizens of the United States of America!"

And suddenly, as I watch the second of my two daughters receive her own honor six years later, her high school diploma, I realize I've had the answer to the question raised in that dream all along: My story is the doorway, and truth is the key to opening it. With it, I will help those struggling to make their way inside.

In just a couple months, Natsanet will leave us to attend university. She wants to study cognitive sciences. She follows her older sister, who just finished her third year at university as a business major with a focus on international commerce. How proud I am of their accomplishments. Between them, they've tutored their fellow peers in English, a language they themselves mastered just a few short years before, held offices in their high school student councils, took jobs in retail while preparing for their college entrance exams. They'll leave here. They have their own paths to follow, and, in due course, their own stories to tell.

It's true, what I've written, all of it. I know some people would rather it not be. One of them was once a hero of my people. Let him hear the truth. Let it gather my enemies. They can't hurt me now. My story is already told.

This chapter of it, anyway.

ACKNOWLEDGMENTS

My story is neither unique nor identical to any other immigrant's story. Each and every one of us overcame endless hurdles and risky situations before we arrived at a destination of peace and hope for their children's future.

I would like to express my gratitude to all people who had a hand in my family's journey to migrate to the United States of America from my homeland of Eritrea. They include, first and foremost, my family and the innumerable friends (unnamed for their safety and security) who pushed the needle in the huge process getting us from one point to another. You encouraged me to push on whenever I was ready to give up. You celebrated with me whenever I made progress. My sister and her husband played a huge part by finding a sponsor for my daughter's surgery. You covered our expenses until my family landed in a good place. I am greatly indebted to the hospital that performed the surgery and arranged for follow-up care, including the staff that saved my daughter's life without asking for a dime in return. You were so gracious in happily providing such excellent care. Also, I would like to extend my gratitude and appreciation to my American friends and fellow church members who supported me throughout the years, helping me raise my children so that we could plant our roots here in America and flourish. As the African saying goes, "You need a village to raise a child." It is true here in America, too.

Also, a huge thank you to my co-writer and publisher, Kenneth Howe, whose expertise and patience were essential to telling my story.

Finally, I reserve my greatest praise and glory for the Almighty God, author of all life in the universe, including my own tiny part of it, for everything He has done for me and my family. He is as much the author of my story as everyone in it.

GOD IS ALWAYS GOOD!!!!!

Thirty years of conflict with a powerful enemy never broke the spirit of the Eritrean people. After winning freedom from Ethiopia, a young Eritrean man dreams of starting a new life, building a home, and teaching his children what it means to be the masters of their own fate. But all too soon, the fighting resumes. Rounded up and forced into military conscription, subjected to inhumane conditions, and made to serve a despotic leader in an army fighting a war nobody wants, he will have to sacrifice much just for a chance to get back what he lost - his family, his freedom, his birthright. But will he succeed? Or will he simply lose everything in the end?

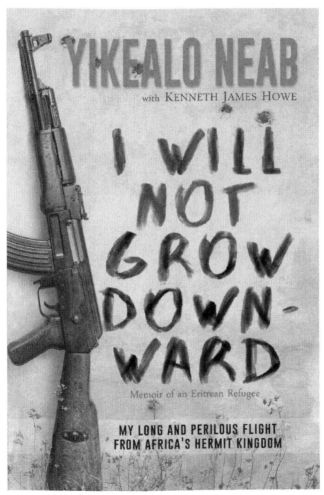

I Will Not Grow Downward offers an exceedingly rare glimpse inside the highly secretive and brutally repressive regime known as Africa's North Korea.